A Fresh Look at Psychoanalytic Technique

This collection of selected papers explores psychoanalytic technique, exemplifying Fred Busch's singular contribution to this subject, alongside the breadth and depth of his work.

Covering key topics such as what is unique about psychoanalysis, interpretation, psychic truth, the role of memory, and the importance of the analyst's reveries, this book brings together the author's most important work on this subject for the first time. Taken as a whole, Busch's work has provided an updated Freudian model for a curative process through psychoanalysis, along with the techniques to accomplish this. Meticulous in providing the theoretical underpinnings for their conclusions, these essays depict how Busch, as a humanist, has continuously championed what in retrospect seems basic to psychoanalytic technique but which has not always been at the forefront of our thinking: the patient's capacity to hear, understand, and emotionally feel interventions. Presenting a deep appreciation for Freudian theory, this book also integrates the work of analysts from Europe and Latin America, which has been prevalent in his recent work. Comprehensive and clear, these works focus on clinical issues, providing numerous examples of work with patients whilst also presenting concise explanations of the theoretical background.

In giving new meaning to basic principles of technique and in reviving older methods with a new focus, *A Fresh Look at Psychoanalytic Technique* will be of great interest to psychoanalysts and psychoanalytically oriented psychotherapists.

Fred Busch, Ph.D., is a Training and Supervising Analyst at the Boston Psychoanalytic Society and Institute. This is his fifth book, his last three being with Routledge: *Creating a Psychoanalytic Mind* (2013), *The Analyst's Reveries* (2019), and a book he edited, *Dear Candidate* (2020). He has published over seventy papers in the psychoanalytic literature and his work has been translated into many languages.

A Fresh Look at Psychoanalytic Technique

Selected Papers on Psychoanalysis

Fred Busch

Routledge
Taylor & Francis Group

LONDON AND NEW YORK

First published 2022
by Routledge
2 Park Square, Milton Park, Abingdon, Oxon OX14 4RN

and by Routledge
605 Third Avenue, New York, NY 10158

Routledge is an imprint of the Taylor & Francis Group, an informa business

© 2022 Fred Busch

British Library Cataloguing-in-Publication Data
A catalogue record for this book is available from the British Library

Names: Busch, Fred, 1939- author.
Title: A fresh look at psychoanalytic technique : selected papers on psychoanalysis / Fred Busch.
Description: Abingdon, Oxon ; New York, NY : Routledge, 2022. | Includes bibliographical references and index. Identifiers: LCCN 2021008970 (print) | LCCN 2021008971 (ebook) | ISBN 9780367621810 (hbk) | ISBN 9780367621841 (pbk) | ISBN 9781003108252 (ebk)
Subjects: LCSH: Psychoanalysis--Case studies. | Psychoanalysts.
Classification: LCC BF173 .B93 2022 (print) | LCC BF173 (ebook) | DDC 150.19/5--dc23
LC record available at https://lccn.loc.gov/2021008970
LC ebook record available at https://lccn.loc.gov/2021008971

ISBN: 978-0-367-62181-0 (hbk)
ISBN: 978-0-367-62184-1 (pbk)
ISBN: 978-1-003-10825-2 (ebk)

Typeset in Bembo
by MPS Limited, Dehradun

To my wife, Cordelia Schmidt-Hellerau, whose careful reading of all my work, along with nudging me towards the European psychoanalytic literature, has broadened my understanding and allowed me to clarify my thinking. She is a tough editor, a wonderful supporter of my ideas, and a distinguished contributor to the literature herself.

It is a great gift to have one's work appreciated by other psychoanalysts whose thinking and writing one admires. I've been fortunate to have this experience with Otto Kernberg, Stefano Bolognini, Elias de Rochas Barros, and Michael Diamond. My dear friend Cecilio Paniagua has been a keen critic and enthusiastic admirer.

Contents

Permissions

"'Can you push a camel through the eye of a needle?' Reflections on how the unconscious speaks to us and its clinical implications" *The International Journal of Psychoanalysis*, Busch (2009) Reprinted with permission of Taylor and Francis

"Conflict Theory/Trauma Theory," *The Psychoanalytic Quarterly*, Busch (2005) Reprinted with permission of Taylor and Francis

"'I noticed': The emergence of self-observation in relationship to pathological attractor sites," *The International Journal of Psychoanalysis*, Busch (2007) Reprinted with permission of Taylor and Francis

"Distinguishing Psychoanalysis from Psychotherapy," *The International Journal of Psychoanalysis*, Busch (2010) Reprinted with permission of Taylor and Francis

"The Search for Psychic Truths," *The Psychoanalytic Quarterly*, Busch (2016). Reprinted with permission of Taylor and Francis

"Searching for the analyst's reveries," *The International Journal of Psychoanalysis*, Busch (2018) Reprinted with permission of Taylor and Francis

"A shadow concept," *The International Journal of Psychoanalysis*, Busch (2006) Reprinted with permission of Taylor and Francis

Introduction

Articulating and extending principles of psychoanalytic technique based upon Freud's neglected structural model has been my passion for the last 30 years. This is, I believe, my most important contribution to psychoanalysis. I think the psychoanalytic method hasn't developed as one might have expected had there been a serious attempt to build upon the therapeutic principles inherent in Freud's second model of the mind. Instead, technique has most often focused on bringing unconscious conflicts into consciousness, without taking into account the need to analyze the powerful forces that prevent this from occurring, which was one of the main discoveries (i.e., unconscious resistances) that led Freud to the structural model.

In retrospect, my pre-analytic training as a psychologist had more of an influence on my understanding of psychoanalytic technique than I realized at the time. Learning to do psychological testing via the brilliantly conceived method devised by (the misunderstood) David Rapaport, who emphasized that form, not content alone, was the deciding factor in making differential diagnosis. What this meant was that in responding to projective tests, a borderline and a neurotic may see similar content, but the manner the content conforms to the Rorschach ink blots, for example, is very different, with the neurotic's perception following more closely to the form of the blots. Thus, when I began psychoanalytic training, learning to focus on the content alone puzzled me. What I mean by this is that the content of interpretations did not take into account the form in which it was given, or how closely it matched the capacity for receiving it. This was especially the case when in my work as a child psychologist, trained by child analysts, content interpretations were often suggested that I knew the child would have no way of understanding. In beginning my psychoanalytic practice with adults, I worked the way I was taught, but felt my interpretations of buried content wasn't helping my patients. I kept trying to give what I now think of as "aha" interpretations. These are interpretations meant to uncover some buried secret, which the patient would respond to with an "aha," leading to all her secrets being revealed. It reminds me now of an old *New Yorker* cartoon, around the time when "walk" signs first became prevalent on busy New York streets. In the cartoon there is a man on crutches waiting to cross the street. When the sign changes to "walk," the man throws away his crutches and begins to walk across the street. In short, my "aha" interpretations were designed to have a similar effect with my patients. Most of the time these interpretations brought about a "huh?" reaction rather than "aha." However, I had no way of understanding at the time how to change my way of working. My psychological testing experience led me to understand something wasn't right in my way of interpreting buried content, but it didn't help me to think about how to work differently.

Of course, I had studied two crucial texts in Freud's move from the topographical model (i.e., "The Ego and the Id," and "Instincts and their Vicissitudes"), as part of my psychoanalytic training. However, with instructors who probably didn't grasp the technical innovations inherent in these papers, as most didn't at the time, I couldn't see their meaning myself until much later. Further, as you will see in my early papers, Freud himself was ambivalent about the potential changes in technique suggested by his new findings, and the same was true for those who followed. This is somewhat understandable in that once one experiences what seems like the power of an interpretations of deeply buried material (probably based on a number of factors other than working through a central conflict), it is difficult to re-learn the slower methodical process of working through the Ego's unconscious resistances via their preconscious derivatives.

I've told this story before, but it's worth repeating. At a meeting of the International Psychoanalytic Association, an analyst spoke from the audience about a case that had been presented, and a lightbulb went on in my mind. He was saying things that gave me a glimpse into what I'd been trying to understand. As I briefly collared him before he ran off to another meeting, he suggested I read the work of Paul Gray. When I returned to the United States, I avidly started to read Gray's work, which was the starting point for the next 30 years of my writing. While there were many things I learned from Gray's writing, central for me was his perspective that one component of a successful interpretation was to connect to something the patient can understand in spite of ongoing resistances. For the next ten years Gray's work influenced my writing. As an aside, the analyst who led me to Gray's work was Cecilio Paniagua, who was supervised by Gray, and later moved back to his home city of Madrid. He became a life-long friend.

The next phase of my work, beginning around 2000, was inspired by my wife, the psychoanalyst Cordelia Schmidt-Hellerau, herself a highly regarded writer. Trained in Switzerland, reading authors unfamiliar to us in United States at the time, she opened my mind to new ways of thinking. I started to write on what happens in the mind of an analysand in a "good enough" analysis, and what are the analytic methods that might best bring this about. This led to discoveries of the importance of the analyst's words, building representations, paying attention to the analytic *process* and not just the content, new ways of thinking of transference, a model for understanding the patient's words as actions (i.e., language action), etc. This resulted in my 2013 nook, *Creating a Psychoanalytic Mind*. In addition, I've questioned aspects of the relational approach, and also explored the Bionion and post-Bionian concept of the analyst's reveries.

Throughout my psychoanalytic life I've met many wonderful people, and many writers who inspired me. It was fascinating to read the early work of Heinz Hartmann and David Rapaport to see how they struggled to expand the purview of psychoanalytic thinking at the time. However, the new area they built, called "Ego Psychology," was greeted with antipathy outside the United States, was difficult to apply to clinical technique, and disappeared shortly after their deaths until revived by Gray, whose primary focus was clinical. Besides the work of Gray and Paniagua in my earlier work, and Schmidt-Hellerau in my later work, the writings of Andre Green, Marilia Aisenstein, and French psychoanalysts as exemplified in the editorship of Dana Birksted-Breen et al in their volume, "Reading French Psychoanalysis" opened new vistas for me. Otto Kernberg, Stefano Bolognini, Elias and Elizabeth Rochas de Barros, and Michael Diamond are amongst my most admired thinkers, along with Michael Feldman.

A word about the organization of this book. The role of the Ego as the arbiter of what is allowed in the patient's mind is the centerpiece of my thinking, along with its function in modulating anxiety. I don't always refer back to these concepts in my later work, as I attempt to find some common ground with seemingly disparate theories. Thus, I have started this selection of papers with two of my recent publications before returning to my earliest ones, to give a broader picture of my work. I have rarely re-read my papers once they were published, as I've always had another writing project I wanted to pursue. In reading these papers again now, I was pleasantly surprised they've stood the test of time. Today, I would say that when I described consciousness in some early papers I was really talking about the preconscious. I describe my understanding of the preconscious in Chapter Nine, "A Shadow Concept: Preconscious Thinking."

I have not included early papers that didn't deal with issues of technique as I believe my most important contributions have been in the area of the psychoanalytic method. I have included a full list of my published work for those interested.

Finally, when I've presented my ideas as papers and clinical workshops throughout the world, analysts trained in very different psychoanalytic cultures can see the wisdom in my ideas. It has been gratifying and a bit surprising. I hope the reader will find in these pages something new and interesting, maybe surprising, but most of all something that opens one's eyes to a fresh way of thinking about psychoanalysis.

Fred Busch
Chestnut Hill, MA, USA

1 Our vital profession

We've all heard the depressive views of our profession: the impossible profession; our dying profession; the pain of being an analyst; a dangerous profession, etc. Today, I am here to present our profession in a different light—the vital profession. I will not be Pollyannaish in presenting my view, as at times, our work is painful, and seemingly impossible. However, when we forget the vital nature of what we do, it can sometimes feel even more painful, impossible, dangerous, and daunting, and we forget about the endless possibilities of the mind.

From its beginning to the present, psychoanalysts have been working to help their patients find or re-find the core of what it means to be alive and human—that is, the human mind. No matter what our theoretical perspective, we are all trying to open up spaces in a patient's mind that were previously closed off, and in this way, we help them re-find their mind. Our colleague, Marilia Aisenstein, captured this vital nature of our endeavor when she stated:

> Analysis is uncompromising in relation to other therapies because it alone aims … at aiding our patients to become, or to become again, the principal agents in their own history and thought. Am I too bold in insisting that this is the sole inalienable freedom a human being possesses? (2007, p. 149)

One of Freud's great discoveries, not put in these terms, was to help us realize that we all are living in a movie, with ourselves as writer, main character and director, driven by unconscious forces and the many defenses against them. However, like in Woody Allen's movie, *The Purple Rose of Cairo*, where the character steps out of the screen to try and create a different life, we try to help our patients discover the movie they've been living, the forces that led them there, the dangers they fear in changing, and in this way help them to live the story of their choosing. It is one of the most important goals of psychoanalysis to help the patient gain the capacity for story-telling, and momentarily step outside the story and observe it as her story. The process of initiating this change is what I've called Creating a Psychoanalytic Mind (Busch, 2013b), which is unique to psychoanalysis. We try to set in motion a creative process that only the patient can complete, and in this way change the inevitability of actions into the possibility of reflection. What a momentous gain!

I think most of us have had the experience I will describe. It was early in my analysis when a song repeatedly came to mind. It was the Beatles singing, "Here Comes the Sun." In words, music and the Beatles' ability to capture a joy in living, the song indicated the lifting of my depression; the emergence of memories unavailable for many years; and the happiness associated with them. The thoughts and feelings were not something I could have consciously put in words at the time. Over the years this song reappeared throughout my analysis. What I want to highlight with this memory is that a song came to mind in analysis, persistently and unbidden, when I was ready, that helped me re-find a part of my mind, my experience, and my feelings—that had been lost to me. My mind had been closed off to a part of me that was the essence of who I was, who I could become, and who I then became. This is why I see psychoanalysis as vital. We try to give back to our patients the one indispensable component of being human—their mind—and the freedom and creativity that come along with it.

So yes, while psychoanalysis is, at times, an impossible, painful, and dangerous profession, let us not forget its vital nature. It offers our patients a new vigor in living.

The vitality of our method

Regardless of which Freud we follow, the important differences we have in our models of the mind, and some of the specific variances we have in analytic technique, there have been paradigm shifts in some of the most basic ways we approach our patients that serve as a new common ground among seemingly disparate points of view (Busch, 2013a).[1] These changes are based upon insights from colleagues from different perspectives over the last 40 years. Yet the profundities of these breakthroughs seem hardly to have been noticed. I think this is because these changes have been the result of an evolutionary process that led to their gradual incorporation into clinical practice, rather than the revolutionary methods some newer theories proclaim.[2] What we see are changes based on clinical practice within a broadly defined Freudian-based model,[3] while incorporating other views of psychoanalytic technique. Let me start with a story.

The girl on the beach

Sitting on a beach I notice a young girl, looking for seashells about 15 feet from the water, in a place where there are very few shells. After a while her mother, who is there quietly helping her, says, "Would you like to go closer to the water, where there might be more shells?" The little girl says "yes," but for some time continues looking in the same spot. A while later she moves closer to the water where she begins to pick up numerous shells.

I would suggest this observation might serve as a model for a current view of psychoanalytic technique. First let us deconstruct the event. The young girl is searching in a place where it is difficult to find what she seeks. She is like our patients who, caught up in unconscious conflict, keep looking for something to solve their problems, but end up searching in the same place and finding the same problems. The mother doesn't tell her daughter to stop what she's doing or get frustrated with her but wonders with the girl if it might be helpful to search for what she seeks somewhere else. In the mother's wondering I would like to highlight the following. The little girl is not told what to do, she isn't forced to search elsewhere, she isn't told where she's looking is wrong, but rather given a choice to explore somewhere else, someplace she hasn't thought of yet, or might never have thought of on her own. In this way she is given agency to make her own decision. The little girl apparently thinks this is a fine idea but keeps searching in this same area that has not led to promising results. There is some resistance to moving away from her spot. The mother doesn't make any further suggestions or give any other ideas, but after a while the little girl decides on her own, to move towards more fertile ground, and ends up with her desires fulfilled.

An everyday clinical moment

The patient, a 50-year-old literature professor, began a session by talking about the difficulty he had this morning in presenting to a committee on funding and in relating with his graduate students. For example, when talking with members of the committee he realized he wasn't being specific enough, and in going over the work of his graduate students he realized they knew much more about the literature in their subjects than he did. He rationalized this at first by saying, of course he couldn't know the literature in depth on every topic but realized that this was a problem he had in general—that is, getting into the literature. He then told of his secretary coming into his office to inform him of some changes in the university's retirement plan, and he felt angry that she was bothering him with this. He had a sense there was something connecting all these events but couldn't quite get it.

This difficulty in connecting his associations had been a prominent issue in the analysis for a while. The analyst then said to the patient, "It's my impression that in these situations there is something about getting into details that you find aversive." The patient replied, "I knew there was something like that, but I just couldn't get into…(there was a pause as the patient searched for the word)…the details (he laughs)." The patient then said, "I just remembered a part of a dream. Pause. This is embarrassing. In the dream I had a bowel movement, and I couldn't get myself clean. I can't remember anything else. I always want to be so clean." The analyst then said, "Maybe the dream is telling us why."

Like with the mother of the "girl on the beach," the analyst isn't telling the patient to look somewhere for his problem with an interpretation, rather he first helps capture the patient's problem expressed in his associations via a new representation (i.e., problem with details). The patient then remembers a dream, which suggests that by not getting into the details he is enacting a fantasy of making a shit mess. He then defends against this by saying how clean he has to be, like the girl taking her time before going closer to the water. The analyst doesn't try and force him back into the mess, but helps the patient see that his defense of being clean is related to the wish to make a mess.

There are two additional, related factors about this clinical vignette that I'd like to draw your attention to. The first is that I think it would be difficult for many to guess the analyst's theoretical perspective, and the second is the analyst's approach integrates certain changes in how we think of technique to be elaborated in the next sections. As a preview, in his first intervention the analyst follows the patient's associations to make an unsaturated (Ferro, 2002), analyst-centered (Steiner, 1994), clarification (Bibring, 1954) in the here and now (Gray, 1994; Joseph, 1985) to represent a preconscious (Green, 1974) defense in the manner of Anna Freud (1936). It leads to a dream that elaborates the unconscious meaning of the defense, followed by an undoing, which is brought to the analysand's attention with another unsaturated, analyst-centered intervention.

Our changing methods

The two most significant paradigm shifts in clinical psychoanalysis came about with a change in focus from working directly with the unconscious, and searching for what has been repressed, to the general recognition across theoretical perspectives that it is important to work more closely with what is preconscious, and the emphasis on building representations of what was previously un-thought, or under-represented, as well as what was repressed. These changes are designed to make our interventions more understandable and emotionally meaningful to our patients, based on our increasing understanding of the mind from a variety of psychoanalytic sources. For too long we've labored under the belief that we needed to interpret in a way that the patient directly experienced his unconscious (Strachey, 1934), without taking into account all that needed to occur before unconscious ideation or feelings could be meaningfully taken into awareness.[4]

Preconscious thinking

We have moved from primarily confronting the patient with what the analyst gleans from the patient's unconscious, to working more closely with what the patient is able to hear, understand, and potentially integrate. In this way we've realized that in order to help a patient grasp how they are ruled by unconscious fantasies, self-states, conflicts, etc., these have to first become understandable.[5]

Except for the French school, preconscious thinking has remained a "shadow concept" (Busch, 2006), if a point of consideration at all. In 1915,

Freud tried to strictly distinguish between unconscious and preconscious thinking on the basis of "word presentations" and "thing presentations." However, buried in this paper is Freud's puzzlement over the fact that "A very great part of this preconscious originates in the unconscious, has the characteristics of its derivatives, and is subject to censorship before it can become conscious" (1915, p. 191), and that there are thoughts that had all the earmarks of having been formed unconsciously, "but were highly organized, free from self-contradiction, have made use of every acquisition of the system Cs., and would hardly be distinguished in our judgment from the formations of that system" (1915, p. 190, my italics). Thus, in contrast to everything else he'd written in this paper, Freud briefly conceives of complex preconscious thinking with infusions of unconscious elements. In these few sentences, Freud, still in his topographical model, presents a view of preconscious thinking that goes from a permeable border of the system Ucs. to the permeable border of the system Cs.[6]

If understood in this way, there are various levels of preconscious thinking at which we are working that make our task more complex. For example, the sexual derivatives that appear early in the treatment of a hysterical patient would be worked with differently compared to similar derivatives that appear in the later phases of an obsessional patient. While the hysterical patient's sexually tinged associations may seem like they are close to consciousness, they are more often closer to the unconscious border and hence more difficult to bring to awareness. The sexual derivatives in the obsessional's associations are more likely the result of the hard work of analyzing defenses, and thus more easily interpretable.[7] As we are dealing with two different levels of psychic organization, we adjust our interventions to the ego's functioning, or to put it in Bionian terms, we metabolize for the patient what he can then further metabolize.

Building representations

As noted by Lecours (2007) and many others, what is represented can continue to build structure and enhance the ability to contain psychic energies. This leads to what Green (1975) called "binding the inchoate" (p. 9) and containing it, thus giving a container to the patient's content and "content to his container" (p. 7).

Anytime we name a vague something that was, as yet, unnamed we attempt to represent it with a word. Any ime we discover and enhance meaning that previously resided in a suspended space, or capture meaning in a meaningful way to the patient, that seemed meaningful (to the analyst) but without meaning at the time (to the patient), we are on the way to building a representation. The representation we build can be as delineated as a word, as complex as a metaphor, or as fleeting as an Ogden waking dream. Whether it becomes something that is representable for the analysand, depends on many factors, including how close it comes to what is tolerable at that exact clinical moment (i.e., the patient's capacity to transform the elements of his familiar thinking into a new gestalt). After each intervention we see what the patient can make of it at that moment. We can call it the work of the alpha function or his ego function. Decisive is whether the patient can allow our interventions to work on his mind.

Representations are not absent or present but are there in a variety of forms. In broad brushstrokes when we talk about building representations in psychoanalysis, we are talking about separate but related issues. The first is building a more nuanced, complex representation out of a highly saturated,[7] simple one. The second is developing a beginning representation from its more primitive, non-symbolic representational origins. Further, one can think of representations as having multiple dimensions: they may range from deeply unconscious to close to the preconscious (Busch, 2006); from simple to complex with varying degrees of saturation. In this model, building representations means attempting to make representations more complex, bring them closer to consciousness, and less saturated (or more nuanced). For example, at times we try to build a representation from one that is conceptually primitive (e.g., somatic representations). With a rigid, highly saturated, simple representation that is close to consciousness (i.e., all men are animals, ego psychology is superficial), we attempt to make the representation more complex and less saturated (e.g., some men are thoughtful and sensitive, maybe there is a valid contribution to be made by the contemporary ego psychologists' approach to the method of psychoanalysis). With a more complex representation that is unconscious, we would attempt to bring the representation to increasingly higher levels of preconsciousness.

Clinical implications

There are certain changes in our methods of working that flow directly from the paradigm shifts I've noted above. All have to do with how we enable the patient to build and accept new representations and bring what has been warded off and under-represented to preconscious awareness. Increasingly we have paid attention to the manner in which we bring our observations and interpretations to the patient's awareness, and the profound effect this has on the patient's ability to use what we say. It is another way of looking at the two-person nature of psychoanalysis, while holding on to our understanding that it is the inner life of the patient we can help change. In what I'll describe, you will find the innovative ideas of psychoanalysts from different perspectives that have contributed to the vitality of contemporary psychoanalysis.

Interpreting "*In the Neighborhood*" (Busch, 1993)—Freud first articulated this principle when he warns a young physician on the uselessness of wild interpretations, by which he meant interpretations the patient wasn't ready for:

> If knowledge about the unconscious were as important for the patient as people inexperienced in psycho-analysis imagine, listening to lectures or

reading books would be enough to cure him. Such measures, however, have as much influence on the symptoms of nervous illness as a distribution of menu-cards in a time of famine has upon hunger … Since, however, psycho-analysis cannot dispense with giving this information, it lays down that this shall not be done before the patient must, through preparation, himself have *reached the neighborhood of what he has repressed*. … (1910, pp. 225–256, italics added)

By introducing the concept of the analysand needing to be "in the neighborhood," Freud is noting, amongst all the principles of clinical technique, the centrality of the preconscious. No matter how brilliant the analyst's reading of the unconscious, it is not useful data until it can be connected to something the patient can be preconsciously aware of.[8]

Listening to discussions of the clinical process, one is impressed with how many interpretations seem based less on what the patient is capable of hearing, and more on what the analyst is capable of understanding. Maybe it's only that the presenter didn't bring the audience into the neighborhood of what he did, but maybe we too often confuse our ability to read the unconscious with the patient's ability to understand it. We are frequently not clear enough on the distinction between an unconscious communication and our ability to communicate with the patient's unconscious. What the patient can hear, understand, and effectively utilize—let alone the benefits of considering such an approach—are only gradually entering the foreground of our clinical discussions.

Green explained it this way: "I support the Freudian concept of the ego in which the patient's freedom is respected and which allows one to proceed according to what the patient is able to understand of what we are saying to him at that point in time of the treatment, i.e., permitting him to elaborate and integrate in a regression-progression process, and so to proceed from the most superficial to the deepest level" (1974, p. 421). In fact, as I've noted previously (Busch, 2013a), analysts from widely varying theoretical perspectives (e.g., Ferro, 2003, pp. 189990; Baranger, 1993, p. 23; Ikonen, 2003, p. 5; Bion, 1962, p. 87) are increasingly attentive to the ways we think about the "neighborhood" as a guide to the patient's capacity to understand and utilize an intervention in an emotionally and cognitively meaningful manner, and the ways the analyst functions that may foster or hinder this process.

Clarification—Edward Bibring's (1954) introduction of this concept never received traction as a defined method of psychoanalytic technique. I think it was because in his writing he limited the use of clarification to material that was close to consciousness. However, in reading the examples he provides, what he describes are actually clarifications of derivatives of unconsciously motivated thinking that are preconsciously organized. This latter way is an important use of clarification, as well as the need to clarify the patient's unconscious use of words as actions (i.e., language action). This differs from an interpretation, where we try to raise unconscious meaning to awareness. Betty Joseph emphasizes a similar process when she suggests the elucidation of those ways in which the patient (for example) creates tone and atmosphere for understanding or against understanding. She argues that only when this is clarified, which often takes repeated demonstrations, is it helpful to move toward understanding the reasons or motives for such behavior.

The reason for the need for clarification is simple—in the midst of conflict a patient's thinking is concrete (Busch, 1995, 2009).[9] He can only think about what is immediately present. For long periods of time, and even when the patient is freely associating, he is incapable of keeping track of the sequence of his thoughts while talking. It requires a great deal of time before we can make an interpretation that may be a word, or metaphor, capturing in a short form the essence of a reverie, and have some hope the patient will understand it in a non-intellectual fashion. What is missing earlier in treatment is the patient's capacity to follow his own thoughts, and integrate them at a higher level of abstraction (Busch, 1995, 2009).[10] Most analysts would agree that this is the level on which an analysand is functioning through much of his analysis—he *thinks, but he cannot think about his thinking. (added) What is this number 7?*Thus, in order to make progress, the patient needs to experience an interpretation, but to do this we need to clarify what he's been doing or saying that led to our interpretation.

Countertransference—The discovery of the importance of countertransference thoughts and feelings as a crucial source of information in the psychoanalytic situation has been one of our most significant advances. Beginning with the pioneering work of the Kleinians on projective identification and followed by so many others, we've come to realize its significance in understanding every patient at some point in their analysis, and its importance in understanding other patients from the moment they walk into our consulting room. After a time of fierce debate change took place, and now I know of no theory that dismisses the importance of countertransference feelings in understanding our patients. However, we also need to heed Hanna Segal's (Hunter, 1993) warning that countertransference is our best servant and worst master. As essential as it is as a tool in our analytic work, it also provides data that is difficult to sort out and translate. In response to the patient we may grow anxious, impatient, or withdrawn. If we have a psychoanalytic mind we can notice and reflect on these occurrences, without having to act, while re-cognizing that a certain amount of acting on our countertransferences is in-evitable (and sometimes useful in understanding).

A particular problem that analysts face is that we often feel forced by the patient into what seems like an alien position, which can drive us to push back and force the patient to accept his own unconscious. At these times the countertransference interpretation seems to result from a wish to expel what is transferred back onto the patient. "You feel this way, not me" we seem to be saying, while meaning to be exploratory or interpretive. It is a way of the analyst getting rid of something uncomfortable stirred in his own un-conscious.[11] Another problem we face is when we seem to treat our coun-tertransference reactions as an unerring guides to the patient's behavior—what

I call "the Descartian Somersault" (i.e., I think therefore you are). Further, it can be a formulaic way of warding off deeper, more conflicted feelings,[12] which is understandable given that countertransference reactions are first registered unconsciously.

In the face of a countertransference reaction it takes considerable restraint, narcissistic balance and an ongoing self-analytic capacity to maintain our role of empathic and reflective participant-observer and forestall the pull towards enactment. Without a capacity for introspection and self-inquiry about these countertransference feelings it is difficult to see how one could sort out these unique moments created by the two participants.

Interpsychic Communication—Bolognini (2011) introduced the term *interpsychic*, to capture the conscious and unconscious dialogue of two interacting people—patient and analyst—"a territory for which we have only barely been able to find words—despite all the words that are in use for it" (Schmidt-Hellerau, 2011, p. 447). Diamond (2014) shows the contributions and acceptance of this term, *interpsychic*, from a wide variety of psychoanalytic cultures (although not labeled as such). In short, this term *interpsychic* broadens the field for the analyst to include a number of states of mind, often thought of as separate, to both understand the patient and demonstrate, without teaching, how the analyst is thinking. In working with the interior of one's mind in response to the patient, there are important ethical and clinical considerations that aren't always noted.

Diamond warns,

> As with every technical innovation, especially the current emphasized use of the analyst's mental experience, there is an ever-present danger of misuse as well as possible ethical transgressions. When taken to extreme, this can lead away from the patient's psychology and center on the analyst's or the dyadic process per se. (2014, p. 531)

Therefore, it is wise to keep in mind that this method is only part of our analytic method to be used. We need to listen to the analysand and ourselves polyphonically to appreciate how best to listen. Finally, how we translate our inner thoughts into usable interpretations is something that is still to be fully understood.

Analyst-Centered Interpretations—Steiner introduced an important clinical term—"analyst centered interpretations"—for working with more disturbed patients where, "The priority for the patient is to get rid of unwanted mental contents, which he projects into the analyst. In these states he is able to take very little back into his mind" (1994, p. 406). He goes on to say that the patient feels threatened if the analyst continues to tell him what he (the patient) is thinking or feeling, as this is what is projected on to the analyst as a way of getting rid of these feelings. I would suggest this is in sync with a solid ego psychological position where the paranoid-schizoid patient's regressed ego functions are taken into consideration.

I would add that analyst-centered interpretations are useful in the full spectrum of pathologies, especially early in the treatment, and throughout the treatment when new regressions emerge. This is because all of our patients are dealing with unconscious thoughts and feelings that are terrifying to know about, as they are associated in the patient's unconscious mind with the most frightening terrors known to man. Therefore, any way we can work to ease these terrors while analyzing them will benefit the patient.

Learning from Steiner's basic idea but modifying it from his work with borderline and psychotic patients within a Kleinian perspective, I have often found the following approach central to help patients open their minds to a new way of thinking of themselves. The basic premise of the method is to wonder with the patient about the analyst's impressions rather than telling the patient they are something, or what she's truly feeling or thinking. This latter way seems more common in clinical practice, as when the analyst says, "You are angry at me, and cannot tolerate it, so you imagine me as angry." An analyst-centered approach seems to help the patient observe something about herself without the sense of being told she is a particular way, which may be harder to internalize in the early phase of treatment as it can often bring a severe super-ego reaction. This is especially true with moments that are clearly important, but more difficult for the patient to observe because of their in-effable quality. Later in treatment an analyst-centered interpretation is useful when something unconscious is about to emerge, which if addressed too directly, would lead to it being repressed again.

Language Action—First identified by Freud (1914), this concept captures a patient's way of talking that is unconsciously meant to do something. At these times words become attempts to bore, seduce, anger, or excite the analyst. This was evocatively captured by McLaughlin when he stated words, "become acts, things—sticks and stones, hugs and holdings" (1991, p. 598). While it seems like the patient is describing a dream, an upsetting event, or complaining about a spouse, the analyst feels mocked for his interest in dreams, blamed for the patient's bad luck, or faced with a demand for unconditional love.

We've been aware of the consequences of language action for some time, as it often leads to the analyst's countertransference reaction. However, the significance of clarifying how language action is expressed before identifying its effects or its unconscious meaning has only become evident more recently (Busch, 2009, 2013b; Joseph, 1985). We can hear this approach in Feldman's (2004) description of Joseph's work when he says, her assumption is "that real psychic change is more likely to be promoted by the detailed description of how the patient is using the analyst, using interpretations, or using her mind in a given session, and then to move on to the way the patient's history, and unconscious phantasies express themselves in the immediacy of the processes and interactions in the session" (Feldman, 2004, p. 28). That is, we try to understand what a patient is doing with us in their words, tone, phrasing of sentences, and ideas expressed. Once we recognize our countertransference reaction to language action, and reflect upon it, this action has already begun to be transformed, that is, represented within the mind of the analyst. From here the analyst can translate the language action into words, which gives the patients increasing degrees of freedom to think and feel.

It is important to remember that the entire range of psychic states can be expressed in language action. My sense is that in our countertransference re-action to language action, we've overemphasized what the patient is doing to the analyst, rather than what he might also be doing for himself (e.g., repairing a fragile self- state).

Working in the Here and Now—In 1914 Freud observed, "we must treat his [the patient's] illness not as an event of the past, but as a present-day force" (p. 151). How often this insight was employed, and the manner in which it was used, has varied over time. However, many analysts now view the psy-choanalytic session as primarily a series of psychic events happening before the patient and us, and therefore as the ideal time to intervene (e.g., Joseph, 1985). As the patient is most often thinking in a concrete "before the eye" reality (Busch, 1995, 2009, 2013b), it is easiest for him to potentially observe himself in the immediacy of what is happening in the session (i.e., in accordance with the level of his ego functioning). Much of what we work with (i.e., asso-ciations, language action, affect shifts, etc.) is most accessible for the patient as it is occurring in the session. As the patient is able to contain more, and becomes a better observer of himself, the analyst is freer to move comfortably between present and past sessions, while interpretations become more meta-phorical or enigmatic.

I want to make clear I am not suggesting we restrict psychoanalytic work to the dynamics of what is present in the analytic situation. Understanding the past in the present is crucial to enliven our patients' sense of who they were and who they are. Understanding the past in the present helps build more complex re-presentations. Additionally, we often see how working in the here and now leads to a memory from the past that sheds light on the present, while what is going on in the present gives depth to how the past affects the present, further differentiating what is there from what used to be. Finally, Bell's (2014) timely caution on this topic is important to note: "Focus on understanding of psychic reality can at one moment serve to deepen understanding, whilst at another can become, in a subtle way, an enactment, creating an illusion that history and life outside the consulting room are of little importance."

Points of difference

In spite of our growing commonality, there are, of course, significant differ-ences in how psychoanalysts from various cultures practice. At our best we confirm Schafer's observation, "our differences show us all the things that psychoanalysis can be even though it cannot be all things at one time or for any one person" (1990, p. 52). I will briefly mention only a few areas (i.e., transference, countertransference, and defense analysis), and then focus on the problems we have in talking with each other.

• Transference: The major differences we have revolve around the following: While at an unconscious level the transference may always be in the room, how useful is it to interpret it at this level while the analysand defends against it?—How necessary is it to bring it into the room and when?

   • The viability of working in displacement.

• Countertransference—One significant difference in psychoanalytic cultures is the degree we view countertransference reactions as the result of the patient's projective identification, or a number of other possibilities. The ways we use our countertransference reactions also vary. Some use it to interpret directly back to the transference, while others share their reactions as part of the interpretive process, or to confront the patient, etc. I tend to agree with Jacobs' view that "our understanding of countertransference, a complex, multiply determined entity that has multiple and complex effects on our patients, is still quite incomplete" (2002, p. 24). Further, since countertransference reactions are primarily unconscious, our understanding only can occur over time.

• Defense analysis—Significant differences exist between those who believe the feelings or fantasies that cause a defense can be interpreted directly, versus those who believe that the fears underlying a defense need to be understood first, before the feelings and fantasies can be brought to the fore. While most often not specified, the differences underlying these methods depend upon belief in Freud's first or second theory of anxiety (Busch, 1993).

Engaging the other[13]

Our field has recently worked diligently to try and overcome regional bias via the introduction of CAPSA programs pioneered by Claudio Eizirik and re-instated by Stefano Bolognini, and the invitation to colleagues from other perspectives to discuss our clinical material at local and inter-regional meetings. Being inclusive in this way, we've learned a great deal about how others think, and we've come to respect the value other perspectives bring. However, we still have a ways to go. How often have we been at a meeting where there is a panel where clinical material is presented from one perspective, and a first discussant reinterprets the material from his perspective, and the second discussant does the same, and then the panel is over after a few comments from the audience. Often the audience is left baffled, as there is little attempt to discuss why one way of looking at the material might be an improvement for this or that reason, at this point or another in the analysis that could then be discussed. Depending on one's predilections, we root for one view or another. It is my impression that for too long, each "school" has tended to guard the purity and effectiveness of its own position. We only quote those from our same team and go to meetings where members of our team are presenting. For practical and transferential reasons we find it difficult to leave our home base, and to try to do so is sometimes interpreted as an attack. The danger we face is demonstrated in a well-known experiment, the invisible gorilla (Chabris & Simms, 2010), where subjects were asked to watch a short video in which six people—three in white shirts and three in black shirts—pass basketballs around. While they watched the video, they were asked to keep a silent count of the number of passes made by the people in white shirts. At some point, a man in a gorilla suit strolls into the middle of the action, faces the camera, thumps his chest, and then leaves, spending nine seconds on screen. Over 50% of people missed seeing the gorilla. In short, if we hold to our theories too tightly, we might miss seeing the multiple gorillas in the room.

So, in the end we have to acknowledge that even for us well-analyzed psychoanalysts, change can be difficult. After working for years to master a particular way of thinking about the psychoanalytic method, our comfort zone can be threatened when faced with different perspectives. It is my impression that it is still rare for someone in these groups to be moved by the views of another. I am well aware of my own resistances to engaging with (for me) new thinkers, even though I had the benefit of a gentle, thoughtful guide, trained in European psychoanalysis, who happened to be my wife. My recent work is a testament to our ongoing exchange.

It is my impression that the most promising changes in our field will come from our attempts to overcome our anxieties and engage with each other on the nitty-gritty of clinical work. This would require what our gifted colleague and president said when he noted that we have to come out of our own "shadow zone," where we hold on to excessive simplification of the theoretical field. "The symptom of this shadow zone is precisely the incapacity for an interchange with the "non-self," which is unconsciously feared as dangerous and too disturbing" (Bolognini, 2011, p. 11). In order not to succumb to the danger of petrification we would do well to heed the wise words of Eizirik, "that our training never ends, and that, among other wise counsels, Freud left us the idea that from time to time we need to return to the analytic couch and be helped to regain the closeness with our unconscious" (2010, p. 375).

So here we are again as psychoanalysts from around the world, trying to learn and talk to each other, while trying to learn how to talk and listen to each other. But why do we continue, I wonder, when it seems so difficult for us? I think it's because what binds us together is our passion for psychoanalysis. We've seen what it can do for us, and our patients, and in spite of the antagonism we face from other perspectives, we deeply care about this legacy from Freud, and our sometimes, perilous journey as we look into the future at this congress.

Notes

1 This follows in the tradition of the work of Wallerstein (1988) and Kernberg (1993), which was based "on the increasing attention given to the actual principles of technique

that flow from alternative psychoanalytic theories, in contrast to 'clinical theories' derived from these various formulations" (Kernberg, 1993, p. 659).

2 It is interesting that often, when one of us discovers a new perspective on psychoanalysis, it is presented as a replacement theory rather than an addition to be integrated with what is already known.

3 I am referring to those models in the international community that use Freud's view of understanding the unconscious interior of the analysand's mind as the basis for treatment, although not the only factor.

4 In this same journal Sterba (1934) presented a view of reaching the unconscious via analyzing resistances, more in line with Freud's second theory of anxiety, where dangerous thoughts or feelings threatening to become conscious set off anxiety in the unconscious ego. It is a method that is based on analyzing the unconscious anxiety as a part of bringing the unconscious into awareness.

5 Green was one of the earliest proponents of the importance of the preconscious in our interpretive work. This perspective was captured succinctly in his statement, "There is no point in the analyst running like a hare if the patient moves like a tortoise" (1974, p. 421). As I've noted previously (Busch, 2013b), similar statements can be found in the diverse work of Paul Gray, Betty Joseph, Nino Ferro, and the Barangers.

6 Freud remained ambivalent in clinically moving from the topographic model, and his first theory of anxiety, to the structural model and his second theory of anxiety (Busch, 1992, 1993; Gray, 1994; Paniagua, 2001, 2008).

7 In my use of Ferro's (2002) concept, if a thought or feeling is highly saturated with meaning it has a highly cathected, specific meaning. In contrast, a thought or feeling that is less saturated refers to it being not so limited by a specific meaning, allowing for greater freedom to play with it.

8 However, as I've noted elsewhere (Busch, 1992, 1993), Freud struggled with holding to this principle throughout his writings.

9 As I understand it, Marty (Aisenstein & Smadja, 2010) uncovered a very similar way of thinking in psychosomatic patients, which changed the way these patients were treated. However, we've learned since then that this type of thinking is characteristic of most patients in areas of conflict.

10 This way of thinking has been described as "pre-symbolic" (Basch, 1981), "pre- conceptual" (Frosch, 1995), "concrete" (Bass, 1997; Busch, 1995, 2009; Frosch, 2012) and "preoperational" (Busch, 1995, 2009).

11 This may be especially true at those times Grinberg called "projective counter-identification" (1962, p. 346).

12 Schwaber's perspective is one that is always important to keep in mind. "We must employ our view, or experience—even vigorously so—as an avenue to finding the patient's—as long as we recognize ours for what it is—how it seems from within our vantage point—and listen with this realization" (1998, p. 659).

13 In this paper I've only engaged with those theories in the Freudian tradition, where the emphasis is primarily on the transformation of what is unconscious into representable form. Although other theories like self-psychology and relational psychology have added a great deal to our understanding of the analytic situation, placing themselves as separate paradigms has made it harder to include them in this discussion. I believe with Rangell (2004) that the paths of reform sometimes "eschew adjustment and turn instead to an opposite extreme, with a disregarding of gains won in the past, and a depreciation of many of the original assumptions and goals of psychoanalysis" (p. 6).

References

Aisenstein, M. & Smadja, C. (2010). Conceptual framework from the Paris Psychosomatic School: A clinical psychoanalytic approach to oncology. *Int. J. Psychoanal.*, 91:621–640.

Aisenstein, M. (2007). On therapeutic action. *Psychoanal. Q.*, 76S:1443–1461.

Baranger, M. (1993). The mind of the analyst: From listening to interpretation. *Int. J. Psychoanal.*, 74:15–24.

Basch, M. F. (1981). Psychoanalytic interpretation and cognitive transformation. *Int. J. Psychoanal.*, 62:151–175.

Bass, A. (1997). The problem of concreteness. *Psychoanal. Q.*, 66:642–682.

Bell, D. (2014). *Knowledge as fact and knowledge as experience: Freud's constructions in analysis.* New York: Presentation to the Contemporary Freudian Society.

Bibring, E. (1954). Psychoanalysis and the dynamic psychotherapies. *J. Am. Psychoanal. Assoc.*, 2:745–770.

Bion, W. R. (1962). *Learning from experience.* London: Tavistock.

Bolognini, S. (2011). *Secret passages.* London: Routledge.

Busch, F. (1992). Recurring thoughts on the unconscious ego resistances. *J. Am. Psychoanal. Assoc.*, 40:1089–1115.

Busch, F. (1993). In the neighborhood: aspects of a good interpretation and a "developmental lag" in ego psychology. *J. Am. Psychoanal. Assoc.*, 41:151–176.

Busch, F. (1995). Do actions speak louder than words? A query into an enigma in psychoanalytic theory and technique. *J. Am. Psychoanal. Assoc.*, 43:61–82.

Busch, F. (2006). A shadow concept. *Int. J. Psychoanal.*, 87:1471–1485.

Busch, F. (2009). Can you push a camel through the eye of a needle? *Int. J. Psychoanal.*, 90:53–68.

Busch, F. (2013a). Changing views of what is curative in 3 psychoanalytic methods and the emerging, surprising common ground. *Scand. Psychoanal. Rev.*, 31:27–34.

Busch, F. (2013b). *Creating a psychoanalytic mind: A psychoanalytic method and theory.* London: Routledge.

Chabris, C. & Simms, D. (2010). *The invisible gorilla.* New York: Crown.

Diamond, M. (2014). Analytic mind use and interpsychic communication. *Psychoanal. Q.*, 83:525–564.

Eizirik, C. (2010). Analytic practice: Convergences and divergences. *Int. J. Psychoanal.*, 91:371–375.

Faimberg, H. (1996). Listening to listening. *Int. J. Psychoanal.*, 77:667–677.

Feldman, M. (2004). Supporting psychic change: Betty Joseph. In: E. Hargreaves & A. Varchekver (eds.), *In pursuit of psychic change* (pp. 20–35). London: Routledge.

Ferro, A. (2002). *In the analyst's consulting room.* Hove: Brunner-Routledge.

Ferro, N. (2003). Marcella: The transition from explosive sensoriality to the ability to think. *Psychoanal. Q.*, 72:183–200.

Freud, A. (1936). *The ego and mechanisms of defense.* London: Karnac.

Freud, S. (1910). "Wild" psycho-analysis. *SE* XI.

Freud, S. (1914). Remembering, repeating and working through. *SE* XII:145–156.

Freud, S. (1915). The unconscious. *SE* XIV:159–215.

Frosch, A. (1995). The preconceptual organization of emotion. *J. Am. Psychoanal. Assoc.*, 43:423–447.

Frosch, A. (2012). *Absolute truth and unbearable psychic pain.* London: Karnac.

Gray, P. (1994). *The ego and analysis of defense.* Northridge, NJ: Jason Aronson.

Green, A. (1974). Surface analysis, deep analysis (The role of the preconscious in psychoanalytical technique). *Int. Rev. Psychoanal.*, 1:415–423.

Green, A. (1975). The analyst, symbolization and absence in the analytic setting (On changes in analytic practice and analytic experience): In memory of D. W. Winnicott. *Int. J. Psychoanal.*, 56:1–22.

Grinberg, L. (1962). On a specific aspect of countertransference due to the patient's projective identification. *Int. J. Psychoanal.*, 43:436–440.

Hunter, V. (1993). An interview with Hanna Segal. *Psychoanal. Rev.*, 80(1):1–28.

Ikonen, P. (2003). A few reflections on how we may approach the unconscious. *Scand. Psychoanal. Rev.*, 26:3–10.

Jacobs, T. J. (2002). Secondary revision. *Psychoanal. Inq.*, 22:3–28.

Joseph, B. (1985). Transference: The total situation. *Int. J. Psychoanal.*, 66:447–454.

Kernberg, O. (1993). Convergences and divergences in contemporary psychoanalytic technique. *Int. J. Psychoanal.*, 74:659–673.

Lecours, S. (2007). Supportive interventions and non-symbolic mental functioning. *Int. J. Psychoanal.*, 88 (4):895–915.

McLaughlin, J. T. (1991). Clinical and theoretical aspects of enactment. *J. Am. Psychoanal. Assoc.*, 39:595–614.

Paniagua, C. (2001). The attraction of topographical technique. *Int. J. Psychoanal.*, 82(4):671–684.

Paniagua, C. (2008). Id analysis and technical approaches. *Psychoanal. Q.*, 77(1):219–250.

Pickert, K. (2014). The mindful revolution. *Time Magazine*. 3 February.

Rangell, L. (2004). *My life in theory*. New York: Other Press.

Rizzuto, A. (2002). Speech events, language development and the clinical situation. *Int. J. Psychoanal.*, 83(6):1325–1343.

Schafer, R. (1990). The search for common ground. *Int. J. Psychoanal.*, 71:49–52.

Schmidt-Hellerau, C. (2011). Secret passages: Review of Bolognini's book. *Psychoanal. Q.*, 81:443–455.

Schwaber, E. A. (1998). From whose point of view? The neglected question in analytic listening. *Psychoanal. Q.*, 67:645–661.

Steiner, J. (1994). Patient-centered and analyst-centered interpretations: Some implications of containment and countertransference. *Psychoanal. Inq.*, 14:406–422.

Sterba, R. (1934). The fate of the ego in analytic therapy. *Int. J. Psychoanal.*, 15:117–126.

Strachey, J. (1934). The nature of the therapeutic action of psycho-analysis. *Int. J. Psychoanal.*, 15:127–159.

Wallerstein, R. S. (1988). One psychoanalysis or many? *Int. J. Psychoanal.*, 69:5–21.

2 The search for psychic truths

> What is new about analysis is that it is the only discipline which considers the search for truth itself therapeutic. Not truth with a capital "T" because you can't find that, and it changes. But the fact is that the search for truth, for *psychic truth*, is the therapeutic factor. (Segal quoted in Hunter, 1993, pp. 9–10)

Hanna Segal's pithy summation raises many issues germane to the intriguing question posed by the Editor of *The Psychoanalytic Quarterly*, "Is truth relevant?" in psychoanalytic treatment. For example, Segal shifts the target of inquiry from *truth* to *psychic truth*. Further, she sees the search for psychic truth—not finding truth—as *the* therapeutic factor in psychoanalysis. Segal also believes there is no single "truth," but rather changing truths that we find in psychoanalysis. I generally agree with Segal's views and will elaborate my own reasons for this position.

However, certain questions come to mind. For example:

- What is psychic truth?
- To whom is the question about truth directed—the patient and/or the analyst?
- What type of truth are we talking about—e.g., historical truth, unconscious truth, or some other type?

As one can see, in trying to discuss truth in psychoanalysis the investigator can quickly feel as though he is falling down the rabbit hole with Alice, or, depending on one's metaphorical preference, engaging in a conversation with Abbott and Costello regarding "Who's on first?"

As a general guideline to what follows, I view psychoanalysis as a way to understand the *psychic* truths that guide a patient and the conflicts they cause, and this is the basis of the curative process. At a very basic level, there are many "truths" in psychoanalysis to be wondered and reflected on. Overemphasis on "known" truths can inhibit thinking rather than freeing it. Further, as Collins (2011) concluded after a thorough review of the literature: "There seems to have emerged a broad understanding that historical truth cannot be unequivocally known due to the role of unconscious fantasy and due to it being constructed in a temporality with its own current influences and perspectives." (p. 1406)

Interpretations from the analyst assigning truth (e.g., "you are angry because you see me as…etc.) may interfere with the patient's own search for psychic truths. In certain psychoanalytic cultures, the analyst's approach has gradually shifted so that the analyst attempts to *create the conditions* in which insight is possible, rather than giving insight per se. It is an important part of a new paradigm for psychoanalytic treatment. (Busch, 2013)

In my way of thinking, the search for psychic truths is *the* domain of psychoanalysis. Uncovering the significance of psychic truths in the minds of our patients, ones that lead to painful inhibitions and self-destructive behavior, is our heritage from Freud, and it is the search for these psychic truths I see as the one indispensable part of a psychoanalytic treatment aimed at helping patients lead a fuller life.

What are psychic truths?

A patient begins a session by talking about her interaction with her colleague, Harold, with whom she has had a flirtatious relationship. Does it matter how the interaction *really* went? I do not think so! In my mind, what matters psychoanalytically is *how she has thought of the interaction* (i.e., is she excited, guilty, rejecting, etc.) and why, *and* (possibly) *what it means to the patient that she is telling me this story*. This is what I think of as *psychic truth*.

With modifications (to be elaborated later), I have the same point of view when a patient tells me something from his past. In fact, I think that the search for "real" truths in psychoanalysis can lead away from psychic truths. The tendency to seek out past events and interactions as the sole cause of our patients' fears, rage, and unhappy relationships can turn the focus away from the fantasies that also drive patients' reactions (Busch, 2005). Further, the search for truths—rather than *psychic* truths—can lead patients to look for Answers with a capital *A,* which often stops thinking, rather than doing what I see as one important component of what psychoanalysis has to offer: i.e., fostering the capacity to think freely about whatever comes to mind, observe it, and play with it. The creativity needed to deal with the inevitable enactments and psychic inhibitions after psychoanalysis terminates is blocked if one can search for answers only in what on has learned in analysis.

There are many other important factors necessary for a successful psychoanalysis to take place; I see these as *necessary but not sufficient*. In my way of thinking, the search for *psychic truths* is *the* domain of psychoanalysis. Uncovering the significance of psychic truths in the minds of our patients, ones that lead to painful inhibitions and self-destructive behavior, is our heritage from Freud, and it is the search for these psychic truths I see as the one indispensable part of a psychoanalytic treatment aimed at helping patients lead a fuller life.

Psychic truths are embedded in *the stories a patient has in her mind that impel her to certain ways of being.* It is what leads her to come to an analyst for help. Inherent in these stories are facts and fiction, reality and fantasy that speak about the patient's experiences and how she thinks of them. Thus, it is through stories that psychic truths appear in psychoanalytic treatment. Compromise formations and other psychic mechanisms inform these stories and disguise their truths. Yet in whatever way they appear, it is the patient's *inner world* that holds her psychic truths, which in turn show us how she experiences and relates to the world.

In fact, patients come to us with all kinds of stories in mind. These are the stories of who they are and how they came to be that way. They also come with stories about important people in their lives and what kind of people these are. Soon in treatment, we ourselves become part of their stories. Some of these stories are conscious; some are not. Some have become unconscious because they were too dangerous and repressed. Other stories have been stored only through varying degrees of pre-representational thought, so that they cannot be put into words. Some stories started as actions driven by dimly perceived, exciting urges (e.g., a four-year-old boy poking his mother with a toy gun, stick, or other pointy object) or have evolved into other reactions when what drives the action comes close to awareness.

Another way of formulating this issue is that we are always dealing with stories remembered but never integrated—the stories experienced but never formulated, the stories experienced and remembered only in the language of action, the stories of unconscious fantasy and defense, and the importance of all these in every other story. Another, more technical categorization might be that these are the stories of compromise formations and screen memories (representational thought)—stories enacted due to unstable structures or to thoughts represented in pre-operational terms. In short, these are the stories of lives interrupted, manifested analytically in rigidly held and fearfully unknown or incomplete stories.

One does not hear much about what I consider a fairly typical analytic experience: that is, the repetition of key stories throughout an analysis, where something new is added that allows for greater understanding of the stories within a story. For example, a small kitchen utensil was involved in a story that ran through the analysis of one patient, Ian. Early in our work, Ian, a 20-year-old undergraduate, told me of having asked his mother what this utensil was and of being told to leave her alone. Within the context of the analysis at that time, it seemed to represent how neglected he often felt by his mother as she struggled with depression. Later, though, Ian told me how furious his mother became when he and a friend played with this utensil. At that time, we understood it as an example of his mother's difficulty in appreciating his curiosity. Still later in the analysis, after I had interpreted Ian's growing provocativeness with me, he remembered that his mother had not gotten mad at him until he and his friend started playing soccer with the utensil. Later still, after a sexual dream that took place in a kitchen, Ian finally identified the kitchen utensil as a V-shaped slicer. The last part of the story emerged as the analysis was ending, when Ian remembered that this slicer had been a present from his father to his mother.

We can see that, over the course of this analysis, the "kitchen story" became the "kitchen *stories*." Altogether they made up some of the stories of Ian's difficulties in forming relationships with women. The emerging stories were not the result of repressed memories coming to consciousness; Ian always knew the different parts of his kitchen stories. But the parts emerged in analysis only in the context of current concerns. This is why I use the plural in speaking of the stories that compose psychic truths. Further, there is nothing more inhibiting to the patient's freedom of mind than for patient and analyst to believe that they have

I believe the view of psychic truths outlined above is now the dominant one in most psychoanalytic cultures (Busch, 2013). It is a different way of thinking about this issue from the past. Our way of deepening these stories has changed in that, for the most part, we now *search for what is there in the patient's words and actions,* rather than *primarily searching for what is not there.* One of the most compelling moments in my psychoanalytic training occurred when, after a scientific presentation by a senior analyst, one of the training analysts present asked if the patient had an undescended testicle. A gasp arose from the audience, and the now slightly befuddled presenter acknowledged that this was indeed the case.

In one way or another, the search for the truth of what was deeply hidden (not necessarily what was unconscious) was, for many of us, the guiding light of our own analyses and of the cases we analyzed. Over time, however, it has been my sense that this approach is not helpful because, while the patient often appreciates the analyst's brilliance, his internal experience is one of being caught or found out and he becomes wary of what else the analyst might see that he is hiding, resulting in increased defensiveness. In such cases, it is often the patient who ends treatment while in the throes of an unanalyzed, idealized transference, feeling no better about himself than when he began treatment.

Kleinian analysts have been the group most associated with psychic truth. As described by Blass (2011), this means *deep unconscious truth* (or *unconscious truth of the mind*), and uncovering it is portrayed as *the* work of psychoanalysis. While I see this as one important part of psychic *truths*, I think it is more accurate, as well as more parsimonious, to consider *levels of psychic truth.* Further, I think it is not helpful to the analytic work if we speak only to what we believe to be the patient's unconscious truth. For example, if a patient believes she admires the analyst, but the analyst believes the patient unconsciously hates him, we need to take into account both sides of the situation in order for the patient to accept an interpretation along these lines. As Paniagua (1991) noted, we are always working with three surfaces: what the patient thinks is on his mind; what the analyst is thinking this means; and what is the *workable surface* (i.e., an amalgam of what the analyst is thinking and what the patient can be aware of in the analyst's thinking).

Others have pointed out that the most effective *interpretive truths* are those that are *preconsciously* available (Busch, 2013; Green, 1974; Kris, 1950). Blass (2006) describes how Joseph worked closer to the preconscious, and as Feldman (2004) pointed out, Joseph showed "continuing efforts to clarify and formulate the experience that is actually available to the patient at the moment" (p. 23). In fact, over the last few decades, it has become clear that most schools of thought consider the work of analysis to take place at a variety of levels of psychic truth (Busch, 2013). As another example, writing from a Bionian perspective, Ferro (2005) highlights that "there is not *an unconscious to be revealed,* but a capacity for thinking to be developed, and…the development of the capacity for thinking allows closer and closer contact with previously non-negotiable areas" (p. 102, italics in original).

What about trauma?

The issue of truth in working with trauma patients raises many challenges. Most of the patients I have worked with have experienced cumulative trauma, primarily in the parents' lack of attention to the developing, healthy narcissistic needs of the patient (Kohut and Wolf, 1978). As most of the memories I hear have a consistency over many years, and are of events that occurred at an age when memory is reliable, and as these memories are repeated in the transference-countertransference, I do not often doubt the veracity of the narcissistic deprivations that my patients tell me about. I agree with Collins (2011) when she concludes that it is most useful to think of whether an experience had authenticity: "that is, whether it possesses *emotional genuineness that originates within the unique analytic encounter*" (p. 1403, italics in original).

Kris (1956b) famously pointed out that autobiographical memories often serve a defensive purpose and may become heir to unconscious fantasies. In my clinical work, I have noted that I have never seen a patient in psychoanalysis in whom there has not been some form of interference in healthy narcissistic development that has led to *unconscious fantasies of causation and solution, resulting in intrapsychic conflict* (Busch, 2005). For example, a child's egocentric view of the world leads him to experience his depressed mother's inability to nurture and mirror his healthy demands as evidence of his excessive needs. Thus, the ongoing trauma of a lack of mirroring leads to his needs becoming associated with unconscious fears of deadness, abandonment, and guilt. In analysis, when he begins to feel needful toward the analyst, these internal dangers pull him back to an inhibited emotional stance.

Thus, in my experience, it is not only the trauma itself that remains traumatic. Inevitably, the *feelings and fantasies stimulated by the trauma* become part of a dangerous intrapsychic truth. In this way, *a trauma also becomes part of an intrapsychic conflict.* Thus, it seems to me that analytic work has to be informed by attunement to empathic breakdowns, past and present, and to their effects on the patient's psychic life both within and outside the analysis, *while the analyst also listens for the resultant unconscious fantasies and intrapsychic conflict*—i.e., the psychic truths.

Grand et al. (2009) sum up the current position of many when they state their view that:

> Traumatic experience requires both a narrative and a historical excavation. Neither, alone, is sufficient to the nature of trauma. When we oppose these two epistemological perspectives, we are engaging in a false, and inadequate, polarity. I think we are slowly evolving toward a new epistemological Zeitgeist, which will allow us a better way to reckon with trauma. This shift will find a new term, which will embrace (and surpass) historical and narrative truth. (p. 11)

Over time, I have changed my way of evaluating patients for psychoanalysis, and whether the patient and I are a good fit, in that I no longer ask about the patient's history. For the most part, I find that if the analysis is going well enough, a patient brings up a piece of history when it is relevant to what is on her mind. Further, I have found that inquiring too much about the patient's history often gives her a stereotyped vision of psychoanalysis: that is, that the analyst is searching for something in the patient's past that will provide an answer to her problems. I have also come to realize that a patient will often use his history as a defense against further explorations of what is on his mind. Statements such as "That must be because of my depressed mother" often signal an end to a line of thought, rather than leading to more thoughts.

I will not enter into the thicket of *recovered memories*. Articles by Brenneis (1994, 1996) and Good (1996, 1998) portray the complexity of this issue. My understanding is that recovered memories from the child's very early life have questionable validity. Among his main arguments against the role of "remembering" in psychoanalysis, Habermas (2014) points to the fact that the first two or three years of life are the "dark ages of every subjective life story" (p. 952). What he means by this is that these experiences are not linguistically encoded and cannot be remembered except via action tendencies (Busch, 2009; Freud, 1914) or in vague sensations or affect states. The patient is subject to being convinced of a cohesive story put together from these elements, but it cannot be remembered. Further, Oliner (2012) cogently argued that because an event seems as though it would be traumatic does not make it so. In my own work, I have never rarely helped a patient recover a memory of trauma; rather, when a patient brings up a new memory in analysis, it is always something the patient has always known, but it is the changing landscape of what is allowed into the patient's mind that leads to the "new" memory.

Psychic truths from the patient's perspective

A reader might observe at this point, "So far you've given us *your* definition of *psychic truths*, but what about the question of whether the patient's psychic truths are *true*, and does it matter?" My simple but definitive answer is, "It depends!" Let me explain! From the perspective of psychoanalytic treatment, *the patient's psychic truths are always true*. No matter what the analyst's feeling about it may be, or how contradictory it might appear from other things the patient has said—or even that what the patient says may be an objective distortion of reality (e.g., the patient is sure the analyst was ten minutes late for a session)—the task of the analyst is to understand how this psychic truth has come to be, not to question its existence. Whether a psychic truth is real becomes a more complicated issue when reality is cited as a basis for this truth, especially the reality of the patient's feelings about the analyst's way of being.

To elaborate on these issues, let me present a clinical example.

Alex is in his fourth year of analysis. He has made great strides, professionally and personally. A central transference has been his coming into sessions with the feeling that I would give him a grade, and his eventual graduation from analysis depended upon his grade point average. Another important transference was Alex's frequent reinterpretation of the analyst's interpretations, so that the meaning was either changed or only vaguely reflected.

In a pivotal session, Alex says:

You were really hard on me yesterday. Well, not really. Afterward I felt this explosion in me. I could see how I really do this thing we talked about—disregarding someone else and taking over.

What Alex seems to be responding to is that, in the previous session, he described how a junior member of his firm had gotten mad at him after Alex rewrote his report; Alex had misunderstood some of the report's background data. Alex realized he had only a vague idea of what the report was for but felt he wanted to help out, as he frequently does with others.

His description of this led me to say the following, also in the previous session:

> While you're appreciated in your firm for how helpful you've been to junior members, your description of this interaction reminds me of the situation here with me and how we've talked about your tendency to take what I say and only vaguely remember it or change it into something different.

This led him to realize that, as with me, he was unable to listen carefully to what this junior colleague was saying, getting only the gist. His thoughts then went to a meeting in which a colleague had misunderstood *him*, and how much this had pissed him off.

Was it true that I was hard on Alex? *From the perspective of his psychic truths, of course it is true.* This is *his* story of what happened the previous day and the meaning he made of it. While he seemed responsive to what I said at the time, did it end up feeling too wounding to his self-image as a "nice guy"? Was I, in his mind, the junior person who did not need to be listened to? I also wondered if, in his use of the phrase *hard on,* Alex might have experienced my reflection of the previous day as part of an exciting sado-masochistic interchange. This was an element of the ongoing transference. *There is no way of knowing a priori whether any of these ideas were related to Alex's psychic truth; we can learn more only by continuing to listen.*

On the other hand, was it true in reality that I was hard on him? While this is an important issue for the analyst to reflect upon, I have found that the analyst also needs the patient's help in understanding the psychic truth for the analyst when something like this happens. *But is the truth of Alex's statement relevant here?* I would say "yes," primarily because it has significant consequences if it is representative of an aggressive countertransference stance on my part.

In short, when Alex says, "You were really hard on me yesterday," it is important to appreciate the statement's psychic truth—and also to consider the truth of what happened in reality when the analyst conveyed his ideas, because of its counter-transferential significance. In reflecting upon what I had said in the previous session, I had a sense of triumph when I realized that what Alex described as happening with his junior colleague was similar to what frequently happened in our work together, which I was often puzzled by. But why triumph, I wondered? I felt frustrated at times by Alex's bland denials of any transferential meaning when he changed what I said into vague generalizations. In my early training as an analyst, as was typical at the time, there was a quality of "gotcha" to the kind of interpretations that were recommended... i.e., the analyst not only found something the patient was trying to hide, but it was often something not pleasant about the patient. Hidden aggressive motives were a favorite. But why had I regressed to this earlier way of working? What came to mind was that earlier in the day I heard about an article I had written and submitted to a journal that I thought the editorial reviewers had misunderstood, and I was irritated. I could see now that hearing about Alex's misunderstanding of his colleague's work and the subsequent "editing" he did potentially set off an unconscious response of irritation in me. However, over the years I have become aware of how easily we can fall into the trap of false positives in evaluating our countertransference reactions, even when our own reflections seem so convincing. Thus, I feel I have to wait to explore the patient's psychic truth before forcing my own psychic truth onto him.[1] I agree with Spillius's view (Roiphe, 2000) that "not all the analyst's thoughts during the session are evoked by the patient, and not all of the analyst's self-understanding will be clinically relevant" (p. 575).

To return to my session with Alex, we can see how the patient immediately negates his feeling about the analyst, when after saying I had been hard on him, he adds, "Well, not really." An inner "explosion" (his word) follows, leading Alex to say that he understands the analyst's interpretation and can see it working elsewhere. However, his next thoughts go to a colleague who misunderstood him and his resultant anger.

At this point, I say: "I have the impression that, while you're trying to be reasonable about what I said yesterday, it seems like it felt harsh and misguided."

There are, of course, many psychic truths that one might try to identify and reflect upon in any session. In general, in my interventions, I try to speak to a psychic truth that will aid the patient in feeling the freedom to explore and reflect upon what is going on in his mind. In this interchange with Alex, I am responding to a conflict that he seems to be having in exploring the idea that I was hard on him.

Alex remembers having felt shaken up on leaving the prior session. He thought a lot about what I had said, and while he can see something in it, as he drove home, he found himself getting angry with other drivers who were blocking his way. He then found himself surprised by what he thought of next: he pictured himself in his parents' living room, terrified that he would spill something on the carpet and his mother would become enraged.

After Alex describes this, we have the following interchange.

F.B.: Given your reaction to the drivers after the session, it sounds like you felt like exploding at me, but to step out of line is to bring on an attack, leading you to temper your feelings.

Alex: [after a long pause] This is surprising. I'm thinking about the time in business school where I had these great discussions with this professor. I remember telling you how he invited me to his apartment and then made these moves on me. [pause] I wonder if I felt like your remark was like a sexual attack. [He laughs.] Wow! Now I remember that we've talked about this recently—how a "fuck you" can turn into a "fuck me." I have been able to feel recently how much I want to control things and have people do things my way—"it's good to be the king."[2]

The development of Alex's capacity for freer thinking in this session is captured by his ability to have a "surprise" thought. He finds himself thinking of the sexual advances of an older professor, which leads him to think in a particular way about what I said the day before (that there had been an aggressive sexual attack), and then in another way (a projection of his wish to sexually attack me). Alex then owns his dominating, controlling side without having to condemn himself, and in fact seems able to get some pleasure from being able to see it.

Is this one of those *blessed moments* (Aisenstein, 2014) in analysis, when the patient can find pleasure in his thoughts and enjoy parts of himself that were previously shut off from awareness, because they were experienced as unpleasant in threatening to come into awareness? Or was it a masochistic surrender?

What we can learn about psychic truths from this clinical example

While one example cannot be generalized to a truth, I think we can see that my acceptance of Alex's psychic truths (i.e., I had been hard on him, there was an "explosion," he was uncomfortable with negative thoughts about me) allowed him the freedom to consider other possibilities about what had happened in the previous session (i.e., that his wish to say "fuck you" could lead him to feel "fucked"). This freedom to think what was previously defended against is a central component of what is curative in psychoanalysis, as I have noted (Busch, 2013).

However, approaching the patient's psychic truths as *true* is different than considering them *real* (i.e., this is what really happened). the standpoint of my countertransference, I can see the possibility that I might have been "hard on him," and from his associations, we can see that there may have been an urge to see me in that way. Both may be true. Some analysts may have taken my countertransference reaction as an explanation of what really happened and told the patient about it. But it is my impression that this shifts the focus from the patient's experience to the analyst's, which can distort the session.

As noted earlier, all patients come to psychoanalysis with thoughts about certain events that were experienced as traumas and that helped form who they are. Of course, tragic events happen to us, and these events certainly shape who we are. We never doubt the traumatic effect of the sudden death of a parent at an early age, for example. However, as also noted earlier, what we cannot know before an analysis begins is *what the person makes of her trauma or its role in her subsequent life*.

Is truth revealed?

The goals of psychoanalysis have evolved in the last 40 years (Busch, 2013) in that: the patient's capacity to *know how to know* her mind has gained importance in comparison to *knowing what is in her mind* (Busch, 2009); there has been a shift in emphasis from what the patient thinks to the way in which she thinks (Ogden, 2010); the emphasis has changed from reconstructing history to building re-presentations (Green, 1975; Lecours, 2007); and we have learned the necessity of speaking to what may become preconsciously available (Busch, 2006; Green, 1974), rather than focusing on direct interpretations of the unconscious.

Together these changes have led to a paradigm shift such that the focus is now on psychic truths that emerge *in the here and now* of the session. In broad brushstrokes, all we need to know to help the patient comes from listening to his free associations and language action while reflecting on our own affect states and reveries. *The truth we now hope to reveal is what is going on in the patient's mind*. We remain interested in the possible forces that have led the patient to think or act in this way, but we no longer think of the revelation of such background data as curative in itself, but rather as a particular part of the curative process to be discussed in what follows.

I think it is preferable to think of the importance of *accuracy* rather than truth in what is revealed in psychoanalysis. That is, the analyst must be as accurate as possible in her understanding of what is going on in the patient's mind in order for her to have an effect on the patient. To elaborate, *accuracy means to bring something to the patient's mind that can be preconsciously felt and thought about,* without raising undue anxiety leading to defensive withdrawal. If not ex-perienced in this way, the analyst's words may be taken in by the patient as stilted knowledge…i.e., the patient now knows something, but it leads to nothing new.[3] The importance of the accuracy of an intervention plays a role in building more complex representations, which in turn gives a new way of understanding why experienced insight helps a patient function in new ways.

The slow demise of "you are…" interpretations

Previous generations of analysts saw their role as telling the patient who the patient *is*, especially with regard to the patient's unconscious. The analysand would come to know these unconscious *truths*, which would allow for "re-integration by the rational ego," in Blum's words (1979, p. 52). Blum saw this as a necessary part of structure building, which I also see as an important part of the psychoanalytic curative process.

However, there were a number of problems with such an approach. First of all, it did not help the patient to experience analysis as a process in which one comes to understand *how to know*. The analyst presented interpretations as facts, rather than as something to reflect upon and play with in a variety of ways. The patient was left with only what he had learned from the analyst.

There is certainly merit in the position that the more unconscious elements we can bring into awareness, the less likely that they will manifest in action. However, as I stated previously:

> There is another perspective to be considered, which is that the process of knowing is as important as what is known. It is my underlying thesis in creating a psychoanalytic mind that what is accomplished in a relatively successful psychoanalysis is a way of knowing, and not simply knowing. My experience in doing second analyses is that patients often come in knowing a lot, but they don't know how to know. They are stuck in knowing what they learned from their analyst in a previous treatment and can't continue to grow and develop when the exigencies of life arouse variations of previous anxieties. It can lead to a belief in a kind of knowing we might call formulaic intuition. (Busch, 2013, p. 10)

From this perspective, *knowledge* can be the enemy of *meaning*.

A second problem in the way we interpreted was saw ourselves as "truth tellers" about the patient's psyche. Difficulties with such an approach are: The main difficulties with such an approach are:

- The analyst becomes the *arbiter of truth*. He is the one who knows.
- The patient is left in the dark as to how the analyst knows these truths. They must be accepted on the basis of the analyst's authority. If accepted, these truths as understood by the analyst are the only truths the patient can know.

In fact, all we are really capable of communicating is our *impression* of what the analysand is telling us. Modified versions of the psychoanalytic method introduced by Steiner (1994) and Ferro (2002) are important additions in helping us move away from being the arbiter of the analysand's psychic world.

Steiner introduced the term *analyst-centered interpretations*. He described his way of working with more disturbed patients, in which "the priority for the patient is to get rid of unwanted mental contents, which he projects into the analyst. In these states he is able to take very little back into his mind" (1994, p. 406). He goes on to say that the patient feels threatened if the analyst continues to tell him what he (the patient) is thinking or feeling, as this is what is projected onto the analyst as a way of getting rid of these feelings.

Since all our patients are dealing with thoughts and feelings that are terrifying to know about, this method seems applicable to the full range of patients, not only those who are seriously disturbed. The basic premise of the method is to *wonder with the patient about the analyst's impressions,* rather than telling the patient that *she is a particular way,* or *what she is truly feeling or thinking.* This latter way seems more common in clinical practice, as when the analyst says, "You are angry at me and cannot tolerate it, so you imagine me as angry." An analyst-centered approach seems to help the patient observe something about herself without her having the sense of being told that she *is* a particular way.

Ferro describes what he calls *unsaturated interpretations.* He believes that "the interpretation should often be an unsaturated polysemous event that permits opening up of meaning and narrative development. The patient's constructive contribution must always be alive and active" (2002, p. 184). New thoughts need unsaturated space and the possibility to oscillate, as there is always a risk of advancing *stopper interpretations* that impede the development of thought. What I want to highlight here is Ferro's emphasis on interpreting in a way that opens up meaning, not stops it.

These ways of working can be seen in the following example. A patient began a session talking about how he enjoyed riding his motor scooter to his sessions in the summer. He loved being out in the early morning air, and he felt more able to look around and appreciate the scenery than when he drove his car. His thoughts then turned to the danger he sometimes felt when cars passed too close to him.

I said to him, "It seems to me you're saying that to do something you love is dangerous." I could have made a more specific interpretation about how the patient was experiencing the danger of his loving feelings toward me, or his homosexual anxiety, and I believe these statements would have been correct enough. However, this occurred at a point in the analysis when any direct interpretation of the transference that I made caused his mind to freeze. While this in itself was significant, it was not helpful to continue interpreting directly in the transference. Thus, I felt that working in this more *unsaturated fashion* gave the patient the best chance of opening his mind in a way that was acceptable to him.

Further, I began my observation with "it seems." In this way, I conveyed the idea that this was my *impression of* what he was telling me. Early in my career, I was warned about not being definitive enough and thereby giving the patient the impression I was too tentative; however, over time I have found that, by talking about my impression of what is going on—rather than telling the patient, "this is what's going on"—I can give the patient greater freedom to disagree and to follow her thoughts rather than mine.

Is truth revealed?

To return to the central question at hand, "Is truth revealed?" I suggest that a key component of the curative process in psychoanalysis is the discovery of the *multiple psychic truths* that have guided the patient's life, most often outside of awareness. However, it is not the discovery of these psychic truths in themselves that brings about change, but rather the effect that knowledge of these psychic truths (when worked through) *have on psychic structures.*

For example, think of the brilliant scientist who cannot get tenure after attempts at several universities. In his mind, the problem is that all universities are filled with small-minded people who resent his brilliance. While one can imagine that there could be a certain reality to his view, it remains a simple representation (i.e., no tenure = small-minded academics in positions of power). In analysis, we may discover 20 different factors that together have led to his fear of flying too high, and that he is unconsciously driven to shoot himself in the foot.

In short, the discovery of psychic truths allows for simple representations to become more complex ones. In fact, there has been a paradigm shift *across psychoanalytic cultures,* captured by Lecours (2007) as the movement from the goal of *lifting* repression to that of *transformation.* That is, rather than primarily searching for buried memories, we now attempt to transform what is under-represented into ideas that are represented in a more complex fashion. For example, we attempt to build representations as a way of helping the patient contain previously threatening thoughts and feelings so that he can move toward deeper levels of meanings. As noted by Lecours (2007), what is represented can continue to build structure and enhance the ability to contain. This leads to what Green (1975) called "binding the inchoate" (p. 9) and containing it, thus giving a container to the patient's content and "content to his container" (p. 7).

Finally, I would like to return to Segal's observation with which I began this paper: that the search for truth is in itself therapeutic. As noted earlier, this observation has not always been emphasized in our thinking. From my perspective, psychoanalysis is not only about discovered psychic truths; it is also a method of *searching for psychic truths*.

How does an individual find the psychic truths that are creating disturbing feelings when the exigencies of life inevitably turn against him? As I have tried to indicate, it is the understanding that *one needs to search for psychic truths, not merely look for answers* that is a central part of the curative process in psycho-analysis. It is this method that is more likely to lead to self-analysis, rather than identification with the analyst's functioning (which has been the primary way that the development of self- analysis has been hypothesized). I believe this is one of the central lessons that we have gradually learned, as noted by Segal at the beginning of this paper. The same basic idea was put forward some 250 years ago by the German author Gotthold Ephraim Lessing (1779). To paraphrase, he wrote that the true value of a man is not determined by his possession of truth, but rather by his sincere attempt to get to the truth; it is the pursuit of truth by which he extends his powers.

Notes

1 Renik (1995) gives an example in which his patient had a view of him as having been gentle with him the previous session, which Renik refuted with the patient. The problem I see with such an approach is that the analyst replaces the patient's psychic truth with his own, interfering with what I see as the necessity for the patient to feel free to explore his mind in whatever way he may want to. By essentially saying to the patient, "You may think that, but it's not the truth," the analyst becomes the arbiter of what is real, rather than the facilitator of the patient's freedom of thought.
2 This is a line from Mel Brooks modestly titled film *History of the World, Part 1* (1981), which I had used in the recent past to empathize with Alex's emerging pleasure in his success, a topic he was tentatively approaching.
3 I do not mean to suggest that every accurate interpretation (in all its meanings) always leads to a penumbra of associations. New understanding sometimes needs time to be reflected on.

References

Aisenstein, M. (2014). Fred Busch's creating a psychoanalytical mind: A psychoanalytical method and theory. *Rev. Fr. Psychanal.*, 78:1165–1172.

Blass, R. B. (2006). The role of tradition in concealing and grounding truth: Two opposing Freudian legacies on truth and tradition. *Amer. Imago.*, 63:331–353.

Blass, R. B. (2011). On the immediacy of unconscious truth: Understanding in Betty Joseph's "here and now" through comparison with alternative views of outside and within Kleinian thinking. *Int. J. Psychoanal.*, 92:1137–1157.

Blum, H. P. (1979). The curative and creative aspects of insight. *J. Am. Psychoanal. Assoc.*, 27(suppl.):41–70.

Brenneis, C. B. (1994), Belief and suggestion in the recovery of memories of childhood sexual abuse. *J. Am. Psychoanal. Assoc.*, 42:1027–1053.

Brenneis, C. B. (1996). Cause for skepticism about recovered memory. *Psychoanal. Dialog.*, 6:219–230.

Busch, F. (2005). Conflict theory/trauma theory. *Psychoanal. Q.*, 74:27–46.

Busch, F. (2006). A shadow concept. *Int. J. Psychoanal.*, 87:1471–1485.

Busch, F. (2009). Can you push a camel through the eye of a needle? Reflections on how the unconscious speaks to us and its clinical implications. *Int. J. Psychoanal.*, 90:53–68.

Busch, F. (2013). *Creating a psychoanalytic mind.* London: Routledge.

Collins, S. (2011). On authenticity: The question of truth in construction and autobiography. *Int. J. Psychoanal.*, 92:1391–1409.

Feldman, M. (2004). Supporting psychic change: Betty Joseph. In: E. Hargreaves & A. Varchekver (eds.), *Pursuit of psychic change.* (pp. 20–35) London: Routledge.

Ferro, A. (2002). Narrative derivatives of alpha elements. *Int. Forum Psychoanal.*, 11:184–187.

Ferro, A. (2005). *Seeds of illness, seeds of recovery.* New York: Brunner-Routledge.

Freud, S. (1914). Remembering, repeating and working-through (further recommendations on the technique of psycho-analysis, II). **S. E.,** 12.

Freud, S. (1915). The unconscious. **S. E.,** 14.

Good, M. I. (1996). Suggestion and veridicality in the reconstruction of sexual trauma, or can a bait of suggestion catch a carp of falsehood? *J. Am. Psychoanal. Assoc.*, 44:1189–1224.

Good, M. I. (1998). Screen reconstructions: Traumatic memory, conviction, and the problem of verification. *J. Am. Psychoanal. Assoc.*, 46:149–183.

Grand, S., Newirth, J., Stein, A., Itzkowitz, S., Pines, D., Sirote, A., & Sussillo, M. (2009). Violence and aggression in the consulting room. *Psychoanal. Perspect.*, 6:1–21.

Green, A. (1974). Surface analysis, deep analysis (the role of the preconscious in psychoanalytical technique). *Int. Rev. Psychoanal.*, 1:415–423.

Green, A. (1975). The analyst, symbolization and absence in the analytic setting (on changes in analytic practice and analytic experience): in memory of D. W. Winnicott. *Int. J. Psychoanal.*, 56:1–22.

Greenberg, J. (1996). Psychoanalytic words and psychoanalytic acts: A brief history. *Contemp. Psychoanal.*, 32:195–213.

Habermas, T. (2014). Dreaming the other's past. *Int. J. Psychoanal.*, 95:951–963.

History of the World, Part 1. (1981). A film written and directed by M. Brooks. Produced by Brooksfilms; distributed by 20th Century Fox.

Hunter, V. (1993). An interview with Hanna Segal. *Psychoanal. Rev.*, 80:1–28.

Kohut, H. & Wolf, E. S. (1978). The disorders of the self and their treatment: An outline. *Int. J. Psychoanal.*, 59:413–425.

Kris, E. (1950). On preconscious mental processes. *Psychoanal. Q.*, 19:540–560.

Kris, E. (1956a). The recovery of childhood memories in psychoanalysis. *Psychoanal. Study Child*, 11:54–88.

Kris, E. (1956b). The personal myth—a problem in psychoanalytic technique. *J. Am. Psychoanal. Assoc.*, 4:653–681.

Lecours, S. (2007). Supportive interventions and nonsymbolic mental functioning. *Int. J. Psychoanal.*, 88:895–915.

Lessing, G. E. (1779). *Nathan the wise.* London: Macmillan, 2004.

Loewald, H. W. (1975). Psychoanalysis as an art and the fantasy character of the psychoanalytic situation. *J. Am. Psychoanal. Assoc.*, 23:277–299.

Ogden, T. H. (2010). On three forms of thinking: Magical thinking, dream thinking, and transformative thinking. *Psychoanal. Q.*, 79:317–347.

Oliner, M. M. (2012). *Perspectives on psychoanalysis, personal history, and trauma.* London: Karnac.

Paniagua, C. (1991). Patient's surface, clinical surface, and workable surface. *J. Am. Psychoanal. Assoc.*, 39:669–685.

Renik, O. (1995). The ideal of the anonymous analyst and the problem of self-disclosure. *Psychoanal. Q.*, 64:466–495.

Roiphe, J. (2000). Countertransference, self-examination, and interpretation. *J. Am. Psychoanal. Assoc.*, 48:571–580.

Schwaber, E. (1983). Psychoanalytic listening and psychic reality. *Int. Rev. Psychoanal.*, 10:379–392.

Steiner, J. (1994). Patient-centered and analyst-centered interpretations: Some implications of containment and countertransference. *Psychoanal. Inquiry*, 14:406–422.

3   In the neighborhood

The phrase "IN THE NEIGHBORHOOD" comes from Freud's (1910) paper, "'Wild' Psycho-Analysis." In this paper, Freud tells of a woman consulting him after having gone to a young physician for problems with anxiety after a recent divorce. The physician diagnosed the women's problems as due to lack of sexual satisfaction and suggested various sexual activities as a remedy. Freud chided the physician for assuming that the woman's primary problem was a lack of information and providing this would result in cure.

> If knowledge about the conscious were as important for the patient as people inexperienced in psycho-analysis imagine, listening to lectures or reading books would be enough to cure him. Such measures, however, have as much influence on the symptoms of nervous illness as a distribution of menu-cards in a time of famine has upon hunger ... Since, however, psycho-analysis cannot dispense with giving this information, it lays down that this shall not be done before two conditions have been fulfilled. First, the patient must, through preparation, himself have reached the neighborhood of what he has repressed, and secondly, he must have formed a sufficient attachment (transference) to the physician for his emotional relationship to him to make a fresh flight impossible. (pp. 225–226)

By introducing the concept of the analysand needing to be "in the neighborhood" Freud is noting the centrality, among the principles of clinical technique, of the preconscious ego. The patient must be able to make some connection between what he is aware of thinking and saying, and the analyst's intervention. No matter how brilliant the analyst's reading of the unconscious, it is not useful data until it can be connected to something the patient can be preconsciously aware of. From this perspective the young physician Freud described did not consider what his patient might understand, let alone if she might find his intervention objectionable. The potential difficulties with this approach are succinctly captured by Freud (1910) in the following:

> Attempts to "rush" him at first consultation, by brusquely telling him the secrets which have been discovered by the physician, are technically

objectionable. And they mostly bring their own punishment by inspiring a hearty enmity towards the physician on the patient's part and cutting him off from having any further influence. (p. 226)

While few analysts would disagree with the necessity of their comments being in the same neighborhood as the patient's thoughts, it is my impression that this is a rule more honored in the breach. As with resistances, there is what Gray (1982) aptly describes as a "developmental lag" between our understanding of the concept at an intellectual level and an affective, clinically useful one. The analysand's fear of and unfamiliarity with unconscious thoughts and feelings (i.e., resistances), along with the importance of including the conscious ego in the working-through process, seem not to have been well integrated within our analytic empathy. Listening to discussions of the clinical process, one is impressed with how many interpretations seem based less on what the patient is capable of hearing, and more on what the analyst is capable of understanding. We too often confuse our ability to read the unconscious and the patient's ability to understand it. We are frequently not clear enough on the distinction between an unconscious communication and our ability to communicate with the patient's unconscious. What the patient can hear, understand, and effectively utilize—let alone the benefits of considering such an approach—are rarely in the foreground of our clinical discussions. Getting to the "real" unconscious fantasy still seems to be our primary therapeutic goal. This appears to be a remnant of the topographic theory we still struggle with.

Greenson is one of those psychoanalysts who offered generously of his clinical work. His wisdom and humanity were evident to all those fortunate enough to have heard his presentations, while his clinical examples elucidate and challenge us. It is in this spirit that I shall introduce an extended example from his work.

In the first year of his analysis, a young man comes into a session angrily denouncing a professor who lectures "without thinking of whether the students can follow." As he continues in this vein, he slips and says that he hates "to have him treat—I mean, teach me." He then challenges Greenson with the comment, "I suppose you will make something of that." When the patient continues to complain about the professor, Greenson makes a semi-resistance interpretation (i.e., where the resistance is noted but the intent is not to explore it but to get to what is being resisted). Greenson asks him, "Aren't you trying to run away from your anger toward me?" The patient acquiesces with some expressed doubt but returns with thoughts about feeling sorry for the professor because of rumors that his wife had recently committed suicide. He then returns to complaining about the professor as a "big shot," who "doesn't give a shit for me."

Greenson intervenes with the following comment: "Aren't you angry with me for going on my vacation next week?" The patient angrily denies this, accusing Greenson of sounding like he looked this up in a book, and making a universal analytic comment. Greenson notes his anger but tells the patient his "real" anger is over his vacation. The patient reluctantly agrees and presents some confirmatory data.

From the beginning of this vignette, Greenson seems not to consider what the patient may preconsciously accept. As with the analysand's complaint about his professor, he does not consider "whether the students can follow." The slip, which indicates the patient has already made the preconscious connection between his feelings about Greenson and the professor, is challenged. It is clear the patient is in a feisty mood, and connections between Greenson and the professor will not be welcome. This is the resistance that seems most closely available to consciousness. Greenson raises it but takes the further step of telling the patient that it is his anger toward the analyst that he is avoiding. Greenson clearly has something in mind, which he finally gets to, when he tells the patient he is angry about the analyst's upcoming vacation. However, there is nothing in the data to suggest that the patient might have any awareness that one might work with, except in the resistance, that he is really angry at Greenson, or that the reason has to do with Greenson's vacation. In bypassing the resistance, the patient's preconscious participation is left out of the analysis, except to passively accept the interpretation. Greenson's explanation for his remarks is that he saw the slip as an indication of the patient's anger, "but he refuses to accept this consciously" (p. 300). This is just the point. Where a patient is consciously and why he is there are also a crucial part of the analytic task. Consciousness is not something to be run roughshod over. Greenson's explanation is, "I believe it is necessary to pursue the resistances until one mobilizes a reasonable ego in the patient" (p. 300). In this one sees Greenson's tendency to confuse the resistance with the feelings behind the resistance. What he pursued were the patient's feelings of anger. What he did not pursue was the patient's reluctance to make a connection between Greenson and the professor (i.e., the most observable component of the resistance at that time). Furthermore, for patients, their conscious ego is always the most reasonable one. If we believe a patient is warding off something from consciousness, it is not our task to only bring this to their awareness. From the side of the ego, there is a perfectly good reason why it is being warded off; understanding this reason is a first step toward conscious acceptance of that which is being warded off.

This paper will be about the importance of paying attention to what Myerson (1981) aptly describes as the *analysand's ability to hear our interpretations*. It does not appear that this component of the analytic enterprise has been fully integrated into consistent usable techniques. Herzog (1991) notes that throughout Freud's work there is no systematic elaboration of consciousness, while Joseph (1987) concludes that Freud did not consider consciousness as particularly worthy of study. Possibly this situation might have been righted if we had access to Freud's missing metapsychological paper on consciousness. However, what we have been left with is a situation where, at best, we have taken as given the complex, detailed preconscious processing that goes on in psychoanalytic work. At worst, the importance of analysands' preconscious readiness to accept and use our interventions remains relatively ignored. I suggest that this developmental lag in integrating a central component of the interpretive process into clinical technique is, in part, a response to Freud's struggle with the integration of his clinical observations with theory, and the relative neglect of the clinical ego in the development of ego psychology. I shall elaborate on the importance of being "in the neighborhood" in the hope that this contribution might prove to be a step in conceptualizing an important but unfinished task in psychoanalysis—the illumination of the role of the ego in the psychoanalytic process.

Freud, his ambivalence, and some that followed

In his 1910 paper on "wild" psychoanalysis, Freud gently chides a young physician for his intemperate interpretation. The primary technical error Freud cites is the belief that the patient suffers from a type of ignorance, and that by informing the patient one will have cured the neurosis. Freud then highlights the significance of combating the resistances for the success of the analysis. However, toward the end of this article, Freud offers the following surprising caveat,

> "wild" analysts of this kind do more harm to the cause of psycho- analysis than to individual patients. *I have often found that a clumsy procedure like this, even if at first it produced an exacerbation of the patient's condition, led to a recovery in the end.* Not always but still often. (p. 227; italics added)

In this one passage Freud seems to renounce everything he has said heretofore. He now comes down on the side of the usefulness of even "clumsy" efforts to bring the unconscious wishes to consciousness, even if the initial effect is deleterious. The importance of being "in the neighborhood" now seems insignificant as an interpretive guideline. The emphasis on the patient's readiness to consciously accept an interpretation and all that it implies seems now to be disavowed. This is done even though most of what he said previously cautions against taking such an approach and expresses doubt about the usefulness of such a technique. The reason Freud gives for this turnaround is that he believes the young physician's remarks *"forced her attention to the real cause of her trouble, or in that direction, and in spite of all her opposition this intervention of his cannot be without some favorable results"* (p. 227). Freud's view now is that bringing the unconscious wishes into awareness has a generally positive, long-term effect on the patient, no matter how the wishes might be brought to the patient's attention. The beneficial outcome is seen as due to the conscious attention of the patient being directed toward the unconscious, even in the face of the resistances. The resistances are reduced to factors which "intensify the prejudices...against the methods of psycho-analysis" (p. 227).

How do we understand these contradictory views? One useful way is described by Lear (1990) as the contradiction between Freud the clinician, "who helped himself to empathic understanding," and Freud the theorist who "tried to fit psychoanalysis into the scientific image of his day" (p. 5). Freud the clinician understood early on that thoughts were kept out of awareness because of their being associated with frightening and overwhelming feelings. Therefore, his clinician side understood that analysands might be upset with the approaching awareness of unconscious thoughts, because of the unpleasurable affects associated with them. Thus, Freud's earliest clinical description of the ideas that fell prey to censorship is a complex amalgam of feelings and dangers. He states (1895) of thoughts that are censored, "they were all of a distressing nature, calculated to arouse the affects of shame and self-reproach and of psychical pain, and the feeling of being harmed; they were all of a kind one would prefer to have not experienced, that one would rather forget" (p. 269). This is the Freud who would understand the uselessness of attempting to bring an idea to consciousness until the intense negative feelings surrounding the idea had been ameliorated in some way. This is the Freud who instantly understood the folly of the "young physician's" remarks. This is the Freud who empathically understood the nature of resistances and kept them at the center of his clinical theory throughout his work.

Freud the theorist held three views in 1910 that are germane to our discussion. The first of these was that anxiety was the result of dammed-up libido. The psychic corollary to this was that only if a wish remained unconscious could it become pathogenic. The final view was that consciousness and unconsciousness existed at two different levels of representation, and only by joining these two levels could an unconscious idea become conscious. The characteristic of consciousness specific to our discussion is that it is represented by "word presentation." This is in contrast to the unconscious represented by "thing presentations." In this model the road to consciousness involves connecting the "thing presentations" to "word presentations." Thus, Freud the theorist could see how the "young physician" could reduce anxiety by putting into words, and thus making conscious, unfulfilled unconscious wishes. From this perspective it was the putting ideas into words that would remove them from the unconscious, and ultimately unblock the dammed-up libido. In short, Freud the clinician was drawn one way while Freud the theorist was drawn in the opposite direction. This distinction is one useful way to understand the contradictory advice Freud seems to be giving in this article on the handling of material in relation to being "in the neighborhood."

Throughout the rest of Freud's early technical papers there are references to this same topic, with Freud oscillating between his clinical and theoretical views. In "The Dynamics of the Transference" Freud's (1912) views are dominated by the necessity of bringing the unconscious thoughts to consciousness. He suggests that if the patient falls silent, this stoppage can be eliminated by assuring the patient that he is holding back thoughts about the analyst. "As soon as this explanation is given, the stoppage is removed, or the situation is changed from one in which the associations fail into one in which they are being kept back" (p. 101). In this we can see that the necessity of being in the same neighborhood as the patient is replaced by a more authoritarian stance. A year later Freud (1913) repeats what happened in the paper on "wild" psychoanalysis. At first, he repudiates the importance of bringing an idea to consciousness without first taking into account how objectionable it might be to consciousness. He notes "there was no choice but to cease attributing to the fact of knowing, in itself, the importance that had previously been given to it and to place the emphasis on the resistances which had in the past brought about the state of not knowing and which were still ready to defend that state (p. 142). However, by the end of this same page, Freud states, when referring to bringing repressed material into consciousness, "At first it arouses resistances, but then, when these have been overcome, it sets up a process of thought in the course of which the expected influencing of the unconscious recollection eventually takes place." This same oscillation occurs in later technical papers (Freud, 1914, 1916–1917).

While Freud does not specifically return to the topic of being "in the neighborhood" in later papers, the underlying issues are crucial to later theoretical developments. The importance of resistances being unconscious is a central component in the development of the structural theory (Freud, 1923). The analysand's readiness to accept interpretations into consciousness, and its relation to the unconscious resistances, become a central factor in the structural theory. Freud's (1926) second theory of anxiety comes much closer to capturing his earliest (1895) observations on those affects associated with keeping thoughts from awareness. However, it was left to others to continue to work on the clinical significance of this new integration of clinical empathy and psychoanalytic theory.

In Ann Freud's (1936) pioneering investigation of the ego, she notes, "we have realized that large portions of the ego institutions are themselves unconscious and require the help of analysis in order to become conscious. The result is that analysis of the ego has assumed a much greater importance in our eyes" (p. 25). From this perspective the centrality of the ego's ability to become aware of its own thought processes is highlighted and continues the thrust of Freud's attempts to integrate clinical observations with the theory of the analytic process. Searl's (1936) paper on technique is a clear integration of what was understood to that point on the importance of considering the patient's ability to "hear" interpretations, while anticipating many of the themes Gray was to return to some 35 years later. Her description of the importance of taking into account what the analysand is capable of becoming aware of, while pointing to the dangers of interpreting "absent content," shows a subtle and complex understanding of the implications for technique of the new ego psychology which was not consistent at the time (e.g., Reich, 1933). Fenichel (1941) succinctly described the principles under discussion here when he stated:

> Analysis must always go on in the layers accessible to the ego at the moment. When an interpretation has no effect, one often asks oneself:

"How could I have interpreted more deeply?" But often the question should more correctly be put: "How could I have interpreted more superficially?" (p. 44)

However, this line of thinking, which started out in such a promising fashion, soon reached a barrier. There are only scattered references to the concepts implied in the interpretive technique of being "in the neighborhood" over the next 30 years. E. Kris (1951) states that in second analyses interpretations that are closer to the surface often lead to significant improvements. Eissler (1965) highlights the importance of interpretations not being isolated from a patient's previous knowledge, while Loewenstein's (1972) concept of identification with the analyst's function is influenced by notions of the importance of autonomous ego functions in the interpretive process. Similar influences can also be seen in the work of Loewald (1960) and Myerson (1960). Why there was this long barren period seems partly related to Freud's ambivalence, and partly related to issues discussed in the next section.

However, it was not until the work of Gray (1973, 1982, 1986, 1987, 1990a, 1990b) that the centrality of the conscious ego in the interpretive process was returned to. No one to that point had approached Gray's meticulous attention to actual techniques in the interpretation of resistances that took into account the conscious ego. Inspired by his work a number of psychoanalysts have recently explored an area that has come to be known as the "analytic surface" (Davison et al., 1986; Levy & Inderbitzin, 1990; Paniagua, 1985). While the emphasis varies slightly, the analytic surface generally refers to behaviors that are observable and demonstrable to the patient. In these investigations the benefits of using the surface, especially in the understanding of resistances, are delved into and elaborated on in a way that gives increasing weight to the work of Gray. Thus, we seem to be on the verge of multiple explorations into the role of the conscious ego in the analytic process. However, before going further into our own investigation, it is important to look at another factor that may have inadvertently hampered psychoanalytic inquiry into the role of the ego in the psychoanalytic process— the development of ego psychology.

Hartmann's legacy

Possibly no one has captured Hartmann's place in psychoanalysis as well as Schafer (1970):

Heinz Hartmann's contributions to psychoanalytic theory (1939, 1960, 1964) rise up before the student of psychoanalysis as a mountain range whose distant peaks with their immense vistas and rarefied atmosphere it is scarcely possible to reach. And yet the student must not only attempt the arduous climb, he must try to get above that range so that he can include Hartmann's work within his own vision of psychoanalysis, for that work is not the whole of psychoanalysis, nor can it be the last word on psychoanalytic theory; it is and can only be part of the terrain of scientific psychoanalysis and of science generally. (p. 425)

While agreeing with Smith's (1986) view that we still need time to fully evaluate Hartmann's contributions, one is inevitably drawn to his work with regard to the topic at hand. In fact, in this area Hartmann's work has proven to be both an important contribution and an unwelcome diversion. While his work stimulated studies that added significant depth to our understanding of subtleties in ego functioning, his emphasis on psychoanalysis as a general psychology may have inadvertently contributed to a diversion from in-depth attention to issues of psychoanalytic technique.

Our understanding of human behavior was radically changed by Hartmann's views of early ego development and his call for research in child development. His view of the ego as an inborn adaptational structure with predetermined strengths and weaknesses interacting with and affected by an environment which was growth-producing or inhibiting, all since shown to be essentially correct by studies of early development, forever changed our view of the infant/child. This, in turn, opened the potential for a new way of understanding patients. To illustrate further, let me turn to a brief example.

A 35-year-old man came for a consultation because he felt life was passing him by. He did not actually "feel" this but knew from a distance that he had chosen a different life than peers and other family members. While super-ficially pleasant, he was restricted in what he could allow himself to talk about, and in the range of feelings he was able to show. He was able to talk fairly freely while picking and choosing his topics, but any question seemed like an unwelcome intrusion. At these times he would show flashes of anger which quickly faded and remained unobserved. His life was severely restricted. He was in a routine job in the family business, far below his seeming potential. He lived at home, had few friends, and had dated only sporadically since college.

Hartmann's influence looms large in how one might think of this brief vignette from an initial consultation. The restricted nature of the patient's ego functioning is most striking. The need for structure and control both in and out of the consultation is noteworthy, with the flashes of anger a seeming response to threats to his ego integrity. One begins to think of an ego under siege. Questions are raised about the patient's analyzability. Will he be able to tolerate the regressive components of the analytic situation? Will he be able to give up enough control to participate in the process of free association? With such severe, long-term restrictions in his ego functioning, is it not more likely these are due to developmental interferences rather than neurotic conflicts? Were there some interferences in his early "average expectable environment" that may have had a profound influence on early ego functions? Such ques-tions come directly from the work of Hartmann and the psychoanalytic in-vestigations into early development he spawned. The importance of the relationship between the infant/child and its caregiver for psychic survival, as well as a sense of self, cohesion, autonomy, individuation, along with tolerance for affects and affect regulation, have all been well documented by now (e.g., Emde, 1988; Mahler et al., 1975; Stern, 1985; Spitz, 1945).

Hartmann's work set the stage for a subtle approach to the understanding of those factors in the ego which affect acceptance into consciousness. The effect on conscious receptivity of thoughts to such things as: changes in ego states (e.g., fragmentation), regressions in levels of thinking (e.g., from formal operations to preoperational thought), and the degree to which communication is dominated by action are more easily comprehended because of the work of Hartmann. His inquiries and encouragement of others to map the developmental outline of the ego, have had the potential to provide a significant impact on our understanding of what is allowable into consciousness. However, it is not clear this potential has been realized as of yet. Much of the work of integrating alterations in ego functioning and their effects on the analytic work have taken place outside the structural theory, most notably in the studies of narcissistic and borderline pathology dominated by the self-psychological and object-relations theorists. As Apfelbaum and Gill (1989) conclude, the technical implications of the structural theory seem not to have been noted and implemented. The heart of the structural theory, that in analyzing the ego resistances one must consider different levels of consciousness, still seems not to be a part of general clinical thinking. To help understand this I think we need to take a look at Hartmann's work from another dimension.

It has been noted that Hartmann's heavy emphasis on metapsychology, which was presented in a way that was removed from clinical data, has had a deleterious effect on clinical theory and technique (Apfelbaum, 1962; Schafer, 1970; Shaw, 1989). The same might be said, in the short run, for his championing the necessity of studies in child development as a way of understanding ego development. The result has been that Hartmann remains a giant in the psychoanalytic pantheon, but as Wyman (1989) notes, his ideas seem to have vanished from the literature. While in the long run I believe his concepts will prove eminently usable, it is clear that in the last 50 years psychoanalysts have found it difficult to integrate Hartmann's work with clinical technique. The abstractness of his theorizing, while forsaking clinical examples, has left a generation of analysts in awe of Hartmann's intellectual powers, while shaking their heads when considering its relevance to their last patient. The importance of the clinical ego in ego psychology was pushed aside for a more abstract theorizing. This trend continued for many years, as noted by Arlow (1975) and Joseph (1975). That Hartmann had a sophisticated clinical view of the ego that took note of such issues as levels of the conscious ego, and the importance of ego analysis, can be glimpsed in the following:

> Defenses (typically) not only keep thoughts, images, and instinctual drives out of consciousness, but also prevent their assimilation by means of thinking. When defensive processes break down, the mental elements

defended against and certain connections of these elements become amenable to recollection and reconstruction. Interpretations not only help to regain the buried material, but must also establish correct causal relations, that is, the causes, range of influence, and effectiveness of these experiences in relation to other elements. I stress this here because the theoretical study of interpretation is often limited to those instances which are concerned with emerging memories or corresponding reconstructions. But even more important for the theory of interpretation are those instances in which the causal connections of elements, and the criteria for these connections, are established. (Hartmann, 1939, p. 63)

In this one can see the importance for Hartmann, in the interpretive process, of what is allowable into consciousness. He alerts us to the significance not only of the memories associated with repressed trauma, but also to the importance of elements of ego functioning associated with defenses and connected to these traumas. He underlines the importance of the expanding awareness of the workings of the conscious ego in the interpretive work and emphasizes the various "mental elements" which are connected to the defenses which become available for entry into consciousness once the defenses become less rigid. We see here the Hartmann that sounds like other voices who have championed expanding awareness of the conscious ego as a primary interpretive goal (Gray, Kris, Searl). Kafka (1989) also suggests that Hartmann was interested in the shadings of conscious experience.

The quandary posed by Hartmann for the psychoanalytic clinician is captured in the following sentence: "Permit me a digression on the nature of thinking in the psychoanalytic situation, in which the predominant object of thought is the subject himself" (Hartmann, 1939, p. 62). That Hartmann considered thinking about the psychoanalytic situation a "digression" is evident in his theorizing. This approach hampered the translation of ego psychology into a viable component of clinical psychoanalysis. While ego analysis was championed in print, its translation into understandable, workable approaches in the clinical situation lagged behind. Thus, the clinical issue of availability to consciousness as one consideration in the analyst's interpretive stance, which began in conflict between Freud the empathic observer and Freud the scientist, once again was obscured behind Hartmann the theoretician. Thus, Hartmann's legacy is that while he opened a window to the possibility of subtleties in understanding ego functions, the shade remained drawn on the clinical ego.

Importance of being "in the neighborhood"

The centrality of being "in the neighborhood" for the analytic process is emphasized in Gray's (1973, 1982, 1986, 1990a) pioneering work on resistance analysis, where he champions the importance of the conscious[1] ego in the analytic process. In a twist of Freud's adage, Gray (1990a) points to the usefulness of looking at the goals of the psychoanalytic process in terms of, "where unconscious ego was, conscious ego shall be" (p. 1095). He believes that "the therapeutic results of analytic treatment are lasting in proportion to the extent to which, during the analysis, the patient's un-bypassed ego functions have become involved in a consciously and increasingly voluntary co-partnership with the analyst" (1982, p. 624). In a series of articles over the last two decades Gray has given us a clear methodology for analyzing the unconscious ego resistances while helping analysands become aware of their mental activity. His emphasis is on helping patients gain greater access to consciousness via unconscious ego activities that lead to resistances. For Gray a successful interpretation has, as one component, a direction of the patient to something he can understand in spite of ongoing resistances. Gray (1990a) asserts that by including the conscious ego in our interpretive stance we encourage and strengthen more mature ego functioning.

The significance of the analysand's conscious awareness of his own thoughts is also seen in the work of A. O. Kris (1982, 1983, 1990). Kris, who considers the conscious ego from a somewhat different perspective, uses the method of free association as the frame of his analytic perspective, and suggests there are inherent satisfactions with freedom of associations. His concept of a pathological process, within the context of the analytic setting, involves inhibition of the pleasure in being able to conceptualize and become aware of one's thought processes. Using interferences with the method of free association as a basis of pathology, Kris takes the position that a definition of health needs to take into account the ability to become consciously aware of one's thoughts, with a corresponding decrease in unconscious resistances to this process. *In the work of both Gray and Kris one sees a view of pathology that is defined within the analytic process as an interference with the ability to become conscious of one's thought processes.* Both use consciousness as a basis of understanding resistances. A corollary to this from the interpretive side is that the analyst's task is to help make conscious the unconscious resistances in a way that allows analysands to have greater access to their mental life. To do this is to keep in mind at all times that: "The interpretive task is to estimate sensitively the patient's ability to comprehend, in order to make a formulation that is not too superficial yet does not stimulate more reactive defenses" (Gray, 1986, p. 253). In this same vein, Gray states: "The effectiveness with which patients can use their capacity for observing ego activities depends primarily on the nature of the burden the analyst's interventions place on them" (Gray, 1986, p. 253). This burden can be decreased by focusing on the unconscious resistances via the analysand's communications and interferences with the free-association method. By directing comments to the "neighborhood" the patient presently occupies, in a way that demystifies the basis of our remarks, we go a long way toward inviting conscious participation in the therapeutic process.

What has not been sufficiently emphasized in the literature to this point are the problems inherent in not being "in the neighborhood." Simply put, given the centrality of the unconscious ego resistances in the analytic process, it is futile to be any place else. If one primary purpose of a resistance is to keep thoughts and feelings out of awareness, to fail to take into account what can be allowed into awareness when making an intervention is to risk our comments falling on deaf ears, at best, and potentially arousing more resistances. Since Freud's (1926) elaboration of his second theory of anxiety it has been clear that resistances are, in part, the ego's response to some experienced danger or threat. If a resistance is in operation, it indicates that the analysand is experiencing his thoughts or feelings as a danger. The purpose of the resistance is to keep the dangerous thought or feeling from awareness. The particular type of resistance is an adaptation, from an earlier time, to this threat. Interventions that do not respect the analysand's resistance to certain thoughts and feelings becoming conscious will be either irrelevant or potentially overwhelming. This basic component of the analytic process has been muddled by our "developmental lag" (Gray, 1982) in understanding the resistances (see also Busch, 1992; Schafer, 1983).

A different perspective on the futility of interpreting outside "the neighborhood" is presented in the work of George Klein (1976). He shows that the basic purpose of any defensive process is to take the meaning out of behavior that is drive-dominated. Thus, the person with exhibitionistic wishes is aware only of feeling self-conscious that people are staring at him, while someone in the throes of an oedipal rivalry knows only about his discomfort around older authority figures. Wishes have an active, ongoing influence on behavior, while the individual has no understanding of the behavior or feeling associated with the wish. The critical accomplishment of defenses is the establishment of a gap between behavior and conscious comprehension of that behavior. The meaning of wishes can be lived out without any conscious understanding. The individual who can "barely" go out in public due to vague feelings of shame and embarrassment when others are looking is living out an ongoing expression of exhibitionistic wishes. The crucial component of the defense is that the individual can live out the wish without any conscious comprehension. One important goal of an interpretation, then, is to fill out gaps in meaning (and not necessarily gaps in memory). The bridge must be made between unconscious wishes acted upon in behaviors and their conscious meanings, along with the reasons for their being kept apart (i.e., the resistances). Until such a bridge is made, behaviors remain unresponsive to feedback, and thus not modifiable. The exhibitionist cannot think of leaving the house while fervently believing he is avoiding pain and discomfort by staying home. The conscious understanding that behaviors have meaning, that there are reasons for our keeping a gap between the behavior and its meaning, and finally what the behaviors mean, become the significant steps in an analysand obtaining understanding of his behavior. By not taking into account the analysand's conscious readiness to grasp the meaning of his behavior, we are missing one of the basic points of the defenses, which is to keep meanings outside awareness. Only by gradually making behaviors consciously meaningful can we hope to modify the basic defensive structure. Defenses are instituted in such a manner that wishes can be lived out without comprehension. With our interpretations, we hope to bring meaning to this lack of comprehension, while increasing comprehension. Without participation of the patient's conscious ego, we subvert our own goals.

A more subtle, and potentially more insidious problem is the enfeebling and undermining of the ego which occur when the analysand's conscious awareness is not taken into account. This can be seen most frequently in what Searl (1936) calls the interpretation of "absent content" (i.e., the interpretation of a fantasy or feeling that the analysand is unaware of), an example of which can be seen in the Greenson vignette cited above. In outlining some of the problems with such interpretations, Searl notes:

> If on the other hand, we say to a patient, "You are thinking so and so," "You have such and such a fantasy," and so on, we give him no help about his inability to know that for himself, and leave him to some extent dependent on the analyst for all such knowledge. If we add "The nature of this thought or fantasy explains your difficulty in knowing it for yourself," we still leave the patient with increased understanding related to a particular type of thought and fantasy only, and imply "one must know the thought or fantasy first before one can understand the difficulty about knowing it." The dynamics about the patient's disability to find his own way have been comparatively untouched if the resistance was more than the thinnest of crusts and will therefore still be at work to some extent and in some form whatever the change brought about by the absent content. (pp. 478–479)

By including the conscious ego in our interventions, we encourage the analysand to take a more active role in his treatment. This is in contrast to those interpretations geared toward absent content which, as Searl demonstrates, enforce a passivity on the patient. Such interpretations encourage a belief in the analyst's omniscience, while stimulating the patient's omnipotent fantasies and reinforcing a belief in magical thinking. Searl's work also suggests that by interpreting content outside of an analysand's awareness we may participate in a bypassing of resistances to independent self-analysis (i.e., the dynamics of the patients' inability to find their own way). This fear and/or distortion of the ability to observe one's own thought processes is a significant resistance in every analysis, but it has been obscured by gaps in our understanding of ego analysis. How frequently have we heard what seem to be relatively successful treatments which are in their final stages where the patient "associates," and the analyst "interprets." The patient's participation in the process of analyzing is too infrequently analyzed, partly because we are not paying attention to the nature of what would be most helpful to the analysand in understanding the analytic process. Is it the understanding of his unconscious fantasies, or is it the increasing conscious awareness of his own thought processes and the barriers to this awareness? I do not in any way rule out the centrality of understanding unconscious conflicts and the resulting compromise formations in symptom resolution. Inevitably, all resistances to self-awareness are intertwined with persistent fantasies which dominate unconscious thoughts. It is simply a question of the best way to show these to the patient so that the analytic process is furthered. The analyst's task is a daunting one. Translating the analysand's action thoughts while understanding unconscious components of a communication from the side of the id, ego, and superego is difficult enough. Communicating this to patients so they can hear what they have been talking about, while also being relevant to concerns they are aware of struggling with, is a never-ending test of our cognitive and empathic abilities.

While recently listening to a colleague interpret, for what seemed like the umpteenth time, the patient's passive homosexual wishes as a defense against his active strivings, I thought of our tendency to interpret, and if the patient is not able to use what we say, to interpret again—like trying to give directions to someone who does not speak our language. Invariably in these situations we tend to speak louder and slower, as if by doing this the foreigner will understand better. Our repetitions of the absent unconscious fantasy in its various forms has the same quality. By continuing to focus on absent content, we may be engaging in a process that undermines the ego while, via our empathic disruption with what the analysand is capable of hearing, we may increase the sense of danger and thus intensify resistances.

I have focused on the dangers of not being "in the neighborhood." Yet the question remains as to what the benefits are of including the conscious ego as part of the intervention process. Inviting the analysand's more active participation supports the enlistment of certain ego pleasures which have not been well integrated into psychoanalytic technique. These pleasures are well known to observers of children. Klein (1976) outlined some of these pleasures associated with ego activities as: functioning (i.e., the activity itself is pleasurable); effectance (i.e., changing a course of action through one's behavior); synthesis (i.e., establishing a sense of order and wholeness). These are similar to ego activities noted by Erikson (1959) and White (1963) as well as by many others. In a similar vein, Emde (1988), in reviewing early childhood research, concludes that two of the basic motivations for behavior are activity and self-regulation. It is clear in observational research that from very early on we are driven by, and find pleasure in, a number of ego activities. These have been called by various names over the years (e.g., a drive for competence, a need for mastery); further clarity is still needed. However, what cannot be doubted are the active ego needs and pleasure in them. In our daily analytic work, we are much more impressed with how the ego becomes compromised by resistances, and unconscious fantasies. Stereotypical, repetitive, restrictions in characteristic ego activities, for much of an analysis, is the observational fare of most analysts. The numbing effect of an ego caught in conflict should not be confused with its potential resilience. We should not, in a countertransference acting out, treat our adult analysands as cognitively impoverished as they appear when a threatened ego is temporarily restricted. With a respectful eye on the conscious ego and its pleasures, one can point to the way ego functioning becomes compromised by conflict, thus removing pleasure in ego activities. Working with analysands in this way often leads them to a feeling that they have "found a part of themselves" or they consider their thoughts more "their own."

Gray (1982) observed that an important distinguishing element among analysts is their "forms of attention" (p. 621) during the analysis. This can be said both about the type of material listened for and how the analyst communicates his understanding to the patient. In terms of the latter, one hears variations in style from analysts who always seem to "assert" what is going on at any moment in the analysis, to those who seem to believe that it is only the patient who can come to his own understanding and thus say almost nothing. Gray's (1973, 1986, 1990a) method of sharing the data that led to his conclusion invites the analysand's conscious ego to participate in the process. It not only has the advantages associated with including the conscious ego in the analytic process, but also helps to focus in a minute way on resistances to the process. This is essential in analyzing resistances to the self-analytic function which seems crucial for post-termination success.

Weinshel (1984) suggests that a useful way of distinguishing among analysts is that there are those who focus on the goal of analysis, and those who focus on the analytic work. Different ways of interpreting to analysands highlight these differences. Inherent within the position of the analyst who "asserts" his interpretations is the goal of bringing unconscious thoughts to consciousness. Thus, this analyst would be working within a topographic model where the therapeutic benefit of analysis is viewed in terms of goals. By sharing with patients, the reasons for our inferences, we emphasize the process. We are saying to our patients, "In your use of the method we can learn such and such from what you are saying." It is not that there are no goals with such a method, it is that the goals are reached by focusing on the method. Implicit in one's approach to interventions, there are hidden assumptions about the nature of the analytic process. The approach I have been suggesting is concisely captured in Gill's (1954) felicitous, oft-quoted comment that we still recognize our friends after they have successfully completed an analysis. If one believes that the work of analysis centers on continuing the work of analysis, rather than obliteration of conflict, then including the conscious ego in a variety of ways becomes a necessary component of the process.

In follow-up studies of completed psychoanalyses by Schlessinger and Robbins (1983), there are clear indications that core conflicts are not dissolved. Instead, what one sees post-termination is an emergence of, and then a working on, issues that were central in the analysis. Under periods of stress (i.e., as in the stimulation of the ever-ready transference fantasies arising in a post-termination interview) old conflicts arise, but this time to be handled far more swiftly and with less disruptiveness. Analysis neither obliterates resistances or the gratifications surrounding conflict. Instead, what analysis accomplishes, from this one perspective, is help in making accessible to consciousness the resistances which are fed by anxiety and accompanied by an array of unconscious fantasies and traumas. Analysis allows for a greater access to consciousness of these myriad components of conflict, allowing for more rapid resolution of the immediate stresses via self-analysis. This capacity for self-analysis, rather than obliteration of conflict, is one of the prime benefits one sees from successfully completed analyses (Schlessinger & Robbins, 1983). As Calef (1982) noted, the outcome of analysis may be most influenced by whether the analysand has been able to identify with its process.

Finally, it is at least important to note there are resistances to including the conscious ego in the interpretive process that lead both analyst and analysand away from the importance of being "in the neighborhood." Gray (1982) and I (Busch, 1992) have commented on the magnetism of unconscious fantasies for the analyst in resistances to analyzing the resistances, and the same can be said here. Universal trends from childhood also tend to pull the analysand toward a regressive relationship where the analysand "associates" and the analyst interprets. This can include such wishes as the desire to remain in a dependent position in relation to an omniscient, omnipotent figure; the narcissistic pleasure of being at the center of another's attention, who is observing and attempting to make sense of whatever one is saying; and the pleasure of letting one's mind go without believing there is the need for any structure or control. Furthermore, there are regressions in ego functioning concomitant with development of the transference neurosis which preclude the analysand from observing his own thoughts. For example, a patient functioning under the influence of preoperational thought feels neither the compunction to justify his reasonings to others nor to look for possible contradictions in his logic. He is, for example, unable to reconstruct a chain of reasoning which he has just passed through; he thinks but he cannot think about his own thinking (Flavell, 1963 p. 156).

When an analysand is in such a state, his thoughts are closer to actions, and he does not recognize there is a "neighborhood" to be in. Thus, when we observe these resistances to conscious awareness (whether in the form of an ego regression or regression in wish), we need to analyze them as we would any resistance. The danger lies in bypassing an important impediment to self-analysis (i.e., the inability to become aware of one's thought process or the wish not to become aware). This takes on added importance when we consider Loewald's (1971) suggestion that part of the curative process in psychoanalysis rests on experiences coming under the influence of higher-level ego functions which were previously not available to consciousness.

Note

1 It's my belief now that what Gray was describing was the preconscious ego.

References

Apfelbaum, B. (1962). Some problems in contemporary ego psychology. *J. Am. Psychoanal. Assoc.,* 10:526–537.

Apfelbaum, B. & Gill, M. M. (1989). Ego analysis and the relativity of defense: Technical implications of the structural theory. *J. Am. Psychoanal. Assoc.*, 37:1071–1096.

Arlow, J. A. (1975). The structural hypothesis: Technical considerations *Psychoanal. Q.*, 44:509–525.

Busch, F. (1992). Recurring thoughts on unconscious ego resistances. *J. Am. Psychoanal. Assoc.*, 40:4.

Calef, V. (1982). An introspective on training and non-training analysis. *Ann. Psychoanal.*, 10:93–114.

Davison, W. T., Bristol, C., & Pray, M. (1986). Turning aggression on the self: A study of psychoanalytic process. *Psychoanal. Q.*, 55:273–295.

Eissler, K. R. (1965). *Medical orthodoxy and the future of psychoanalysis*. New York: International Universities Press.

Emde, R. N. (1988). Development terminable and interminable: II. Recent psychoanalytic theory and therapeutic considerations. *Int. J. Psychoanal.*, 69:283–296.

Erikson, E. H. (1959). *Identity and the life cycle*. New York: Norton, 1963.

Fenichel, O. (1941). *Problems of psychoanalytic technique*. New York: Psychoanal. Q.

Flavell, J. H. (1963). *The developmental psychology of Jean Piaget*. Princeton, NJ: Van Nostrand.

Freud, A. (1936). *The ego and the mechanisms of defense*. Writings 2. New York: International Universities Press, 1966

Freud, S. (1895). Studies on hysteria *S.E.* 2.

Freud, S. (1910). 'Wild' psycho-analysis *S.E.* 11.

Freud, S. (1912). The dynamics of the transference *S.E.* 12.

Freud, S. (1913). On beginning the treatment (further recommendations on the technique of psycho-analysis) S.E. 12.

Freud, S. (1914). Remembering, repeating, and working through *S.E.* 12.

Freud, S. (1916–1917). Introductory lectures on psycho-analysis *S.E.* 16.

Freud, S. (1923). The ego and the id *S.E.* 19.

Freud, S. (1926). Inhibitions, symptoms, and anxiety *S.E.* 20.

Gill, M. M. (1954). Psychoanalysis and exploratory psychotherapy. *J. Am. Psychoanal. Assoc.*, 2:771–797.

Gray, P. (1973). Psychoanalytic technique and the ego's capacity for viewing intrapsychic conflict. *J. Am. Psychoanal. Assoc.*, 21:474–494.

Gray, P. (1982). "Developmental lag" in the evolution of technique for psycho-analysis of neurotic conflict. *J. Am. Psychoanal. Assoc.*, 30:621–655.

Gray, P. (1986). On helping analysands observe intrapsychic activity In Psycho-analysis: The science of mental conflict. In: A. D. Richards & M. S. Willick (eds.), *Essays in honor of Charles Brenner* (pp. 245–262). Hillsdale, NJ: Analytic Press.

Gray, P. (1987). On the technique of analysis of the superego—An introduction. *Psychoanal. Q.*, 56:130–154.

Gray, P. (1990a). The nature of therapeutic action in psychoanalysis. *J. Am. Psychoanal. Assoc.*, 38:1083–1097.

Gray, P. (1990b). A conversation with Paul Gray Amer. *Psychoanal.*, 24:10–11.

Greenson, R. R. (1967). *The technique and practice of psychoanalysis*. New York: International Universities Press.

Hartmann, H. (1939). *Ego psychology and the problem of adaptation*. New York: International Universities Press, 1958.

Hartmann, H. (1960). *Psychoanalysis and moral values*. New York: International Universities Press.

Hartmann, H. (1964). *Essays on ego psychology*. New York: International Universities Press.

Herzog, P. (1991). *Conscious and unconscious. Psychological Issues Monograph* 58. New York: International Universities Press.

Joseph, E. D. (1975). Clinical formulations and research. *Psychoanal. Q.*, 44:526–533.

Joseph, E. D. (1987). The consciousness of being conscious. *J. Am. Psychoanal. Assoc.*, 35:5–22.

Kafka, E. (1989). The contribution of Hartmann's adaptational theory to psychoanalysis, with special reference to regression and symptom formation *Psychoanal. Q.*, 58:571–591.

Klein, G. S. (1976). *Psychoanalytic theory: An exploration of essentials*. New York: International Universities Press.

Kris, A. O. (1982). *Free association: Method and process*. New Haven, CT: Yale Univ. Press.

Kris, A. O. (1983). The analyst's conceptual freedom in the method of free association. *Int. J. Psychoanal.*, 64:407–411.

Kris, A. O. (1990). Helping patients by analyzing self-criticism. *J. Am. Psychoanal. Assoc.*, 38:605–636.

Kris, E. (1951). Ego psychology and interpretation in psychoanalytic therapy. *Psychoanal. Q.*, 20:15–30.

Lear, J. (1990). *Love and its place in nature*. New York: Farrar, Straus & Giroux.

Levy, S. T. & Inderbitzin, C. B. (1990). The analytic surface and the theory of technique. *J. Am. Psychoanal. Assoc.*, 38:371–392.

Loewald, H. W. (1960). On the therapeutic action of psychoanalysis. *Int. J. Psychoanal.*, 41:16–35.

Loewald, H. W. (1971). Some considerations on repetition and repetition compulsion. *Int. J. Psychoanal.*, 52:59–66.

Loewenstein, R. M. (1972). Ego autonomy and psychoanalytic technique. *Psychoanal. Q.*, 41:1–22.

Mahler, M. S. Pine, F., & Bergman, A. (1975). *The psychological birth of the human infant*. New York: Basic Books.

Myerson, P. G. (1960). Awareness and stress: Post-psychoanalytic utilization of insight. *Int. J. Psychoanal.*, 41:147–155.

Myerson, P. G. (1981). The nature of transactions that enhance the progressive phase of a psychoanalysis. *Int. J. Psychoanal.*, 62:91–105.

Schafer, R. (1970). An overview of Heinz Hartmann's contributions to psychoanalysis. *Int. J. Psychoanal.*, 51:425–446.

Schafer, R. (1983). *The analytic attitude*. New York: Basic Books.

Schlessinger, N. & Robbins, F. P. (1983). *A developmental view of the psychoanalytic process: Follow-up studies and their consequences*. New York: International Universities Press.

Searl, M. N. (1936). Some queries on principles of technique. *Int. J. Psychoanal.*, 17:471–493.

Shaw, R. R. (1989). Hartmann on adaptation: An incomparable or incomprehensible legacy. *Psychoanal. Q.*, 58:592–611.

Smith, J. H. (1986). Dualism revisited: Schafer, Hartmann, and Freud. *Psychoanal. Inq.*, 6 543–574.

Spitz, R. A. (1945). Hospitalism: An inquiry into the genesis of psychiatric conditions in early childhood. *Psychoanal. Study Child*, 1:53–74.

Stern, D. N. (1985). *The interpersonal world of the infant*. New York: Basic Books.

Weinshel, E. M. (1984). Some observations on the psychoanalytic process. *Psychoanal. Q.,* 53:63–92.

White, R. W. (1963). *Ego and reality in psychoanalytic theory. Psychological Issues Monograph* 11. New York: International Universities Press.

Wyman, H. M. (1989). Hartmann, health, and homosexuality: Some clinical aspects of "Ego psychology and the problem of adaptation." *Psychoanal. Q.,* 58:612–639.

4 Thoughts on unconscious resistances

While the analysis of resistances has been a cornerstone of modern psycho-analytic technique, our understanding of the concept remains somewhat confused. One hears it referred to far too rarely in clinical discussions, while published papers dealing with the topic most often fluctuate between its pre- and post-structural meanings and the technical implications inherent in these positions. As Schafer (1983) states, "Certain things about resisting which ought to be well known and are said to be well known and sufficiently appreciated and applied, are in fact not known well enough and not consistently attended to in practice" (p. 66). Gray (1982) charitably calls this muddled understanding of one of our basic concepts a "developmental lag," while reminding us that our understanding of theory informs our clinical stance.

While it might be comforting to think of this "lag" as a thing of the past, it would be erroneous to do so. Many analysts still eschew an ego-psychological approach to resistance analysis in favor of a pre-structural method, with its primary emphasis on unearthing the derivatives of the unconscious fantasy. In the recent definition of resistances given by Moore and Fine (1990) both views are given as if they were part of an integrated perspective rather than alternate points of view. While presenting many ideas on the ego's contribution to the resistances similar to those to be presented in this paper, the authors end their discussion with the following:

> Once the patient's unconscious conflicts have been uncovered and some insight obtained, resistances may lead to delay or even failure to progress, reflecting an unconsciously determined reluctance to give up inappropriate childhood wishes and their maladaptive, defensively distorted expressions in symptoms, character, or behavior. Moreover, the relief or mental equilibrium that the neurotic symptoms achieved for the individual is hard to give up. These many factors contributing to resistance make the process of working through an essential part of analytic work. (p. 169).

In this one sees a return to a drive-dominated view of the resistances. The role of the unconscious ego in the working- through process is underemphasized when compared to the fixated drives. The complexity of understanding and bringing into awareness the unconscious dangers perceived by the ego, as well as the adaptational component of the resistances, are downplayed in the working-through process. Delays in the analysand's changing are primarily seen as sequelae to the difficulty in giving up "inappropriate childhood wishes." This approach to the resistances seems to be an example of what Apfelbaum and Gill (1989) note as a tendency on many analysts' part to see ego analysis as something one does prior to id analysis, rather than throughout an analysis. As we shall see later, the comparative role of the ego vs. the drives in resistances was an issue Freud struggled with, but never successfully resolved. In fact, the struggle is still going on.

Goldberger (1989), in a review of a book on resistance, comments on the pejorative tone that creeps into the discussions. This is a common phenomenon for analysts who view resistances as primarily an impediment to id analysis. One author in this collection goes so far as to suggest that the concept of resistance analysis ought to be abandoned because of its potential harm to the analytic enterprise. Widely varying views of resistance still exist, and changes in technique based on increased understanding of the ego have been difficult for many analysts to integrate into clinical technique. Furthermore, while some of the most useful recent insights into resistance have come from self-psychology, Kohut's (1984) dismissiveness of ego psychology in general, and his misunderstanding of resistance in particular, have made integration of these insights into general psychoanalytic theory problematic at best. What Kohut describes as narcissistic transference can also be seen as resistance based on the fear of ego disintegration (i.e., due to faulty mirroring, over or understimulation, etc.). However, Kohut's view of what he calls traditional treatment is "an *overcoming* of resistances in order to make the unconscious conscious" (Kohut, 1984, p. 111). From this one can see how errors in understanding, perpetuated through the years, can skew the utilization of clinical insight.

Freud (1895) recognized resistances early, often came back to the topic (1913, 1914, 1915–1916, 1926, 1937a, 1937b, 1940), saw resistances as serving many purposes and as due to various causes (e.g., defensive, unconscious gratification, secondary gain, superego guilt, the repetition compulsion-adhesiveness of the libido). In this paper, I shall focus on the defense resistances (unconscious ego resistances). For the sake of simplicity, I shall refer to them only as "resistances." While I shall concentrate on their role in defense, it should be noted at the outset that I see resistances as complex acts with contributions from many sources. The most salient resistances are often found to serve purposes of defense, drive gratification, adaptation, and transference. However, it has been the defense aspect of the resistances that has been the most baffling for analysts to consistently integrate into clinical technique. I shall focus on persistent problems in the interpretation of resistances in the hope that understanding subtle resistances to the interpretation of resistances, which are embedded in our theory and technical approaches, will serve as a useful adjunct to Gray's (1973, 1986, 1987, 1990) work on the technique of resistance interpretation. As with any investigation of persistent resistances, the hope is that expanded ego awareness will lead to greater conceptual freedom in our approach to the resistances.

The resistances I shall refer to are not only the most overt types, such as missed appointments or silences. My perspective is similar to that of other psychoanalytic authors (Glover, 1955; Stone, 1973) who believe anything can be used as a resistance. One can find resistances in the way patients associate—or do not; or the way they tell a dream, or keep bringing dreams, or do not tell dreams—or do not listen; or the way they listen. All can be potential resistances. A patient rushing through his thoughts may be expressing one kind of resistance, while a patient who needs to pause after every thought may be expressing another type. Anything that interferes with the patient's ability to look at what is coming to mind, how it is coming to mind, and why it is coming to mind, may express resistance.

Historical antecedents of current ambiguities

Differences among clinical techniques of resistance analysis are mainly based on how closely the analyst follows Freud's view of "the ego as the sole seat of anxiety, and in one's understanding of the differences between Freud's first and second theory of anxiety. *"Whereas the old view made it natural to suppose that anxiety arose from the libido belonging to the repressed instinctual impulses, the new one, on the contrary, made the ego the source of anxiety"* (Freud, 1926, p. 161; italics added).

It has not been clearly emphasized that it was only with the introduction of the structural theory and the second theory of anxiety that a full psychoanalytic meaning of working with resistances was possible. Before this, the anxiety leading to the resistance was seen as a by-product of dammed-up libido. Therefore, the primary purpose of the psychoanalytic clinician was to free the libido by bringing the unconscious libidinal wishes into consciousness. The resistances were a barrier to be overcome, although not in the old sense, as in the hypnotic phase when the resistances were bypassed completely. Instead, after the resistances were brought into consciousness, the psychoanalyst was called upon to use various methods (e.g., promising the rewards of health, using the positive transference, suggestion) to help the patient push on in the face of resistances. In Freud's second theory of anxiety, the ego is seen as the source of anxiety. That is, anxiety is seen as occurring when the ego perceives danger (i.e., when it fears being overwhelmed), which is further seen as a repetition of an earlier traumatic situation. The resistances are viewed as the ego's response to anxiety. With this conceptual understanding of the underlying psychic mechanisms in place, psychoanalysts could grasp the full meaning of the resistances as the result of the perceived danger to the ego. Thus, the importance of Freud's second theory of anxiety is: (1) for the first time resistances could be understood in a psychodynamic rather than an energic fashion; (2) a psychoanalytic working through of these resistances could truly be undertaken which would center on an understanding of the danger to the ego underlying the resistance.

What is striking is that the clinical implications of Freud's second theory of anxiety seem only to have been episodically grasped in our psychoanalytic history. Although Freud's clinical brilliance led him to understand that resistances were inevitable, necessary, and even useful components of the psychoanalytic method, he never fully appreciated the clinical potential of working with resistances. Even after he realized that the source of anxiety was in the unconscious ego's response to a perceived threat, his clinical approach to the resistances was primarily guided by earlier views. In these works, Freud (1914, 1915–1916) described the necessity for "working through" resistances, but what he meant by this was using suggestion, influence, and interpretation from above in what we would call today attempts to overcome the resistance. This was a working through only in the sense that it did not bypass the resistances entirely. In those earlier papers (e.g., Freud, 1915–1916) where Freud started to recognize the resistance as a response to danger, his interpretive mode remained overcoming the resistance. This technique was consistent with his first theory of anxiety. Even after his discovery of the source of resistance as the ego's experience of anxiety due to fears of being overwhelmed, his technical approach to the resistances, as expressed in an addendum to "Inhibitions, Symptoms and Anxiety," remained essentially unchanged.

> If the resistance is itself unconscious, as so often happens owing to its connection with the repressed material, we make it conscious. If it is conscious, or, where it has become conscious, we bring forward logical arguments against it; we promise the ego rewards and advantages if it will give up its resistance. (Freud, 1926, p. 159)

In line with his understanding of the role of the unconscious ego in resistances, Freud recognized the importance of bringing the resistances to consciousness. However, once the resistances were conscious, he returned to his technical view of using influence or suggestion to enlist the ego's cooperation in dealing with these interferences. Even though Freud had opened the door to a purely psychological approach to the resistances (i.e., helping the patient understand the sources of anxiety and the danger behind this), it was left to others to fully explicate this point of view. I believe that Freud's tie to the economic model and the principles of energy underlying the psychic system made it difficult for him to see the full clinical significance of his brilliant discovery. Thus, while emphasizing the importance of purely psychic factors in the role of resistances, Freud's notions of "working through" were still influenced by the concept of the energic powers of the repressed unconscious, leading to the view of the psychoanalyst as one of a juggler working with metal objects in the face of a giant magnet. From this perspective, the analyst needed an equally powerful force (e.g., suggestion within the context of a positive transference) to counteract the pull from the unconscious. This point of view was still in evidence when Freud returned to the topic of resistances in his later papers (1937a, 1937b, 1940). With an appreciation for the difficulties in working through resistances bordering on pessimism, the threat to the ego as a major factor in these difficulties faded into the background. Instead, contributions based on economic principles (i.e., the death instinct, adhesiveness of the libido, and constitutional differences in the ego), which led to the ego's inability to modify the drives, were advanced (Freud, 1937a, pp. 240–243). "Once again we are confronted with the importance of the quantitative factor, and once again we are reminded that analysis can only draw upon definite and limited amounts of energy which have to be measured against the hostile forces" (Freud, 1937a, p. 240).

Freud's dual view of resistances as something to be over- come versus a psychical act that could be understood is one factor in our muddled understanding of resistances. This same duality keeps appearing in our literature on the subject of resistances. There are those who grasp the psychoanalytic meanings of working with resistances inherent in Freud's second theory of anxiety. However, contemporaneously with these same authors, and seemingly not influenced by them, are those who reflect Freud's ambivalence toward a purely psychoanalytic understanding of the resistances. The latter present the psychoanalytic reader with the confusing task of integrating insights into the nature of resistances with technical suggestions that do not take into account the ego's response to a dangerous situation. What follows are highlights of the above-mentioned trends in the literature which leave one with the impression of a concept in disarray.

Analytic writings on resistance, after Freud's presentation of the second theory of anxiety, started out in a most promising fashion. Reich (1933) was one of the first to grasp the significance of resistances in analytic work, and his ideas are echoed throughout the literature on the topic. Reich's work reflects his understanding of the resistances as the ego's response to danger, and he offers the first technical suggestions based on this premise which reflect a true psychoanalytic working through of the resistances and not simply overcoming them.

> The better way, then, is to approach first the defense of the ego which is more closely related to the conscious ego. One will tell the patient at first only that he is keeping silent because-"For one reason or another," that is, with- out touching upon the id-impulse-he is defending him- self against the analysis, presumably because it has become somehow dangerous to him. (p. 65)

Working on the premise of the resistance as a danger to the ego, Reich elaborates on the procedure for analyzing the resistances. In current terminology, he suggests the necessity of first identifying, and then clarifying the resistance, before the unconscious wishes can be interpreted. We recognize in this the beginnings of ego analysis, of which analysis of the resistance is a major component. However, Reich is not consistent in applying this perspective. As Schafer (1983) notes:

> Reich himself shows in his militaristic metaphors of armor and attack how much one may fall into an adversarial view of the analytic relationship. Despite his rich understanding of the analysand's needing to resist and the complex meaning of function of this policy, he, like so many others, lapses into speaking of it as though it were a motiveless form of stubbornness or belligerence. (p. 73)

It is as if Reich approached the resistances *simultaneously* from two different perspectives: as an ego under threat and as a blockade that must be overcome. It is not the only time we shall come upon such an apparent paradox in our literature review.

Three years after Reich's book, Searl added brilliantly to the beginning psychoanalytic understanding of resistance.[1] Searl (1936) accomplished two major tasks which had not occurred before. She integrates and expands Freud's views of ego resistance into the clinical realm, while also pointing to problems that occur if ego analysis does not take place. She approaches the resistances as adaptive responses that attempt to manage frightening emotions. This leads Searl to suggest, as Reich did before her, that once a resistance is recognized it is not enough to help the patient overcome it with educative measures. She notes the importance of understanding the reasons for its formation (i.e., fear leading to an adaptive response), and the patient's difficulty in emerging from it. She suggests that unless the patient becomes aware of the reasons for feeling he will be overwhelmed, along with becoming aware of the feelings themselves, these will remain unconscious, and no educative measures will have any lasting effect. She goes one step further than Reich in noting that once the resistances have been pointed out and clarified, the specific nature of the danger the patient fears and where it comes from need to be analyzed. Finally, Searl subtly points out the hazards of bypassing the resistances to get to unconscious derivatives the analysand is unaware of. By doing this, she states, we miss the opportunity to work with and strengthen the conscious components of the ego—a significant point only returned to recently in the literature (Busch, 1993; Gray, 1986, 1987, 1990).

Anna Freud's (1936) earliest work on ego psychology, while championing the investigation of the ego as a necessary component of a psychoanalytic investigation and pointing the way to the study of unconscious defenses, does surprisingly show some ambivalence about the necessity of investigating ego resistances. She describes "abolishing" and "destroying" the ego resistances as a way station to analyzing the id. It is a view of the resistances as something to be attacked in order to get to the real work of id analysis. In her theoretical presentation of resistances, she does not show Searl's sophistication in approaching the adaptive side of resistances, nor does she state as succinctly the analytic problems inherent in bypassing the ego. She does not high- light the benefits accruing to the analysand with the expansion of the ego which occurs with careful attention to the unconscious ego resistances. Yet, in her clinical descriptions, there is a clear understanding of how resistances in analysis can be a result of the ego's avoidance of some danger. Thus, in these first writings on resistances, there emerges a familiar pattern. The importance of the resistances is highlighted, while the clinical approach suggested varies between resistances as something to be abolished versus understood. This same theme will recur many times in our literature review, at times within the same article, thus repeating Freud's divergent perspectives.

Two analysts writing contemporaneously (Sterba, 1940; Fenichel, 1941) serve as good examples of how divergent views on resistance analysis could be taken from Freud's writing. Quoting liberally from Freud, Sterba took the position that a transference resistance was just that-a transference *used* for the purpose of resistance. That the resistance might be a by- product of the anxiety raised by the transference seems generally ignored by Sterba. The patient's expression of the transference was viewed as a resistance to remembering. Sterba's technical handling of the resistance, then, was to tell the patient that he had to give up the transference before the analysis could continue (Sterba, 1940, p. 370). Fenichel, on the other hand, saw the implication of Freud's view of resistance as the ego's response to anxiety. He reminds us of the need to understand the affect generating the resistance in the ego, before at- tempting an investigation of the id content. Fenichel highlights the im- portance of analyzing the resistances throughout the analysis, while presenting the reader with what has become an all too familiar cautionary note on our lagging technique in dealing with resistance.

One of the stimuli to the development of so-called "analytic ego psy- chology" was insight into the fact that resistance in the analysis is a real therapeutic agent in that pursuing the aim of analyzing resistance has as a prerequisite a thorough analytic investigation particularly of chronic attitudes of resistance anchored in an individual's character. Here again, the volume of the literature concerning the newly gained psychological insight is in- comparably greater than the number of papers which seek to utilize this insight to contribute to an improvement of psychoanalytic technique (Fenichel, 1941, p. 106).

Little appeared specifically on the topic of resistances until works by Glover (1955) and Greenson (1967). Glover's work is noteworthy in that, like Reich, he highlights numerous subtle aspects of resistances (e.g., resistances can invade all aspects of psychoanalytic work), while ignoring their importance as a re- sponse to danger. Greenson's work is especially intriguing in that he alternately champions, within a single, unified discussion, two separate approaches to the resistances (pp. 59–60, 78). He does this not to highlight the differences, but as an integrated view of resistances.

Stone's (1973) pithy article is worth noting because it returns once again to a view of resistances as multifaceted dynamic constructions erected to ward off potentially disruptive affects. Stone points to the role of the ego avoiding painful feelings as central in resistances but adds some thoughts which have been implicit in the work of others. First of all, Stone believes that analysts need to pay attention to what he calls the *affirmative, functional* aspects of the resistances. In this, Stone highlights what Searl also noted (i.e., resistances are brought into being because they were adaptive at one time). Second, Stone highlights the *self-protective* nature of resistances. He points to what the ego experiences as potentially disruptive affects which are being warded off by the resistances.

In summary, seeds of ambiguity were inherent in Freud's views of resistances. Even after his discovery of the second theory of anxiety and the corresponding view of resistances as the ego's response to danger, Freud found it difficult to give up his economic, drive-dominated view of resistances and the technical implications of this perspective. Following Freud, the literature on resistances frequently reflects his ambivalence. We continually see a return to a drive-dominated view of the resistances, with diminished importance given to understanding the role of unconscious ego responses to danger. Growth in our clinical understanding of resistance has been stunted by confusion over the basic meanings of resistances, while clinical technique has lagged similarly. As both Gray (1982) and Schafer (1983) have intimated, there is something about the ego resistances that leads psychoanalysts to protest their understanding of the concept while continuing to present the same conceptual errors in their thinking.

Resistances and clinical technique—the dual perspective

Since clinical theory informs clinical technique, one would expect our tangled perspective on resistances to be reflected in confusion over the clinical handling of resistances. Nowhere is this seen more clearly than in the work of Greenson (1967). Partly this is because of Greenson's willingness to generously offer us a window into his clinical work. What one sees are numerous examples that perpetuate Freud's dual view of resistances. On the one hand Greenson expresses a perspective that clearly reflects the influence of Freud's second theory of anxiety: "Thus, I have the impression that no matter what the original source of an activity may be, its resistance function is always derived from the ego. The other psychic structures have to be understood as operating through the ego. The motive for defense and resistance always is to avoid pain" (p. 87). On the other hand, numerous statements are made, and examples given, which reflect a tendency to bypass the ego and not take into account the "pain" Greenson sees as crucial in understanding the resistances. I shall expand on this aspect of Greenson's work, since it so accurately reflects the dual perspective of resistances, and also provides an opportunity to explore some general issues of technique in resistance analysis.

One of Greenson's basic edicts is that the nature of what the patient is resisting can be boiled down to *what painful feeling he is trying to avoid* (p. 107). While this perspective seems based on Freud's second theory of anxiety, it leads Greenson to a technique that circumvents resistance analysis. Greenson describes how frequently, despite the patient's resistance, the affect is expressed in nonverbal form (e.g., blushing, hiding, crossing the legs). He states:

> In all these instances, I am trying to detect the nonverbal, bodily reactions that are taking place. They may offer us clues as to what particular painful affect the patient is struggling with. *If I think I can detect the specific affect, I confront the patient with, "You seem to be embarrassed, or afraid, or sad....* (po 108; italics added)

Note that in this Greenson seems less interested in *why the feeling is being avoided or why it is painful,* than he is in what the affect is. He is more intent on picking up on whether the patient is hiding, embarrassed, shy, sad, etc., than on why the patient is not able to be aware of or bring attention to what he is feeling. In this way, Greenson bypasses the resistance rather than exploring it. If a patient is keeping a feeling from awareness, one possibility we need to take into consideration, from the side of the resistance, is that there is some threat associated with the feeling coming into awareness. If we determine that it is a resistance leading to a feeling being kept from awareness, it is the threat we would want to focus on and not the feeling itself in isolation from the threat. In modifying Greenson's approach, I would suggest saying the following, "You seem to be feeling sad, but there is something about becoming aware of this feeling that seems dangerous to you." Here the emphasis is on the threat from becoming aware of the feeling. This is more in line with the nature of what a resistance is. Bringing the affect to light, without focusing on the danger associated with being aware of the feeling, becomes a bypassing of the resistance. It is that the feeling is painful, as Greenson notes, which is leading to its entrance into awareness being resisted. However, by attempting to bring the feeling into consciousness Greenson bypasses analyzing what this pain is about which has led to the feeling being kept from awareness. While stating that the question of resistances can be reduced to what painful feelings are being avoided, Greenson's clinical approach is based on what *feeling* is being avoided, with the fact that it is painful as secondary. However, if this were indeed the essence of resistance, it would be just that the feelings were painful that would lead to their being resisted, and this would need to be the focus of the analyst's attention. Greenson's interpretive approach leaves out the painful part of the resistance.

The problems Greenson gets into with his approach can be seen in the following example.

> A physician in analysis with me for several years begins to speak medical jargon in the middle of an analytic hour. In stilted tones he reports that his wife developed a "painful protruding hemorrhoid" just prior to a mountain trip they were planning. He said the news caused him "unmixed displeasure" and he wondered whether the hemorrhoid could

be "surgically excised" or whether they would have to postpone their holiday. I could sense the latent anger he was withholding and could not refrain from saying: "I think you really mean that your wife's hemorrhoids are giving you a pain in the ass." He replied angrily: "That's right, you son of a bitch, I wish they would cut it out of her, I can't stand these women and their swellings that interfere with my pleasures." This last detail, incidentally, referred to his mother's pregnancy which precipitated his infantile neurosis at the age of five. (p. 66)

By confronting the patient with his latent anger (i.e., the supposed painful feeling he is avoiding), Greenson gives up the opportunity to explore how aware the patient is of his use of "medical terminology," and his thoughts about its use. In short, Greenson does not begin to *explore* what at this time is the most obvious resistance. It is insufficient to answer that Greenson seemed to feel he knew what the resistance was to. It is insufficient because it is still bypassing the resistance, and the chance for ego analysis with an invitation to the patient to participate. The answer to the question of why this patient is fearful of his anger, except in generic terms, is not answerable in Greenson's approach. He is interested more in getting out the strangulated affect than in understanding the reasons for it being kept in.

As Schafer (1983) notes:

> There are many moments in the course of an analysis when analysands seem to dangle unexpressed content be- fore the analyst. These are moments when the analyst is tempted to say, for example, "You are angry," "You are excited," or "You are shamed." But if it is so obvious, why isn't the analysand simply saying so or showing unmistakably that it is so? To begin with, it is the hesitation, the obstructing, the resisting that counts. If the analyst by- passes this difficulty with a direct question or confrontation, the analysand is too likely to feel seduced, violated, or otherwise coerced by the analyst who has in fact, even if unwittingly, taken sides unemphatically. (p. 75)

If one holds that resistances can be boiled down to a painful feeling that is being avoided, it can lead to a superficial approach to the resistances. This is why it is important to keep in mind that, from the perspective of resistance as defense, it is a threat to the ego that leads to resistance. This threat may be experienced as a painful feeling but is not necessarily synonymous with it. Furthermore, looking for the painful feelings behind the resistance and finding some underlying painful feeling easily lead one to fall far short of where one needs to get in working through a resistance. For example, finding out that a patient's restricted associations are due to embarrassment over exhibitionistic wishes is not equal to the uncovering of the rea- son for the resistance, even though the painful affect has been discovered. The affect is a route to un- derstanding the threat to the ego but cannot be considered synonymous with it. Identifying the immediate affect which is causing the patient to be inhibited as embarrassment is a step toward working through the resistance, but a full understanding requires an articulation of the threat as well as its reasons for being there.

Greenson believes that in looking for the unconscious determinant of resistance we are searching out the unconscious drives and their derivatives in thought. As he states:

> After the resistance is demonstrable and clear, we are ready to attempt to interpret the unconscious determinants. That means we try to uncover the hidden instinctual impulses, fantasies or memories which are responsible for the resistance. (p. 112)

Again, Greenson confuses the issue when he describes impulses as the source of the resistances. Impulses, fantasies, or memories in themselves do not cause resistances. Rather, it is the potential threat to the ego that they present which is the source of the resistances. By focusing on looking for the unconscious fantasies one is again prone to bypass the resistances rather than to interpret them. Ultimately one hopes to come to the unconscious impulses and their derivatives which cause the threat to the ego. However, by seeking them out as our goal, once the resistance has been demonstrated, is to miss that the ego is unconsciously reacting to some threat. By bringing the unconscious fantasy to awareness, we do not remove the threat. By focusing attention on the role of the threat to the unconscious ego, we are forced to keep in mind the importance of the ego in determining the form of resistance and its reasons for existence. In this way we can avoid the tendency to bypass the resistance to get to the "real" content.

One of the most important components of the resistance which Greenson leaves out is their *adaptive function*. Resistances are an adaptation to a threat to the ego at an earlier time. Thus, the patient who is silent in the face of emerging sexual thoughts about the analyst is not simply withholding, or derailing the process, or any of the other interpretations of hostility which may be part of any resistance. From the side of the ego resistance, the patient is responding to what is unconsciously experienced as a threat to which silence appears as a solution which mirrors an earlier adaptation (e.g., repression or oppositionalism as a regressive defense possibly designed to make the parents angry and thus deflect the threatening sexual fantasies).

The importance of recognizing the adaptive component of resistances cannot be overestimated. Most obviously, by keeping it in mind, the analyst can help to understand yet another factor in the evolution of what likely will be symptom-related behavior. Furthermore, understanding the adaptive aspect of the resistances allows for an easier acceptance of the behavior for both analyst and patient. It takes some of the accusatory/guilt components out of the interpretive process if it can be seen by both analysand and analyst as a repetition of an earlier adaptation to something frightening.

Some current perspectives

No one has explored the role of resistances in as much depth as Gray (1973, 1982, 1986, 1987, 1990). In his work, resistance analysis is at the center of the psychoanalytic process, with the unconscious threat to the ego as the crucial component. The work of analysis involves identifying the resistance and analyzing the threat, for the purpose of allowing thoughts greater access to consciousness. He has, more than any other analyst, taken Freud's second theory of anxiety and applied it to technique.

The author most frequently mentioned as being aligned with Gray in an ego-psychological approach to resistances is Schafer (1983), and indeed there are many similarities when views dominated by the release of unconscious fantasies are compared. However, there are subtle differences in their views of the resistances which have yet to be explored. Schafer's approach is presented as an antidote to the critical view of resistances that creeps into discussions when the role of the ego is not appreciated. Yet the centrality of the threat to the ego in resistances is noted only in passing in his work. While Gray highlights the significance of identifying the resistances in order to make them conscious, Schafer frets over the implied criticism in such an approach (p. 169). Schafer does not seem as concerned as Gray in keeping closely attuned to what the analysand is consciously aware of in the analyst's interventions (pp. 171–172). How far the analyst can stray from the surface, and still make effective resistance interpretations, is also a point of dispute. Apfelbaum and Gill (1989), as well, trumpet the ego-psychological approach to resistance; many of their perspectives are similar to Gray's and Schafer's. Issues in common include the importance of the analyst's neutrality (p. 1087), consideration for ego syntonicity in resistance interpretations (p. 1090), and the analyst not taking on an authoritarian role (p. 1094). However, what Apfelbaum and Gill focus on is the subtle relation between defense and what is being defended against, with the goal of defense analysis being to clarify the relation between them. Again, some subtle differences from Gray's work appear. Gray's technique of resistance analysis is directed to uncovering and highlighting resistances in a manner that allows for the analysand's greater *conscious* participation. His focus is more on the nature of the threat than the feelings or fantasies causing the threat. Gray's (1987) view is that the primary threat to the ego is from a superego, reexternalized onto the analyst, which was experienced first from an earlier authority figure. This is in contrast to Apfelbaum and Gill's (1989) view "that what is defense at one moment in relation to a given wish may the next moment become the wish defended against" (p. 1076). In their view, the distinction between the resistance and what is being resisted is only momentary; the primary threat is not easily established.

What seems most significant in these current works on resistance is that *the implications of Freud's second theory of anxiety are being explored, and some important questions on the nature of the ego and its consequences for clinical technique are being raised*. For example, Gray's (1990) method of listening for "breaks" in the associative process (p. 1087) to determine the moment of a resistance makes an assumption about the nature of ego functioning which is different from the views of Schafer or Apfelbaum and Gill. Gray (1986) believes there are no inherent barriers to the drive derivatives, which he portrays as constantly seeking access to consciousness. If a resistance develops, it is the result of a conflict in action, and this is the moment when the resistance can be fruitfully brought to the analysand's attention. The analyst must wait until there is evidence of the unconscious ego blocking unconscious drive derivatives, before proceeding. Inherent within this position is a view of an ego which is more passive than Schafer's or Apfelbaum and Gill's conception of it. From this come questions about the ego's ability to observe its own resistances. Are there changes throughout an analysis requiring the analyst to stay closely at-tuned to the moment of resistance at one time, but, at other times, allowing him to let the resistance and associations to it flourish so that a more subtle resistance interpretation might develop? From another perspective, can Schafer's concerns about focusing on the resistances be blunted, as Gray might suggest, via education without becoming intellectualized? These are examples of some of the questions that need to be investigated. What is exciting is that the early promise of ego psychology seems finally to be bearing fruit in these investigations of resistance. Meaningful questions on the role of the ego in clinical technique are being addressed. However, we must also not get too far ahead of ourselves. As noted above, there are still those who view resistances from a drive-dominated position. For some the ego resistances are still a barrier to be breached so that the unconscious drive derivatives behind them can be uncovered.

Writing contemporaneously with the authors just noted, Dewald (1980) starts from the premise that core resistances (what he calls strategic resistances) exist to aid in the maintenance of unconscious gratifications and the avoidance of painful feelings associated with *renunciation of these gratifications*. Dewald sees the ego functioning in what he calls "tactical resistances," which are used to defend against awareness of strategic resistances. Although Dewald does not discuss why it is necessary to defend against strategic resistances, it would seem that this is because of the *pain and grief the patient would feel if he became aware of and needed to give up unconscious wishes*. However, what we see in Dewald's definition of ego defenses is that the ego part is relegated to a secondary role (i.e., protecting of the unconscious wishes). A major clinical problem such a position poses is that it takes the clinician's view from the ego during a time of resistance, to the unconscious wishes. In such a stance, one is drawn to bypass the ego resistances to get to the unconscious libidinal component of the re-sistances. Once again, we see an experienced clinician taking a position on the meaning of ego resistances which would likely lead to their being bypassed. It reflects a regressive view of patients whereby an enfeebled ego is there pri-marily to protect and guard the infantile wishes. The notion that infantile wishes continue to exist, in part, because of fear associated with higher-level functioning leads us to once again recognize that it is, specifically, the threat to the ego which remains unacknowledged here.

Discussion

Why do we need to keep rediscovering a way to work with resistances that takes into account the latter stages of Freud's thinking on anxiety? There are numerous factors that need to be considered in order to understand this phenomenon. Some are historical and some seem to be hazards of the profession.

To start with, Freud's new theory of anxiety did not lead him to any radical rethinking on the technique of resistance interpretation. While phrases from his pre-1926 approach to resistances give the impression of a growing understanding consistent with the new theory on the role of the ego in resistances, reading the entire text allows one to see the primacy of Freud's early theory of anxiety. In fact, Strachey (1959) notes that as Freud expounded on the correctness of his new theory of anxiety, he did not fully abandon the first theory of anxiety. Brenner (1982) points out that Freud needed to keep a purely economic, quantitative explanation for anxiety to explain what he saw as "contentless anxiety" in the actual neurosis. Even while refuting his old theory Freud (1926, p. 109) states, "we see, then, that it is not so much a question of taking back our earlier findings as of bringing them into line with more recent discoveries" (Freud, 1926, p. 141). The student of psychoanalysis in 1926, then, was left with a confusing picture on the causes of resistances. The technical approach to resistances based on economic principles would be quite different than that based on an unconscious sense of danger. The approach to the actual neurosis necessitated a freeing of the repressed drive, while the second theory of anxiety required a careful exploration of the perceived dangerous affects which set off the resistances. These very different approaches continue to find their way into the literature on resistance. While few psychoanalysts would agree today with a view of anxiety based on dammed-up libido, the impact of this view has remained significant in the clinical literature and has left some with the impression that Freud was ambivalent about the role of the ego in resistance (Gray, 1982).

The continued emphasis on the primacy of drives in Freud's view of resistances can be seen in the following statement:

> The dynamic factor which makes a working-through of this kind necessary and comprehensible is not far to seek. It must be that after the ego's resistance has been removed the power of the compulsion to repeat-the attraction exerted by the unconscious prototypes upon the repressed instinctual process-has still to be overcome. (Freud, 1926, p. 159)

One can see in this Freud's view of the power of the drives as an important component in the working-through process. From the side of the ego, however, one can say that working through is necessary to explore the unconscious threats to the ego. Indeed, if one sees working through as a battle against the attraction of unconscious drives, special techniques are necessary to (1) keep the conscious ego's attention on the resistance, and (2) bolster the analysand's attempt to fight off the power of unconscious gratifications. Arguments against the resistances, along with "rewards and advantages" proposed to the ego if it gives up its resistances, are logical extensions of this economic view of the resistances. This view of the resistances, as something to be overcome via the use of what we would now call special parameters, has had a profound effect on psychoanalytic perspectives on the resistances. As Gray (1986) points out:

> the positive transference...is a form of suggestion that is still widely used to overcome resistance. It is usually more accepted in practice than acknowledged in theory. Many analyzable patients have a capacity and a tendency to cling to this particular motivational source. Analysts who depend on it usually assume it will be relinquished near the end of the analysis. This is not necessarily the case. (p. 247)

Another possible reason for our clinical stagnation in approaching the resistances is that the earliest and most influential ego psychologists, following Freud's predilection for theory building, were more interested in the ego as part of a general psychology. Many analysts (Apfelbaum, 1962; Arlow, 1975; Fogel, 1989) have noted the work of these theorists was criticized for being remote from clinical experience. The beginning explorations of the dimensions of the ego were not clinical in nature, but instead turned toward the development of the ego, its autonomous functioning, and especially developmental tasks in conjunction with the environment and their effect on the ego. This line of investigation has germinated a rich harvest of data which ultimately have enriched our clinical work. However, the more strictly clinical investigations into the work of the ego, especially the unconscious ego, have suffered from benign neglect. The result has been that our knowledge of the resistances, as Weinshel (1984) noted, has stagnated. Our clinical work suffers from confusing messages on the correct technique for dealing with resistances, and the more interesting questions in dealing with resistances still need to be addressed.

I believe we also need to look in a direction other than our intellectual educational past to discover the reasons for our neglect of the resistances. The region we need to explore further has to do with the pleasures, disappointments, and hazards of the profession. Stone (1973) and Gray (1982) have described the power or magnetism of the id for most analysts in contrast to the resistances. To support this all I would ask is for the reader to think back to his last discussion of clinical case material, and how many of the comments were directed to the "real" unconscious fantasy (especially if the analysis was stalled). While each of us has our own personal reasons for this predilection to interpret a particular type of material over another, when an entire group shows this tendency, we are dealing with more than an individual phenomenon. The search for a hidden, driving force behind seemingly random events is as old as man himself and is a motivational source for the development of religion and the sciences. To find behind man's suffering a secret, unifying theme which touches on our basic nature is the stuff of man's dreams from the beginning of time. The psychoanalyst's tendency to search for the unconscious fantasy binding together the symptoms, transferences, external reality, and daydreams of the patient is the psychoanalyst engaging in an endeavor which has always captivated man. However, while scientist and philosopher may spend a life-time searching for a small piece of the answer to the great human mysteries, we often feel we come up with our answers daily, if not several times in one day, if we are really cooking. In this context, it is notable that Oedipus's marriage to Jocasta was preceded by two important events. One was the killing of Laius; yet the other was solving the riddle of the Sphinx. It has led me to wonder whether, in part, our attraction to unraveling the mysteries of the unconscious id is a repetition of this timeless ritual, with the fantasy reward and attendant feelings of power, a revival of the wished-for oedipal victory.

There are a number of other factors that tend to draw us away from the resistances. When a patient is in the throes of a prolonged resistance, the "feeling in the session" is that they are working against us. For most of us this raises issues of narcissistic injury and attendant anger, so that we are not at our most empathic. Furthermore, it is a time when the patient is most resolute in his fighting the analysis and analyst, often outside of awareness, in a way the patient is frequently comfort- able with. At such times we need to be most empathic with our patient's earliest anxieties and fears of being overwhelmed. When the patient is most out of tune with the idealized analytic state which serves as a model for participation, we need to be most understanding of his primitive affective states. This then needs to be integrated and presented to the patient in a way that is not threatening. We need to consider whether our desire to explain the meanings behind the resistance, before exploring the resistance itself, is an attempt to defend against the patient's primitive anxieties and our own hostility by being "over-giving." As with any need to be "giving," one has to wonder about the unconscious hostility behind it. In fact, it is not infrequent for patients to associate to violent intrusions or to become more masochistic after a resistance has been bypassed with an interpretation of the unconscious wishes behind it. Furthermore, the intellectualization in-herent in interpreting before the resistance has been clarified and the affect explored, seems to be the analyst's way of defending against the depth of feeling associated with resistances which initially appear wordless or as "action thoughts" (Busch, 1989). In the throes of a resistance even our higher-functioning patients seem more primitive.

Finally, I do not believe we have had a good language for exploring the resistances. Just as with patients where putting things into words brings an alteration in higher-level ego functions (Loewald, 1971), the same can be said for clinical concepts. While most analysts know that interpretations of resistances should take place first, exactly what this means, how it might be done, what one needs to look for, still seem mysterious. As Gray (1986) has noted, Freud's observation on the resistance to uncovering resistances "often results from the analyst's failure to provide the analysand with the best opportunity to perceive the resistance" (p. 254). Gray's (1986, 1987, 1990) articles on techniques for helping analysands learn about unconscious ego resistances are an excellent beginning in this area. However, it may not have been sufficiently emphasized that understanding resistances might take a slightly different type of listening on the analyst's part. In most case reports one hears the analyst listening to the *content* of the associations for the derivatives of the unconscious fantasies. Listening for the resistances sometimes requires greater attention to the *process* of associations. Thus, the heart of Gray's clinical technique revolves around listening for the moment in the psychoanalytic process when a resistance is in operation. He calls these moments "breaking points" (1990, p. 1087), where there is a change in voice. "It may be a blatant, dramatic, sudden difference from what occupies the moment before; or it may be an exceedingly subtle alternative" (p. 1087). At other times, one can hear the resistance in an analysand's "consistency of voice." Take, for example, the patient who rushes from topic to topic in order to ward off a fantasy of being suffocated, or the analysand who keeps spaces between topics, so they do not touch. At these times the analyst may listen primarily for the meaning of *how* the analysand is associating, rather than to the meaning of the associations themselves. The associations may be in the action of associating. While likely this is a familiar manner of listening for many analysts, like the resistances themselves, familiarity should not breed content. This, however, is still another recurring theme.

Note

1 See Busch (1995) For a detailed description of her work, and the tragic tale of what happened to her shortly after she wrote this paper.

References

Apfelbaum, B. (1962). Some problems in contemporary ego psychology. *J. Am. Psychoanal. Assoc.*, 10:526–537.

Apfelbaum, B. & Gill, M. M. (1989). Ego analysis and the relativity of defense: Technical implications of the structural theory. *J. Am. Psychoanal. Assoc.*, 37:1071–1096.

Arlow, J. A. (1975). The structural hypothesis: Technical considerations. *Psychoanal. Q.*, 44:509–525.

Brenner, C. (1982). *The mind in conflict*. New York: International Universities Press.

Busch, F. (1989). The compulsion to repeat in action: A developmental perspective. *Int. J. Psychoanal.*, 70:535–544.

Busch, F. (1993). In the neighborhood: Aspects of a good interpretation and a "developmental lag" in ego psychology. *J. Am. Psychoanal. Assoc.*, 41:151–177.

Dewald, P. A. (1980). The handling of resistances in adult psychoanalysis. *Int. J. Psychoanal.*, 61:61–70.

Fenichel, O. (1941). *Problems of psychoanalytic technique*. New York: Psychoanalytic Quarterly.

Fogel, G. I. (1989). The authentic function of psychoanalytic theory: An overview of the contributions of Hans Loewald. *Psychoanal. Q.*, 18:419–451.

Freud, A. (1936). *The ego and the mechanisms of defense*. New York: International Universities Press, 1966.

Freud, S. (1895). Studies on hysteria. *S. E.*, 2.

Freud, S. (1913). On beginning the treatment. *S. E.*, 12.

Freud, S. (1914). Remembering, repeating and working through. *S. E.*, 12.

Freud, S. (1915-1916). Introductory lectures on psychoanalysis. *S. E.*, 15 & 16. - -

Freud , S. (1923). The ego and the id. *S. E.*, 19.

Freud, S. (1926). Inhibitions, symptoms and anxiety. *S. E.*, 20.

Freud, S. (1937a). Analysis terminable and interminable. *S. E.*, 23.

Freud, S. (1937b). Constructions in analysis. *S. E.*, 23.

Freud, S. (1940). An outline of psychoanalysis. *S. E.*, 23.

Glover, E. (1955). *The technique of psychoanalysis*. New York: International Universities Press.

Goldberger, M. (1989). Review of techniques of working with resistance, eds., D. S. Milman & G. D. Goldman. *Psychoanal. Q.*, 58:295–298.

Gray, P. (1973). Psychoanalytic technique and the ego's capacity for viewing intrapsychic activity. *J. Am. Psychoanal. Assoc.*, 21:474–494.

Gray, P. (1982). Developmental lag in the evolution of technique for psycho-analysis of neurotic conflict. *J. Am. Psychoanal. Assoc.*, 30:621–656.

Gray, P. (1986). On helping analysands observe intrapsychic activity. In: A. D. Richards & M. S. Willick (eds.), *Psychoanalysis: The science of mental conflict-essays in honor of Charles Brenner*. Hillsdale, N.J.: Analytic Press.

Gray, P. (1987). On the technique of analysis of the superego-an introduction. *Psychoanal. Q.*, 56:130–154.

Gray, P. (1990). The nature of therapeutic action in psychoanalysis. *J. Am. Psychoanal. Assoc.*, 38:1083–1098.

Greenson, R. R. (1967). *The technique and practice of psychoanalysis*, Vol. 1. New York: International Universities Press.

Kohut, H. (1984). *How does analysis cure*. Chicago, IL: Univ. Chicago Press.

Loewald, H. W. (1971). Some considerations of repetition and repetition compulsion. *Int. J. Psychoanal.*, 52:59–66.

Moore, B. E. & Fine, B. D. (1990). *Psychoanalytic terms and concepts*. New York: American Psychoanalytic Association and Yale Univ. Press.

Reich, W. (1933). *Character analysis*. New York: Farrar, Straus & Cudahy, 1949.

Schafer, R. (1983). *The analytic attitude*. New York: Basic Books.

Searl, M. N. (1936). Some queries on principles of technique. *Int. J. Psychoanal.*, 1:471–493.

Sterba, R. (1940). The dynamics of the dissolutions of the transference resistance. *Psychoanal. Q.*, 9:363–375.

Stone, L. (1973). On resistance to the psychoanalytic process: Some thoughts on its nature and motivations. *Psychoanal. Contemp. Sci.*, 2:42–73.

Strachey, J. (1959). Editor's introduction to inhibition, symptoms, and anxiety. *S. E.*, 20.

Weinshel, E. M. (1984). Some observations on the psychoanalytic process. *Psychoanal. Q.*, 53:63–92.

5 Some ambiguities in the method of free association and their implications for technique[1]

Freud's method of free association, labeled the "fundamental rule" of psychoanalysis in 1912, and part of his psychoanalytic technique by 1892, remained unchanged as a technical precept from its elaboration in The Interpretation of Dreams:

> We therefore tell the patient that the success of the psychoanalysis depends on his noticing and reporting whatever comes into his head and not being misled, for instance, into suppressing an idea because it strikes him as unimportant or irrelevant or because it seems to him meaningless. He must adopt a completely impartial attitude to what occurs to him, since it is precisely his critical attitude which is responsible for his being unable, in the ordinary course of things, to achieve the desired unravelling of his dream or obsessional idea or whatever it may be. (Freud, 1900, p. 101)

There is little doubt that, at present, most analysts would agree with Kanzer's assessment that, "Free association remains the essential instrument of psychoanalytic investigative techniques" (Panel, 1971, p. 104), or Kris's (1990b) observation that "free association is the hallmark of psychoanalytic treatment conducted by analysts of every stripe" (p. 26).[2] When one is listening to colleagues present clinical data, it does not appear as if there have been significant changes in the intent or tone of the instructions given to analysands since Freud's original description. While the words may be different, Moore and Fine's (1990) description of "free association" some 85 years later defines the expectations for the analysand as essentially the same.

> The patient in psychoanalytic treatment is asked to express in words all thoughts, feelings, wishes, sensations, images, and memories, without reservation, as they spontaneously occur. This requirement is called the fundamental rule of psychoanalysis. In following the rule, the patient must often overcome conscious feelings of embarrassment, fear, shame, and guilt. His or her cooperation is motivated in part by knowledge of the purpose for which he or she is in analysis—to deal with conflicts and overcome problems. (p. 78)

It is difficult to know what to make of Lichtenberg and Galler's (1987) survey of analysts' presentation of the fundamental rule. A skewed sample, giving variable responses (in terms of detail), can only give one an impressionistic view of some analysts' current perception of how they practice. While the authors are impressed with the diversity of responses they received, I am impressed with their similarities to the guidelines suggested by Freud. With some exceptions, the numbers of which are difficult to determine, the intent of the instructions often remains the same. "I hope you will express yourself as freely as possible because the more you can do so, the more likely it is that we will be able to work usefully...I'd like you to tell me as fully as you can everything as it enters your mind, and I will try to help you as best as I can" (pp. 64–65). Lichtenberg and Galler's characterization of the tone of the guidelines given to patients as "gentle exhortation" (p. 63) captures a current dilemma for many analysts. The strident nature of Freud's view of the method of free association seems alien, thus the "gentle" component. Yet we still believe it necessary to "exhort" our patients to hold back as little as possible. One does get the impression from this study, and from informal discussions with colleagues, that subtle changes in the method of free association are being made. However, the reasons for such changes, and their implications for technique, have not been made explicit.

This paper, then, is in the spirit of the conclusion of a panel on this topic which ended with the thoughts, "Free association, so basic to the science of psychoanalysis, is far from being a closed book, and that despite the further delineation of the conceptualization of it, thus far we are still on the threshold of the exploration of its many mysteries" (Panel, 1971, p. 109). It is my contention that there are conceptual contradictions buried in the method of free association as currently practiced, which lead to confusion in the method and goals of psychoanalysis. Recent advances in understanding the ego have given us the potential for a subtly different view of the method of free association from Freud's. But these different views, and why they are necessary, have not been fully explicated. For some, my argument will have a familiar ring in that older and newer models of the method have been blended together and differences between them have become blurred. However, I shall explore the distinction between Freud's view of the method, and the problematic view of the psychoanalytic process it fosters, and some current views of psychoanalytic technique rooted in the structural model which have important implications for the method of free association.

Free association and resistance analysis

Freud's discovery and elucidation of free association stems from a time when he viewed anxiety as the result of dammed-up libido, and views cast a long shadow over the method of free association. The purpose of free association was to get out in the open something that was unconsciously being held back. While Freud understood and appreciated resistances, and wrote about them, at times with a clinical sensitivity enviable even today (see Breuer & Freud, 1895, p. 269), his technical handling of resistances relied primarily on suggestion, education, and the influence accrued to the analyst, via the positive transference, to overcome resistances. The method of free association as first developed was geared to overcoming and not understanding the resistances. In his instructions to patients, Freud (1913) included the following injunctions against holding anything back:

> You will be tempted to say to yourself that this or that is irrelevant here, or is quite unimportant, or nonsensical, so that there is no need to say it. You must never give in to these criticisms but must say it in spite of them—indeed, you must say it precisely because you feel an aversion to doing so. Later on, you will find out and learn to understand the reason for this injunction, which is really the only one you have to follow... Finally, never forget that you have promised to be absolutely honest, and never leave anything out because, for some reason or other, it is unpleasant to say it. (p. 135)

This recommendation was repeated in 1923. "They were to communicate these ideas to the physician even if they felt objections to doing so, if, for instance, the thoughts seemed too disagreeable, too senseless, too unimportant or irrelevant" (p. 195). Freud's view of the technical significance of this prohibition against holding thoughts back is captured in the following: "It is very remarkable how the whole task becomes impossible if a reservation is allowed at any single place" (Freud, 1913, p.135). On another occasion, referring to the prohibition against holding thoughts back, Freud referred to it as his "sacred rule" (Freud, 1917, p. 288).

It becomes clear that the very essence of the method of free association was geared toward overcoming rather than analyzing resistances. When a resistance developed, the patient was instructed to push on in spite of it. Freud saw the work of analysis as "impossible," as long as resistances were in evidence—this, in spite of the fact that he saw resistances as an inevitable part of the analysis. I believe this is another crucial component in the "developmental lag" of integrating resistance analysis into clinical technique that Gray (1982) and I (Busch, 1992) have pointed to, while also contributing to a critical attitude toward resistances on the part of many analysts. While analysts generally agree that resistances are the ego's response to distressing affect as first described by Freud (1923, 1926), and that resistance analysis is a cornerstone of the psychoanalytic method, our technique of analyzing as expressed in our instructions to patients is geared toward bypassing the importance of these affects and the ego's responses to it. This seems to be a factor in why so many analysts persist in seeing their purpose as "getting out" the strangulated affect or unconscious fantasy in spite of seemingly sophisticated views of the resistances (e.g., Greenson, 1967, pp. 299–300). The basic mission of analysis, as defined by the original intent of the method of free association, is to have the patient hold back as little as possible. While this contradiction exists (i.e., we believe the analysand should not hold back anything while considering it crucial to work with those reasons why he inevitably holds back), confusion over goals and methods of analysis must exist. We cannot continue to ask the patient "to say what comes to mind no matter how painful" without acknowledgment of the impossibility of the task, and the importance of understanding the reasons for its impossibility. Our understanding of resistances dictates that instruction in the method of free association needs to be updated.

Until recently there have been few critiques of the method of free association. As Mahony (1979) notes, many of Freud's original ideas on this subject get "reiterated in the psychoanalytic literature with very little advance beyond them" (p. 163). Kris (1992) observed that even through the height of the ego-psychological approach to psychoanalytic technique, insight remained inter-twined with the lifting of repression and the topographic notion of making the unconscious conscious. Thus, the method of free association, when empha-sizing the pushing away of resistances so that the unconscious could be ob-served, was quite compatible with this approach. An exception was the work of Loewenstein (1963) who noted, as Freud did, the "possibility of complying with such a request is severely limited" (p. 455), and quietly changed the focus of the associative process, suggesting, "the patient is expected to observe and express emerging thoughts as well as his reluctance to perceive or verbalize them" (p. 454). With this additional focus, the resistance is brought to center stage in the associative process. The analysand's focus is equally on the emerging thoughts and those barriers to thought. Loewenstein, however, did not note the slight but significant alteration in perspective, seemingly because of his belief in Freud's "insistence on the importance of analyzing resistances" (p. 254). While this is correct from one perspective, as noted above, Freud's view of analyzing resistances relied heavily on suggestion and persuasion.

Some analysts have argued that directing the analysand to hold nothing back exerts a type of superego burden which the patient cannot meet (Blum, 1981; Epstein, 1976; Kanzer, 1972). That the analysand's attempt to meet the de-mands of free association was doomed to failure was well known to Freud. In discussing free association, Freud (1913) states, "Later, under the dominance of the resistances, obedience to it weakens, and there comes a time in every analysis when the patient disregards it" (p. 135). In presenting free association as a demand upon the analysand to "say everything that comes to mind," without any stated modifications regarding this difficult task, we shall likely contribute to the opposite effect than intended. We are consigning the pa-tient's efforts to inevitable failure, with each individual's response based on his or her particular psychology (i.e., some patients will become secretive, some will be rebellious, or passive). This is not to say that giving the correct in-structions will do away with reactions to the associative process. However, as we well know, there are important differences between the reality of being asked to comply with an impossible task and a fantasy that this is what is being asked.

A fresh approach to the method of free association is found in the work of Kris (1982, 1983, 1990a, 1990b, 1992) and Gray (1973, 1986, 1990), 1992). Instead of seeing resistances as a barrier to free association, they see free association as a method by which resistances can become the centerpiece of the analytic process. For Kris (1990a), "the first aim of the method is to help diminish through understanding the unconscious restrictions that limit the associations" (p. 27). The key component of this approach is that "through understanding" the inevitable resistances are worked on, with the goal to increase the analysand's conscious acceptance of his thought. No longer are the resistances an impediment that makes treatment "impossible." "A major goal of the analytic process is to help the analysand gain full access to those habitual, unconscious, and outmoded ego activities that serve resistances" (Gray, 1986, p. 245). In an attempt to correct what Gray (1986) characterizes as a "paucity of methodology for achieving this goal" (p. 245), both authors focus on the process of free association rather than its "hidden content." The heart of their technique involves listening for the moment in the associations when a resistance is in operation. Gray has likened it to an apple picker watching a conveyer belt for bad apples. One's attention is on the flow of material, looking for a change that indicates the flow of thoughts has been blocked. This is the moment of the resistance, and the point at which the analysis of the resistances begins. The advantage of this method over searching for the "hidden content" (i.e., either by directing patients to tell us what they were holding back, or via the analyst interpreting what was not said) have been known for some time (see Searl, 1936), and recently have been brought to our attention by Gray. In essence, investigating the resistances to free association rather than circumventing them, has been shown to be an ego-strengthening rather than weakening technique. While there are significant differences between Kris and Gray in their techniques for investigating the resistances, and in the specifics of how they see this process as helping the patient, both have given psychoanalysts a way of thinking about working with free associations in a manner that corrects one of our oldest methodological inconsistencies, and fits with our understanding of the workings of the mind as modified by our knowledge of the unconscious resistances. Before, analysts had to resolve how we could implore patients to follow the "basic rule," while also believing that working through resistances was a cornerstone of analytic technique. This has had a profound effect on the methods and goals of psychoanalysis.

> Gray's (1986) instructions, which include the expectation that resistances to the method of free association will occur, could serve as a useful model...I make clear that I am talking about an effort toward free association, since interferences regularly take place while we are working to carry out this task. I point out that it is precisely the study of these interferences and the obstacles to putting the observations into words that provides us with greater access to what is now out of reach and which contributes to the patient's problems; and that the nature of the obstacles

to free association will be intimately connected with the nature of the problems or conflicts that brought the patient to treatment. (p. 248)

With this addition to the "basic rule," conveyed in whatever language and with whatever timing the analyst deems best, we tilt the method of free association toward the study of resistances. Kris (personal communication) suggests that "instructions are designed to reduce reluctances, but to highlight resistances, not to circumvent them." This will not solve the problem of what Gray (1982) has called analysts' resistances to resistance analysis, but it is an attempt to correct what Apfelbaum and Gill (1989) note as the difficulty for many analysts to integrate the structural model into clinical technique.

Self-reflection and free association

The role of the analysand's interest in and capacity for thinking about his own thought processes has been confounded from the beginning of the method of free association. Freud's (1900) stated view was that reflecting on one's thoughts, in contrast to observing them (i.e., like a passenger on a train), was antithetical to the method of free association.

> I have noticed in my psycho-analytical work that the whole frame of mind of a man who is reflecting is totally different from that of a man who is observing his own psychical processes. In reflection there is one more psychical activity at work than in the most attentive self-observation, and this is shown amongst other things by the tense looks and wrinkled forehead of a person pursuing his reflections as compared with the restful expression of a self-observer. In both cases attention must be concentrated, but the man who is reflecting is also exercising his critical faculty; this leads him to reject some of the ideas that occur to him after perceiving them, to cut short others without following the trains of thought which they would open up to him…. (pp. 101–102)

Yet shortly after rejecting a reflective mode of thought as an interference to free association, Freud (1900) in quoting the writer Schiller, supports the necessity of self-reflection in order to make sense of associations.

> Looked at in isolation, a thought may seem very trivial or very fantastic; but it may be made important by another thought that comes after it, and, in conjunction with thoughts that may seem equally absurd, it may turn out to form a most effective link. Reason cannot form any opinion upon all this unless it retains the thought long enough to look at it in connection with the others. On the other hand, where there is a creative mind, Reason—so it seems to me—relaxes its watch upon the gates, and the ideas rush in pell-mell, and only then does it look them through and examine them in a mass. (p. 103)

Here Freud is saying that observation of one's thoughts is really not enough. In order to make anything of one's observations, the observations need to be observed. Freud's concern over the critical component of reflection is regarding the first level of observations (i.e., free associations), not the further reflections on the observations. Yet, given Freud's theoretical views and clinical experience at the time, it is not surprising that he would come to focus on the freedom of the free associations as the key to symptom removal. Thus, his instructions to patients were geared toward as little self-reflection as possible, even though Freud (1917) recognized there were patients who could associate perfectly well, yet nothing ever came of it.

While Freud championed the importance of the analysand's associations, the significance of the analysand's contemplation, reflection, or observation of his associations remained in murkier territory—where it still remains. As mentioned elsewhere (Busch, 1992), the primary model for many analyses is that the analysand associates, and the analyst observes and interprets. The analysand's interest and ability to reflect back upon his thoughts, or his resistance to doing so, seems not to be a common part of the analytic field. Yet, as we shall see, the capacity of the analysand to observe his thoughts is seen as an important, yet neglected, part of the outcome of psychoanalytic treatment.

Sterba's (1934) classic paper on the fate of the ego in psychoanalysis brought analysts' attention to the significance of the analysand's observations of the ongoing analytic process. He describes what he calls a "dissociation" in the ego, which develops during the analytic process and becomes the *sine qua non* of the success of the analysis. Freud (1932) had already suggested this when he described the ego's capacity to take itself as an object and observe itself, while also characterizing the goal of psychoanalysis as widening the ego's field of perception. Sterba states that the "dissociation" occurs when, via the analyst's interpretations, an alliance is formed with the ego that helps dissociate it from instinctual and repressive forces. The fate of the analysis is seen as resting with experiences where "the subject's consciousness shifts from the center of affective experience to that of intellectual contemplation" (p. 121). According to Friedman (1992), "Sterba saw it as a variant of the normal, characteristically human capacity of reflection, the sort of thing a Piagetian might describe as operating upon one's operations, or a philosopher might refer to as abstracting from one's abstractions, or a man in the street might say amounts to looking hard at oneself" (p. 3). It is a process whereby the analysand steps back from his experience of the analysis (i.e., his thoughts and feelings), and reflects upon it —just the type of analytic experience Freud seemed ambivalent about.

Surprisingly, Sterba's concept remains "dissociated" from the theory of the psychoanalytic process. It is one of those concepts that, while generally accepted as a necessary component of the process, is not fully integrated into our theory. Friedman (personal communication) calls it "an un-scrutinized presupposition of the psychoanalytic procedure." The centrality of the concept is captured poetically by Gardner (1983) when he states, "Every patient and every psychoanalyst, the first and each after, has struggled and will struggle between aims to advance self-inquiry and aims to obstruct it" (p. 8). While Friedman (1992) points out that it is often confused with the "therapeutic alliance," there seems to be a generally accepted developmental line from self-reflection to self-analysis. The essence of this perspective is caught in the statement by Kantrowitz and her colleagues (1990), "We define self-analysis as the capacity to observe and reflect upon one's own behaviors, feelings, or fantasy life in a manner that leads to understanding the meaning of that phenomenon in a new light" (pp. 639–640; italics added). Others have seen this capacity as an important one that develops during the analysis, and as a criterion for termination (Gaskill, 1980; Novick, 1982). Yet, for the most part, comments in the literature on the significance of patients' capacity to reflect on their association are presented as sidelights to other issues, and not addressed head-on. For example, Loewenstein (1963) notes, "Not only does the analyst pay equal attention to id, ego, and superego manifestations, but even the patient is expected to observe and express his emerging thoughts as well as his reluctance to perceive or verbalize them" (p. 178; italics added). Later (1972) he writes, "What the patient learns from his analyst is to allow certain thoughts to become available to himself, and to look at them from a point of view acquired from the analyst" (p. 221). Similar thoughts (i.e., on the significance of a split-off ego for the success of the analytic process) have been expressed by others (A. Freud, 1936; Fenichel, 1941; Greenson, 1967; Kris, 1956; Nunberg, 1955). Weinshel (1984) highlights the significance of the development of self-reflection to the analytic process in this way: "I would suggest that this organization and these structures—the psychoanalytic process—remain as permanent products of the reasonably successful analysis and that their presence is reflected most immediately and most tangentially in the operation of a more effective and more 'objective' capacity for self-observation" (p. 82). He bolsters his argument for the importance of this development (as do Kantrowitz et al., 1990) by citing data on follow-ups of successfully completed analyses which indicate the importance of the internalization of an observing function. Sonnenberg's (1991) description of his ongoing analysis supports this view. However, for Weinshel, as for those analysts who have considered the subject before him, the development of the observing capacity is not so much a part of the analysis as a side effect. It is most frequently written about as a function of identification with the analyst, or the work of the analysis, but not as an integral part of the analytic work.

The significance of self-observation as part of the analytic process has been most clearly articulated by Gray (1973, 1986, 1990, 1992). In elaborating on Sterba's early views Gray (1986) states: "I believe we can move beyond the implications of the word fate by thinking of the changes in the self-observing ego as more than a kind of inevitable byproduct of the analysis. Systematic attention to self-observation, when clinically appropriate, can become a more explicit aim of analysis of the neuroses" (p. 260). Gray sees self-observation not only as an important goal of analysis, but as the focus of the analysis. Following the work of Anna Freud (1936), he treats the ego as the seat of observation. He reminds us that the ego is under the sway of various forces that influence how an analysand thinks about himself. The primary focus of his technique is helping analysands' observe their unconscious defensive activity designed to keep thoughts out of awareness. By staying closely attuned to conflicts in action that are observable to the patient, Gray works toward strengthening and giving greater autonomy to those ego functions involved with observation and thought. This is in contrast to techniques that rely primarily on the analyst's empathic or intuitive reading of the unconscious, bypassing the ego's participation in the process except as admirer of the analyst's observational capacities. He deplores that, "as a result, the ego's often highly detailed role in enforcing the repression it is less likely to be subject to the important perception, examination, and exploration of its history" (Gray, 1990, p. 1092).

Using Freud's later model of the mind, Gray has shown the significance of the ego's self-observation capacities for the analytic process in resistance analysis, and the growth of autonomy via strengthening those observational abilities. The resistances Gray highlights are those seen in the moment-to-moment observation of the patient's associations. A typical example cited by Gray is when there is a break in the associative narrative after the emergence of a disturbing thought. Gray then helps analysands' to observe the resistances in action, while helping them to understand the causes for the resistances. This is one form of expanding the ego's observational capacities.

Important, also, is the analysis of resistances to thoughts as meaningful (i.e., self-observation as a method for self-analysis). Analysts have long been aware of the dynamic significance of resistances to self-analysis (e.g., self-analysis as a dangerous challenge to the analyst, or as a capitulation; thoughts representing feces that can be presented but not touched or are presented to the analyst for admiration). However, there is a way of thinking, characteristic of an ego caught in conflict, which ensures that the analysand remains oblivious to thoughts about his thoughts. This thinking, which is descriptively unconscious, leads to resistance to the analysis of thoughts, and becomes a crucial determinant of whether self-analysis is possible. At these times, the patient may be accepting of the analyst, seeing meaning in his thoughts, but the patient remains descriptively resistant to engaging in this aspect of the analytic work for himself. Unless one keeps the analysand's capacity for self-observation as an active component of the free association method, an important impediment to self-analysis may not be analyzed. An analysand's acceptance of the analyst's interpretation of meaning is a limited method of judging analytic change. Increasing understanding of the role of the ego in the psychoanalytic process allows us to understand the changes in orientation of the analysand in relation to his thoughts, as aspects of conflict are brought into awareness. While data from follow-up studies indicate the importance of the development of self-analysis, Loewald (1971, 1975) suggests that what one sees in successful analyses in areas of conflict is the move from lower- to higher-level ego functioning. Descriptively, we see this in the way patients can move from total immersion in the affective truth of a transference reaction, to the capacity to step back from it momentarily and wonder why they might be feeling the way they are. In this one sees a movement from thinking based on what Piaget (Inhelder & Piaget, 1958) called "preoperational" thought to that based more on "formal" operations. Developmentally, it is only in adolescence that the capacity for thinking back upon one's thoughts, using a variety of perspectives, is possible. A patient under the influence of preoperational thought feels neither the compunction to justify his reasonings to others nor to look for possible contradictions in his logic. He is, for example, unable to reconstruct a chain of reasoning which he has just passed through; he thinks but he cannot think about his thinking (Flavell, 1963, p. 156). Thus, in the early stages of treatment, one would not expect reflective thought in areas of conflict. The ego in a regressive state is not capable of looking back upon itself, while in nonconflictual areas self-reflection may be highly developed. As more components of the conflicts are brought into awareness, there is a move from actions and thoughts being closely intertwined—as they are in preoperational thought (see Busch, 1989)—to the capacity for objectifying thoughts and reflecting back upon them. Thought now has, "through this new orientation, the potentiality of imagining all that might be there—both the very obvious and the very subtle—and thereby of much better insuring the finding of all that is there" (Flavell, 1963, p. 205). From this perspective, movement toward increasing self-observation is a developmental step in thinking which then enhances the self-analytic process. Self-analysis without self-observation seems a contradiction in terms. How conscious this process need be, however, is not yet clear. Seeing the capacity to reflect as a developmental step in the analytic process, then, changes the view of the free association method. Observing one's thoughts as they are occurring is one developmental step, being able to then think about what one is thinking, is still another developmental step.

In contrast to Freud's initial view of reflection and observation, we now see them as vital for continuing self-analysis. Without the ability to observe thoughts along with the resistances to thoughts in action, it is difficult to see how an analysand may find meaning in them. It is, after all, a major analytic accomplishment when a patient recognizes there is something in his thoughts or actions to understand, and that it can be helpful to understand. This whole process can be seen most dramatically with patients whom we see in a second analysis. These patients will frequently show the capacity for reflective observation, except in areas of unanalyzed conflict where they remain "blind" to the possibility there is something to be observed.

Concluding thoughts

For a variety of historical reasons, our method of instructing patients in "free association" as first explicated by Freud, is designed to circumvent resistances and keep the analyst's ability to understand the associations at the forefront of analytic technique. This is not surprising as Freud's views on the method of free association were developed at a time when his understanding of the psychoanalytic task was very different from our current views. Furthermore, "Freud repeated himself on this important topic, and though he came back to it again and again throughout his life, he never got far beyond some early core ideas" (Mahony, 1979, p. 163). Based on a particular patient population, which contributed to a theory of anxiety and the unconscious heavily influenced by 19th-century views of energic principles, Freud's view of cure was the verbalization of unconscious ideation. Furthermore, his great discovery of "meaning" behind seemingly random thoughts and actions ultimately led to a view of the analyst's role as a type of psychic cryptographer. In conjunction, these two perspectives led to the model of the analysand as provider of primary data on his unconscious fantasy life, while the analyst became the reader of these data. As has been pointed out, Freud never fully integrated his ego psychology with technique (Busch, 1992, 1993; Gray, 1982). Furthermore, later forays into ego psychology tended toward understanding normal development, and not the role of the ego in the clinical process. This has hampered our understanding of the ego in the psychoanalytic process, as exemplified in our uncritical (for the most part) acceptance of the method of free association as first described by Freud.

It seems clear that analysts need to reorient themselves to the method of free association. This would include taking into account Freud's second theory of anxiety, and the growing body of data on what is essentially psychoanalytic in the psychoanalytic process (i.e., follow-up studies showing the significance of self-analysis in successful analyses). Whereas Freud's first theory of anxiety explained symptom formation as due to dammed-up libido, his second theory emphasized danger to the ego as the basis of the sense of threat. What is significant is that Freud's second theory of anxiety seems only to have been episodically grasped in our written history. An analyst's orientation toward resistances to free associations will differ dramatically based upon his stance vis-à-vis the source of anxiety.

One important component of the lag in evaluating the method of free association is the tension that exists between psychoanalysis as the understanding of meaning in memory, and psychoanalysis as the understanding of meaning in process. There is considerable disagreement on the appropriate stance of the analyst when listening to a patient's masturbatory fantasy told with a great many pauses. The psychoanalytic stance from the position of memory is to try and understand the meaning of the fantasy in the context of the general transferential ambiance as a repetition of the past. The psychoanalytic process stance would be interested in the meaning of the pauses, especially within the understanding of ongoing, demonstrable ego resistances. Psychoanalysis, from its very beginning, has been the study of memory. While Freud was well aware of the clinical importance of the psychoanalytic process, this understanding became lost in the ill-fated theoretical link between repetitions in action, the repetition compulsion, and the death instinct. Traditionally, the analysand has been viewed as the purveyor of associations. We have been much slower to integrate the associative process into our work, especially the ego's role in it as seen in surface manifestations of conflict.

Currently differences exist in how free associations are viewed not only by obviously divergent schools, but by those who might be considered similar in persuasion. There are subtle, but important differences in the nature of what the analyst is looking for as seen in the work of Arlow and Brenner (1990), and that of Gray (1992).

> In doing so [demonstrating transference], the analyst helps the patient to distinguish between fantasy and reality, between past and present. It becomes possible to demonstrate to the patient how much his or her thought and behavior are determined by unconscious conflicts and fantasies deriving from the past. (Arlow & Brenner, 1990, pp. 681–682)

> My aim is a consistent approach to all of the patient's words, with priority given to what is going on with and within those productions as they make their appearance, not with attempts to theorize about what was in mind at some other time and place. (Gray, p. 324)

Protestations aside about the many similarities in outlook between these analysts, there is a subtle but significant difference between them in their view of the associative process. Arlow and Brenner are geared more toward the elucidation of the meaning of the associations and their echoes from the past, while Gray is focused more on the immediate conflict as seen in the process of associating. This difference in emphasis reflects continuing tensions between unintegrated components of the topographic model, especially the role of consciousness, that linger in limbo in the structural model. While few analysts would disagree with the importance of elucidating unconscious fantasies, it remains cloudy as to how this is best accomplished in the face of ongoing unconscious resistances, which themselves may become the repository of wishes that are then defended against. Proponents champion one side of the conflict and tend to finesse this issue. I believe this is one factor in why Freud's view of the method of free association has not been sharply contrasted with an approach consistent with his later views on the resistances. That is, we blend these two approaches as we attempt to accommodate clinically to a thorny technical problem. B. Landau (unpublished) suggests the concepts ego synchronicity/dystonicity are more at the core of the structural theory than consciousness. This promising line of thought orients the psychoanalytic clinician to the analysand's associations from the perspective of the ego, a perspective that has been missing in our conceptual understanding of the method of free association. It orients the clinician to the ego in the defense/drive oscillation typical in associations, while providing a new dimension for examining the analysand's view of his own thoughts.

In essence, then, this paper is not so much about the words the analyst uses to describe the method of free association to his patients (although I do not consider the words insignificant), but about the orientation of the two participants toward the process. Our heritage has been geared toward using the method to bypass the ego's participation. Taking advantage of our increased understanding of the role of the ego as mediator of psychic threat, as well as the seat of the observation of conflict, analytic interest in the patient's free associations could most fruitfully be turned (again) toward the ego. Primary use of other orientations to the process of free association has the potential for colluding with the wish to avoid threat by circumventing the resistances and meeting certain regressive gratifications.

Notes

1 Written in honor of Paul Gray's 75th birthday.
2 Things have changed a lot since I wrote these words. From what I read in the literature now, there seems to be little use of free association in the United States, except those still following a Freudian perspective. Throughout the rest of the world the Kleinian and French analysts, and their followers, still seem to see free association as basic to the psychoanalytic method.

References

Apfelbaum, B. & Gill, M. M. (1989). Ego analysis and the relativity of defense: Technical implications of the structural theory. *J. Am. Psychoanal. Assoc.*, 37:1071–1096.
Arlow, J. A. & Brenner, C. (1990). The psychoanalytic process. *Psychoanal. Q.*, 59:678–692.
Blum, H. P. (1981). The forbidden guest and the analytic ideal: The superego and insight. *Psychoanal. Q.*, 50:535–556.
Breuer, J. & Freud, S. (1895). Studies on hysteria *S.E.* 2.
Busch, F. (1989). The compulsion to repeat in action: A developmental perspective. *Int. J. Psychoanal.*, 70:535–544.
Busch, F. (1992). Recurring thoughts on the unconscious ego resistances. *J. Am. Psychoanal. Assoc.*, 40:1089–1115.
Busch, F. (1993). In the neighborhood: Aspects of a good interpretation and its relationship to a "developmental lag" in ego psychology. *J. Am. Psychoanal. Assoc.*, 41:151–178.
Epstein, G. (1976). A note on the semantic confusion in the fundamental rule of psychoanalysis. *J. Phila. Assn. Psychoanal.*, 3 54–57
Fenichel, O. (1941). *Problems of psychoanalytic technique*. New York: Psychoanal. Q.
Flavell, J. H. (1963). *The developmental psychology of Jean Piaget*. Princeton, NJ: Van Nostrand.
Freud, A. (1936). *The ego and the mechanisms of defense. Writings 2*. New York: International Universities Press, 1966
Freud, S. (1900). The interpretation of dreams *S.E.* 4 & 5.
Freud, S. (1912). Recommendations to physicians practising psycho-analysis *S.E.* 12.
Freud, S. (1913). On beginning the treatment *S.E.* 12.
Freud, S. (1917). Resistance and repression *S.E.* 16.
Freud, S. (1923). The ego and the id *S.E.* 19.
Freud, S. (1926). Inhibitions, symptoms and anxiety *S.E.* 20.
Freud, S. (1932). New introductory lectures on psychoanalysis *S.E.* 22.
Friedman, L. (1992). How and why patients become more objective? Sterba compared with Strachey. *Psychoanal. Q.*, 61:1–17.

Gardner, M. R. (1983). *Self inquiry*. Boston: Little, Brown

Gaskill, H. S. (1980). The closing phase of the psychoanalytic treatment of adults and the goals of psychoanalysis: "The myth of perfectibility." *Int. J. Psychoanal.*, 61:11–23.

Gray, P. (1973). Psychoanalytic technique and the ego's capacity for viewing intrapsychic conflict. *J. Am. Psychoanal. Assoc.*, 21:474–494.

Gray, P. (1982). "Developmental lag" in the evolution of technique for psychoanalysis of neurotic conflict. *J. Am. Psychoanal. Assoc.*, 30:621–655.

Gray, P. (1986). On helping analysands observe intrapsychic activity. In: A. D. Richards & M. S. Willick (eds.), Psychoanalysis: *The science of mental conflict. Essays in Honor of Charles Brenner.* Hillsdale, NJ: Analytic Press.

Gray, P. (1990). The nature of therapeutic action in psychoanalysis. *J. Am. Psychoanal. Assoc.*, 38:1083–1097.

Gray, P. (1992). Memory as resistance and the telling of a dream. *J. Am. Psychoanal. Assoc.* 40:307–326.

Greenson, R. R. (1967). *The technique and practice of psychoanalysis*. New York: International Universities Press.

Inhelder, B. & Piaget, J. (1958). *The growth of logical thinking from childhood to adolescence*. New York: Basic Books.

Kantrowitz, J., Katz, A. L., & Paolitto, F. (1990). Followup of psychoanalysis five to ten years after termination: Development of the self-analytic function. *J. Am. Psychoanal. Assoc.*, 38:605–636

Kanzer, M. (1972). Superego aspects of free association and the fundamental rule. *J. Am. Psychoanal. Assoc.*, 20:246–266.

Kris, A. O. (1982). *Free association: Method and process*. New Haven, CT: Yale Univ. Press.

Kris, A. O. (1983). The analyst's conceptual freedom in the method of free asocation. *Int. J. Psychoanal.*, 64:407–411.

Kris, A. O. (1990a). Helping patients by analyzing self-criticism. *J. Am. Psychoanal. Assoc.*, 38:605–636.

Kris, A. O. (1990b). The analyst's stance and the method of free association. *Psychoanal. Study Child*, 45:25–41.

Kris, A. O. (1992). Interpretation and the method of free association. *Psychoanal. Inq.*, 12 208–224.

Kris, E. (1956). On some vicissitudes of insight in psychoanalysis. *Int. J. Psychoanal.*, 37:445–455.

Lichtenberg, J. D. & Galler, F. B. (1987). The fundamental rule: A study of current usage. *J. Am. Psychoanal. Assoc.*, 35:47–76.

Loewald, H. W. (1971). Some considerations on repetition and repetition compulsion. *Int. J. Psychoanal.*, 52:59–66.

Loewald, H. W. (1975). Psychoanalysis as an art and the fantasy character of the psycho-analytic situation. *J. Am. Psychoanal. Assoc.*, 23:277–299.

Loewenstein, R. M. (1963). Some considerations on free association. *J. Am. Psychoanal. Assoc.*, 11:451–473.

Loewenstein, R. M. (1972). Ego autonomy and psychoanalytic technique. *Psychoanal. Q.*, 41:1–22.

Mahony, P. (1979). The boundaries of free association. *Psychoanal. Contemp. Thought*, 2:151–198.

Moore, B. E. & Fine, B. D. (1990). *Psychoanalytic terms and concepts*. New Haven, CT: Yale Univ. Press.

Novick, J. (1982). Termination: Themes and issues. *Psychoanal. Inq.*, 2:329–365.

Nunberg, H. (1955). *Principles of psychoanalysis.* New York: International Universities Press.

Panel (1971). The basic rule: Free association—a reconsideration. H. Seidman, reporter. *J. Am. Psychoanal. Assoc.*, 19:98–109.

Searl, M. N. (1936). Some queries on principles of technique. *Int. J. Psychoanal.*, 17:471–493.

Sonnenberg, S. M. (1991). The analyst's self-analysis and its impact on clinical work: A comment on the sources and importance of personal insight. *J. Am. Psychoanal. Assoc.*, 39:687–704

Spacal, S. (1990). Free association as a method of self-observation in relation to other methodological principles of psychoanalysis. *Psychoanal. Q.*, 59:420–436.

Sterba, R. (1934). The fate of the ego in psychoanalytic therapy. *Int. J. Psychoanal.*, 15:117–126.

Weinshel, E. M. (1984). Some observations on the psychoanalytic process. *Psychoanal. Q.*, 53:63–92

6 What is a deep interpretation?

It is my impression that there is a growing schism among psychoanalysts as to where we believe meaningful psychoanalytic work takes place. One aspect of this schism is our different conceptions of what constitutes a deep interpretation, differences that reflect divergent models of the mind. The word deep, with its two distinct meanings—i.e., distant from a surface, and intense and highly pertinent—nicely encapsulates the dispute. To pose the issue in its most extreme form, there are analysts who judge the depth of an intervention by its distance from the surface of what the patient is capable of knowing, and there are others who judge its depth by how close it is to the surface of the patient's mind while still remaining emotionally meaningful. There are those who believe that the analyst's task is to bring to the surface those elements that are most dystonic and so farthest from awareness, and those who believe that the most meaningful interpretations are those closest to awareness. The differences in these approaches are guided, I believe, by embedded assumptions regarding the presence or absence of mental structure (i.e., definite or fixed patterns of organization) and its role in a theory of interpretation. I don't believe we have fully confronted this issue.

When it comes to content, there is general agreement, among analysts of all stripes, that there is some type of structure to the mind. The persistence of unconscious fantasies or relational models is an example of such structure. Thus, belief in the patient's unconsciously guided fixed view of him- or herself and the analyst, inherent in all models of the mind, is one instance of a type of mental structure we all seem to agree on. Where agreement breaks down is in our models for intervention and the change process in psychoanalysis, and the degree to which these models recognize the role of mental structures in controlling content. To put the matter simply, what I am referring to here are structures that regulate what content can be allowed into awareness, and what understanding of this content is acceptable. For example, there is agreement among widely divergent schools of psychoanalytic thought that resistances occur in psychoanalysis, and that these are the result of an attempt, based on earlier adaptations, to avoid something unpleasant or dangerous (Gray, 1994; Malin, 1993; Renik, 1995; Spezzano, 1993). Only a structuralist perspective, however, suggests that in approaching these resistances it might be useful to think in terms of mental structures, as in the following propositions: (1) An unconscious part of the ego scans thought processes for potential dangers regarding what might be coming to mind. (2) Special techniques taking into account the properties of this unconscious structure may at times be needed to bring it to the attention of the analysand (Gray, 1994; Davison et al., 1990). (3) Because of the way thought processes develop, thinking directed in part by an unconscious ego is concrete; interpretations are therefore most effective when they refer to something the patient can see and understand in a "before the eye" manner (Busch, 1995b, 1999).

Those who believe in the significance of structures that control mental content thus have a view of resistance different from that of those who don't. Structuralists, for instance, often view as bypassing resistances what others consider their working through (Busch, 1992). Even many of those most identified with the structural model have recently been shown to ignore the idea of mental structures in their interpretive approaches (see Busch, 1999; Gray, 1992; Pray, 1994). Brenner's recent repudiation of the structural model (1994) is but confirmation of what has long been evident in his clinical approach (Busch, 1999). Thus, there are significant differences among analysts on the question of whether the mind itself has structure (as opposed to simply having structured content), and these differences have important consequences for how we then view the interpretive process.

Steiner (1996), a Kleinian analyst, describes the importance of mental structure in determining the aims of psychoanalysis. He describes as structures two defenses (splitting and projective identification), the effect these have on patients' ways of thinking, and the need for the individual to reintegrate parts of him- or herself. These are useful concepts for the analyst to keep in mind in defense analysis. However, I would view the defenses as mechanisms established by the ego as protective devices. The structure establishing them is the ego, and what Steiner is describing are certain ways the mind works when these defenses are engaged. Just as we would not call repression a structure, even though it leads the mind to work in certain predictable ways, so there seems little justification for calling splitting and projective identification structures. Further, the clinical method Steiner suggests is very different from that proposed by those of us identified with a structuralist position. For us the basic method of helping patients integrate split-off parts of themselves involves (1) resistance analysis based on close process monitoring and (2) interpretations based on the ego's readiness to understand and integrate them. In contrast, Steiner describes a method based on "the individual's capacity to face psychic reality and in particular to confront the reality of loss and to go through the mourning process that results from this confrontation" (p. 1076). The method is based also on the analyst's capacity "to use his imagination to construct a picture of what he thinks is going on" (p. 1081) and on confronting defenses rather than analyzing them. In summary, it is my impression that the Kleinian concept of structure is different from the one I have been using and leads to different ways of working.

The workable surface

Paniagua (1991), using a structuralist model, designated three surfaces—patient surface, analyst's surface, workable surface—that analysts are always faced with in the formation of an analytic intervention. It would be my contention that effective interventions must of necessity take all three of these surfaces into account. The patient surface includes what the patient is aware of in his or her communications as part of the use of the method of free association. The analyst's surface is an amalgam of the thoughts and feelings the analyst is having in attempting to understand the patient's communications. The workable surface is the plane on which an intervention can be made that is affectively meaningful, thereby ensuring the ego's participation in the process. This surface, an amalgam of the other two surfaces, is designed to take into account both the ego's structure and the unique role played by the ego in the change process in psychoanalysis (Busch, 1996).

Take, for example, a patient who talks, immediately before an extended vacation break in the treatment, about being emotionally abandoned by a friend. The patient surface is that he is upset because he has been left by his friend. The analyst may be thinking that this is about the upcoming vacation. That is the analyst's surface. The workable surface is whatever part of the two surfaces in interaction may be usable by the patient.

What leads to a judgment regarding the workable surface at any moment is an integration of a complex set of variables. In the example above it might include the following considerations: (1) the patient may be narcissistically vulnerable, and this is one in a series of slights that have been expressed in the analysis; (2) this is an unusual foray into feelings by the patient; (3) the story is told in a bored, detached manner, or with icy hatred; (4) the analyst may be moved, infuriated, or detached while the patient is talking. In evaluating the patient surface, one might note the patient using the story as the beginning of an associative process that includes some self-reflection—e.g., "I wonder why this is coming to mind today." This may be said in an inquisitive manner, or as part of a reflexively masochistic pattern of self-recrimination. Though the patient's story may not appear to be a direct expression of psychological-mindedness, it may be brought up during a period of openness to psychological understanding in general, or of a growing appreciation of the ubiquitousness of the transference. Alternatively, the patient may describe the abandonment as a purely external event, with no seeming interest in why the topic has come up. This disinterest may be feigned, sadistic, or masochistic. In short, the variables playing a role in determining the workable surface are part of a complex grid. All of them enter the analyst's judgment regarding the workable surface and are part of an ongoing evaluation of the structural components operating within a dynamic framework at any given moment. Interpreting at the surface requires an assessment of multiple factors and, finally, a judgment an intervention. Faced with an analysand talking about abandonment before a break in the treatment, we are now forced from the comfortable position that we understand as transference what is occurring, to wondering about the relevance to the patient of that understanding (even if correct) when the current state of the patient's mental structures is considered.

Titanic interpretations

Often, I question the usefulness of what some consider a deep interpretation. Here, I think, we need to distinguish depth of understanding from depth of interpretation. While I agree with the need to understand our patients in the most subtle and complex manner, this is very different from interpreting deeply. My understanding of the analytic process is that by the time one makes a "deep" interpretation, it shouldn't seem very deep at all. If we are correctly interpreting the patient's murderous rage toward the analyst, that communication should have been preceded by enough preparatory work that it doesn't seem "deep" to the patient. Ideally, the patient's rage should come to light as a perfectly understandable feeling. For me, the deepest interpretations are those that help patients understand themselves in a way that is emotionally meaningful, that is based on a process they can understand, and that allows for increased appreciation of the power of their own mind. This is a new paradigm of interpretation, one different from current views of the structural model that suggest that interpretation leading to insight "assaults or challenges patients' psychic equilibrium" (Raphling, 1992, p. 354). The latter view is based on what I consider the erroneous assumption that from the patient's perspective "interpretation is opposed as an alien disturbance of psychic equilibrium's status quo" (p. 353). This position does not take into account either the possibility of working through resistances in order to facilitate the patient's acceptance of previously unacceptable ideas, or varying degrees of receptivity.

For many analysts, an interpretation's depth is gauged by the level of its content; for others by its degree of separation from what the patient can be aware of. In this latter view, transference interpretations are often considered the deepest one can go. Such a perspective, I believe, affords a limited view of the psychoanalytic landscape, and may disguise a reluctance to engage fully with the patient at various levels of affect and content within the context of shifting ego states. It privileges the analyst's surface while remaining distant from the workable surface. It is a form of disengagement from aspects of the patient's experience. While it purports to go deeper, it in fact reflects a less complex model of the mind engaged in the analytic process and may lead the analyst to engage the patient in a limited fashion.

A recent article by Lawrence Josephs (1997), "The view from the tip of the iceberg," illustrates some of what I have said. Josephs, while appreciative of the technical innovations developed from the structuralist perspective, worries that they may inhibit the patient from reaching deeper levels of understanding. While he raises important issues that need to be addressed, his critique rests in part on a confusion, common to many theories of technique, between patients' use of the method of free association and their conscious understanding of what they are communicating to the analyst. This confusion in effect equates the analyst's surface with the patient surface. Crucial steps get left out in the working through process, as important resistances are ignored, and behaviors are interpreted before the patient can fully grasp their psychological importance. Patients are forced into a relatively passive position, as the analyst's perspective is privileged.

The critique advanced by Josephs focuses on clinical data I presented from the first two sessions of an analysis to demonstrate the use of free association in establishing an analytic frame (Busch, 1995a). The patient began the analysis by mentioning a conference that would require his missing several appointments. He had forgotten to mention this in our initial consultation and wondered whether he would go. His thoughts then went to a series of incidents in which he now felt he had been recklessly out of control. This was followed by memories of when he was younger and bridling under limitations imposed by his parents. In my interpretation I linked these associations, suggesting that as he began treatment he wondered if I would stop him from going to the conference, as he felt others did not protect him adequately from dangerous situations; but he was also concerned, I pointed out, that limitations might be placed on his freedom. In the following session the patient was aware of feeling anxious coming in. His associations began with his recounting various situations in which he needed to keep his feelings tightly controlled. A memory then followed, still palpably fearful, of believing that he had almost killed his sadistic older brother in a hunting accident when he had acted on instinct. I suggested that his anxiety coming into the session, along with his concerns about going to the conference, were based on a fear that he was dangerous, and that his feelings needed to be kept in check. I suggested further that his beginning analysis was stirring up fears that the treatment might lessen his controls. This led to his recalling a persistent childhood image of a desolate landscape, which I related to his fears of what might happen were his anger to emerge.

Josephs makes what I consider another common error in psychoanalytic technique, that of equating the patient's associations with manifest content. It is an error that fails to take into account the structure of the patient's mind. This view is dominated by what I have called the semiotic method (Busch, 1997), whereby it is assumed that the patient's associations are the manifest content, and that buried within them is the latent content. It is easiest to see this in his understanding of the clinical material:

> The patient presents himself as an impulsive child who is both wishful and fearful of structure and discipline from a strong parental figure. Perhaps the repudiated latent conflict reflects a reversal of this configuration: the patient both wishes and fears to be the authoritarian parent who omnipotently controls others, thereby squelching the defiant attempts of others to assert their own autonomy in the face of controlling behavior. (p. 449)

Josephs suggests that an early interpretation could be made that would point to an even deeper issue—"I wonder if you feel some need to see yourself as someone with questionable impulse control" (p. 450)—to set the stage for what he considers the more significant, ego-dystonic interpretation that "you seem to need to see yourself as someone who needs to be controlled because you are frightened of admitting how much you wish to control others, as you fear they will try to control you" (pp. 450–451).

Josephs believes that the manifest content here is the series of associations in which the patient presents himself as out of control, and that therefore it adds little to be talking with the patient about this self-concept and its offshoots as an important step in beginning the treatment. However, the mere fact that the patient is producing these associations does not mean that he has a conceptual model of himself as an impulsive, dangerous child that he is trying to present to the analyst. We should not regard the course of the patient's associations as a consciously or preconsciously directed process.

From my perspective, the patient does not "present himself as an impulsive child," a characterization that suggests conscious intention. The patient did not seem aware of presenting himself in any particular way. What he did seem aware of at this point, as is typical with most beginning patients, was the request that he present his thoughts as they come to mind. From the patient's perspective, what he presented was a series of disparate thoughts, incidents from his life. Given the concrete nature of thought in areas of conflict, especially at the beginning of treatment, there will be significant interferences with the capacity for observing one's own observations (Busch, 1995b). It is the analyst's interpretation of the associations that leads to the formulation of the patient's ambivalence over control in beginning the analysis. Josephs mistakenly confuses the analyst's understanding of the patient's associations with the patient's intention, a problematic interpretive strategy that elsewhere I have spoken to at length (Busch, 1993, 1995c); he confuses the analyst's surface with the patient surface.

When Josephs suggests interpreting to the patient that he feels some need to present himself as someone with questionable controls, we are very far from what the patient is capable of being aware of. In the patient's mind he does not need to present himself in any way. He is not even aware of presenting himself in a way. The first step is to see if the patient is aware of presenting himself in a way (i.e., of having an unconscious model of himself as an out-of-control child) before determining the factors that lead him to do so. Need is one among a host of possible factors. If the patient needs to present himself as out of control, there will be ample opportunity to discern this in his insistent approach toward the analyst. Remember that we are considering here the first two sessions of an analysis. There is nothing inherent in the ego psychological method I have been writing about that would prevent our observing a need to present oneself as out of control. Unfortunately, the dystonicity of the interpretive process has dominated psychoanalytic thinking from previous interpretations of the structural model to the relational theorists.

Clinical example

I have expressed, with Kamler (in Busch, 1995c, pp. 205–214), the value of isolating a clinical variable and focusing on it as an independent variable. This has been a useful way of demonstrating the power of an ego psychological perspective. However, as it is clear that at times the part has been mistaken for the whole, it may be helpful to give a fuller picture of the range of issues I think about in a typical clinical hour. I see my understanding of human behavior as multi-perspectival, in line with what Pine (1988) has described as the four psychologies of psychoanalysis. There is little in our theoretical mosaic that I find unusable as a way of understanding my patients. It is how the analyst comes to his or her way of thinking about the patient, and how this understanding is communicated to the patient, that I have been writing about.

In the example to follow, careful attention to the fluctuating state of the workable surface leads the patient to deeper material. This approach is what I try to highlight in the material. Though I may be thinking about deeper unconscious meanings (at the analyst's surface), and though I try to show how such thoughts inform my overall understanding of the case, it is my ongoing evaluation of the many factors that determine a workable surface that leads me to intervene as I do.

The patient, Michael, a man in his mid-thirties, had been unable to practice his profession, despite a brilliant academic record. When he came to analysis, he was unclear about what had led him to leave his most recent position. He could cite only vague feelings of anxiety and irritation. Similar problems had occurred through undergraduate and graduate school, but with supportive therapy over many years he finally completed his studies. He came to analysis after having left several positions. His relations with both men and women were superficially pleasant but devoid of any sustained involvement or emotional depth. Over the years we have come to understand his anxiety in a variety of ways. We have discovered (1) a sense of inauthenticity that makes him feel he is about to be found out; (2) a sense of waiting for the rug to be pulled out from under him; (3) an image of himself as a bad seed, deserving to die and not flourish; (4) an underlying sense of rage that, projected, makes the world seem a dangerous place; and (5) homosexual anxiety attendant on his longing to be cared for and loved by a man, as both part of a developmental interference and as a regression from the anxiety and guilt associated with competitive feelings. As one might guess, the patient's early history was dominated by the early separation of his parents, in conjunction with his mother's mercurial temperament and his father's self-absorption. Yet there was a basic structural integrity to the family, with both parents continuing to offer a presence, despite their emotional absence.

Michael is in the fifth year of his analysis. After a rocky start, including frequent absences and moving between the chair and the couch, the analysis has seemed to move productively. His increasing freedom with a range of feelings and thoughts has been accompanied by a sustained, if tumultuous, relationship in which marriage has been proposed, and by steps toward a professional position commensurate with his interests and skills. Recently, for the first time, his anxiety could be understood as related to self-punitive fantasies associated with competitive feelings and wishes in the transference. I have chosen this particular session because it is typical of how I work, and of how I think about my work. I will present not only the clinical material, but my thinking about why at any given point I did or did not intervene. Others might work differently with this same material, and I try to speak to some of these issues as I describe my thinking about the case. In what follows, my thoughts about the case will be interwoven with the clinical material and will be presented in brackets.

Michael's girlfriend was at his place for the entire weekend, which seemed another symbolic step in cementing their relationship. He came in describing how upset he had been most of the weekend. His speech was pressured, with a panicky tone to it. This was unusual at this time in the treatment. The primary conscious focus of his upset was a sore on the side of his mouth that had seemed to get worse over the weekend. He struggled with a tendency toward feeling convinced this was a spreading cancer, the result of an AIDS virus, and noted that there was significant swelling in a lymph node on his neck. Although he knew full well that this was a premature diagnosis, his mind kept going back to the most frightening possible causes of the sore with a sense of certainty that led to a feeling of terror and doom. This alternation between worrying over a potentially fatal illness and assuring himself it wasn't so was repeated in the session. For example, after stating how absurd his concern was at this point, he would go to thoughts that clearly indicated that he needed further reassurance. That he had given blood just last month and thus had been screened for the AIDS virus was one thought he used to reassure himself. He had fooled around with a woman from work a few weeks ago, but neither of them had taken their clothes off. Yet all weekend he had kept feeling the area was rapidly spreading. His girlfriend's assurances were only temporarily comforting.

Noteworthy here is the fluid state of Michael's ego, with a tendency toward more regressed functioning. He is in the grip of a powerful unconscious force that is interfering with his ability to use his objective knowledge. In spite of his "awareness" that it is premature to panic, he keeps being drawn to do so. The regression was notable in that it harkened back to earlier times in the analysis, when he could easily feel panicky. We see the theme that he is being punished for his sexual activity, in that the disease is viewed as sexually transmitted. It is a theme that has gradually been coming into focus as significant. Consideration for Michael's surface is the primary factor in not interpreting his anxiety as a response to sexual thoughts and the guilt associated with them. Given Michael's ego regression at the moment, it would be difficult to interpret in a way that could be meaningfully integrated by him. Michael is not sure at this moment whether his panicky feeling is based on a realistic possibility or is all in his mind. (The diagnosis, made later in the week, was that he had a cold sore.)

An interpretation might alleviate some of his anxiety via acceptance of my perspective (the analyst's surface) on the basis of authority. However, given Michael's general psychological resilience at this point in the analysis, and his growing capacity for and interest in self-exploration, it would seem in his best interest to see what he could do with these feelings on his own—a decision based also on the principle that the analytic process should be viewed as a growing partnership (Busch, 1995c; Gray, 1994). With a patient who was less resilient, if I felt sure of my judgment, I might intervene more quickly as a way of helping him understand that this feeling he was having was potentially understandable. However, I think it is imperative that we not move too quickly to interpret Michael's experience. It is Michael's fear, and we should treat it respectfully and seriously. It should be interpreted when he is ready to have it interpreted, or we run the risk of dismissing the authenticity of his experience. While the work of analysis necessarily includes investigating the analysand's views based on unconscious fantasies and relational models, this is far more subtle than I believe we have considered. Every interpretation can be viewed as an attempt to balance the questioning of perceived meaning in a way that does not iatrogenically undermine the analysand's appreciation of his or her thoughts. We want patients to end up with curiosity about their thoughts, and this goal is compromised by our seeing those thoughts primarily as raw material for content interpretations, and by our not taking their experience into account in considering the workable surface. While at a given moment, it may be necessary to privilege the analyst's perspective, as an un-questioned, constant therapeutic attitude the approach has serious drawbacks.

Michael's thoughts then went to the past weekend, and how he had kept vacillating between thinking he would marry his girlfriend or break off the relationship. Something similar had happened earlier with regard to taking a high-powered position he'd been offered. At times he was convinced he would take it; at others he thought of leaving his profession completely. He then described how, in the midst of sex with his girlfriend over the weekend, he had lost his erection. He then went into familiar obsessional detail about whether, or to what degree, she is sexually attractive to him. He focused on the smallness of her breasts. He then noted, with some irony, that on occasion during the weekend he had found himself thinking longingly about a woman who lives in his neighborhood, and whom he frequently sees jogging in the morning. He was struck by the fact that, when he thought about it, she was built remarkably like his girlfriend, with smallish breasts.

Here in the session we see a beginning shift in ego functioning, whereby Michael can begin to observe his thoughts. He recognizes that the jogger he is attracted to has the same characteristics as his girlfriend, who he feels is not sexually attractive enough. The panic is now gone from his voice, and his whole manner is shifting to a more reflective mode. Given that this shift is taking place, I find it prudent to see what develops next. Such a shift in the ego's relation to its own thoughts often heralds an elaboration of what has just occurred. While at this point, we don't know what has caused the shift, and though an explanation would certainly be of interest, I have opted for privileging whatever area Michael is ready to explore. I am not describing a conscious process. Rather, if one believes that Michael's attempt to use the method of free association involves an unconscious scanning by the ego to determine where it is safest to go in the context of a wish to understand oneself,[1] then analytic listening is best conducted by privileging his use of free association. While the analyst may have many questions or observations, these should take a back seat to Michael's associations. Most often, patients will tell us, if we allow them to, which area they are ready to explore. Thus, the link I had considered making earlier in the session—between his anxiety and sexuality—has now been raised by him. After he talks about his panic, his associations eventually turn toward what occurred sexually over the weekend. In the context of the change in ego functioning we have just observed, why not follow Michael's thoughts to see what he can elaborate?

Michael's thoughts then turned to a time when he was driving with his girlfriend to her mother's home. They had a number of things to do before leaving and realized they would be a few minutes late. He found himself getting very upset. In retrospect, he wondered why. (Another example of an observing ego.) On the ride there his girlfriend indicated, in what he felt was a snide fashion, that she didn't like the radio station he had on. He slammed off the radio, and she got mad at him, which infuriated him even further. Yet he wonders why he turned the radio off the way he did. He must have been feeling angrier than he thought, and sensed he was being provocative. He must have felt criticized by her statement about the radio station, yet he wasn't sure that's what she meant. At this point I intervened: "It seems to be a continuation of what you describe feeling all weekend—that is, someone or something is doing something to you that is threatening or dangerous. This feeling seemed to reach its height in your conviction that you had a fatal illness, although you had some inkling this was a premature diagnosis."

Of all the possible interventions, why would I choose this one? There are two components to my answer. The first is that this issue is one Michael was struggling with all weekend, and it was therefore emotionally alive for him. Second, his thoughts keep returning to this theme, with an increasing capacity to observe them, suggesting an ego that is less regressed and less caught up in conflict. My intervention is an attempt to work with what is most meaningful to Michael, both emotionally and in terms of the ego's openness to new ideas. At this point in the session Michael senses he is reacting to something. This is part of the patient surface. What I judge to be the workable surface in my intervention is based on Michael's readiness to think of himself as playing a role in his reactions, along with the consistent theme of reacting as if something bad were happening to him, whether a fatal illness or his girlfriend's scolding him. In each varying degree, that his reaction might possibly be off base. He was unaware, however, of the consistency, throughout the weekend, of this feeling of being threatened. The linking of the various events is what gives them their power. To this point in the session, Michael is unaware of the connections between his reactions over the weekend. It seems the type of link that Josephs (1997) would see as manifest content, but that I see as Michael's unconsciously organized way of thinking about his experiences. There seems to be no point in suggesting possible causative factors until I can see Michael's reaction to the linked power of these multiple reactions. Will he need to deny the connection? Will it become part of what he experiences as a series of snipes at him? Or will his associations lead us to a deeper understanding, in a demonstrable manner, of the link between his sexual thoughts and the punishment he has been waiting to befall him?

After some reflective moments, Michael stated that it felt like he's been waiting his whole life for some calamity to happen. (I had never heard him say anything like this before.) He reminded me of various times through college and graduate school when he ended up in the emergency room, convinced he had a fatal illness. The strange thing, he now realized, was that he always felt calmest when there was something actually wrong with him. He found himself thinking about a time, after his first year of graduate school, when he was being considered for a prestigious fellowship. He was a basket case until he came down with mono that summer, and all his anxiety seemed to flow away.

His thoughts then turned to his other preoccupation that weekend—what to do regarding his profession. He found himself "disgusted" by all his prospects. He was surprised by his using that word. It wasn't how he was actually thinking about things, and it seemed to be a word that he has more often thought of in relation to sex. As always, he said laughingly, "the plot thickens." Again, I intervened: "There being something terribly wrong about sex seemed prevalent in your feelings over the weekend, especially in your conviction that you were dying from a sexually transmitted disease. You seem to feel you are doing something disgusting and are expecting to be punished for it. This also seems to be affecting your thinking about your professional development." He observed that he was always waiting for something bad to happen to him after sex.

After my earlier intervention, Michael's associations led to confirmation of the interpretation, with the recognition of a lifelong expectation of being punished, along with a beginning elaboration of a feeling (i.e., disgust) that seems part of what triggers the expectation. Michael now feels free to explore his thoughts. My intervention here is intended to synthesize the disparate elements that individually are capable of coming into consciousness, but that remain at the level of individual observation. In the midst of his increasing emotional openness, within the context of an affectively alive conflict, an interpretation is given that offers a set of constructs to organize his thinking while lending further structural clarity to the problem. The intervention tries to respect the structural elements operative at the time, while attempting to build structure. It offers Michael a new way of conceptualizing what happens when he is in particular difficulty.

Discussion

There are deeper meanings to this material that some analysts may have spoken to in the session, and past and future analytic work might have proven such a formulation correct as to the underlying fantasy fueling Michael's anxiety. My view of this material over time is that homosexual anxiety stirred by the weekend separation had led to a fantasy of taking in the analyst's breast/phallus. This stimulated both his feeling of panic over the conviction that he had AIDS, and the loss of his erection during intercourse. In speaking about the latter, Michael focused on his girlfriend's small breast—more like a man's—while he noted feeling turned on by a woman with a similar breast size. While elaboration of this fantasy over time proved important in Michael's understanding, I considered it a significant piece of analytic work first to identify the underlying feeling during the weekend that dominated Michael's associations (e.g., imminent danger) but that was experienced by him as discrete incidents. It is this step of identifying what we can see in a patient's associations (e.g., feelings of pleasure followed by depression, successes undermined by self-sabotage) that are too often bypassed as we look for what is hidden by the associations (Busch, 1997). The power of unconscious fantasy comes alive in the context of patients' first seeing how irrational thoughts and destructive behavior impact on their lives via a close following of their associations. Michael was able to grasp how his weekend was ruined by a persistent feeling of danger, while also discovering an unconscious feeling (i.e., disgust) that was linked to his thoughts and difficulties over the weekend. Such a process, by providing a powerful demonstration of unconscious forces at work, brings the analysis alive for the patient in a way that more abstract interpretations of unconscious fantasy cannot.

Concluding thoughts

If there are indeed structures in the mind that affect how patients think about and integrate their own thoughts, as well as the analyst's—the evidence strongly points in this direction (e.g., Busch, 1995c, 1999)—and if it is the products of these structures that show change in psychoanalysis (Busch, 1996), then it follows that these structures must be taken into account as part of the change process in psychoanalysis. As noted above, this is an area where there are significant differences among analysts regarding what and how we interpret, especially when it comes to "deep interpretations." In my clinical example I have tried to show how I work with a patient's material using a structural model. While I try to consider many levels of meaning, and think of myself as a theoretical pluralist with respect to understanding meaning, the considerations uppermost in my thinking are (1) the patient's capacity to think about, integrate, and internalize interventions from a perspective that is accessible to him or her; (2) how to contribute to the analysand as increasingly participatory in the process; and (3) privileging the patient's experience of his or her thoughts and feelings.

Critics will say this method may be all well and good when things are going smoothly, but what about those times when the patient's associations become actions (Loewald, 1975), when the words themselves are an attempt to actualize (Boesky, 1982) some aspect of the transference? The patient may invite an attack, induce feelings of deadness, of excitement, or love, or pursue any of the myriad purposes that words can be turned to. What about those times when the patient is in an ongoing regressive state, as Michael was at the beginning of his session? I would suggest that the basic principle regarding interventions remains the same at these times, despite what seems a favored strategy, one I have noticed even in my own work—confrontation of the defense or impulse. Much of psychoanalytic work can be characterized as an objectification of the patient's subjective world. However, in clinical moments of the sort I have just described, our initial understanding often comes from our most subjective side. We find ourselves feeling angry with a patient without knowing why, or we note something in the tone of personal information that seems irrelevant. Our thoughts, in defensive retreat from a confusing mass of data, may turn away from what the patient is saying, or we may find ourselves in private reverie. I suggest that the analyst's subjective reactions will hold the most meaning for the patient if they can be objectified. This is best done when our subjective reactions, verbalized or not, are connected to something the patient can see in his or her associations. At these times the task of integrating the surfaces of patient and analyst is daunting, but it can be accomplished if one is oriented to regard the patient's voluntarily verbalized communications as the productions of a structured mind. This principle is an anchor, a reference point, that needs to be incorporated in the interpretive process if our interventions are to be emotionally meaningful and relevant to what our patients can understand. That, after all, is one meaning of the word deep, and what I would consider the *sine qua non* of a deep interpretation.

Note

1 I recognize this is not always the case, and further on will briefly speak to this issue. However, in my experience it is far more frequently the case than seems acknowledged in the literature.

7   Are we losing our mind?

"Dare to know," said Kant, capturing the spirit of the Age of Enlightenment. "Dare to know." It is my premise that this maxim is at the heart of every psychoanalysis. But why "Dare to know"? Why not just "Know!"? Dare—it speaks to the fact that people believe it is dangerous to know about key elements in their mental life, and courageous for them to approach these areas. Thus, "Dare to know." The belief that knowing is dangerous is a fact of analysis that we have lived with uneasily since it was introduced by Freud, and one that is imperiled by some current analytic points of view that emphasize "doing" and de-emphasize "knowing." "Dare to know." It is time to reassert the importance in psychoanalysis of daring to know, along with the significance of a freer mind as a condition for the improvement in symptoms for which patients come to us. How this happens in a psychoanalysis, what it means for clinical technique and the goals of psychoanalysis, and how all this fits within the current climate of psychoanalysis in the United States—this is the topic of my plenary.

In the Unites States, psychoanalysis is drifting into a state of mindlessness. We can see it in the view that analysts cannot know even their own minds, let alone the minds of others. It is evidenced in the lack of interest among some analysts in the individual mind of the analysand, except in interaction with the analyst's. We see it in the belief that analysis is primarily a co-creation of two minds, both in the clinical moment and as the agent of the change process.

A consideration of the co-created mind is useful as one of the many points of view from which analysts can approach the clinical moment. However, as a unitary view of clinical theory and technique it is clinically inadequate, scientifically questionable, and philosophically deficient. It is one among the many clinical perspectives in psychoanalysis that bring some clarity to our clinical understanding and ways of working, but when its adherents espouse the view that the tail of the elephant is the elephant, we need to do some serious zoological investigation. This has been done in the recent work of Jonathan Dunn (1995), Larry Friedman (1999), Charles Hanly (1999), Gil Katz (1998), and Harry Smith (1998), to name just a few.

Mind matters

As a starting point, consider the following example from a prominent writer and clinician who takes the view that "mind itself is a relational construct and can be studied only in the relational context of interaction with other 'minds'" (Aron, 1996, p. 51).[1] This is a point of view common to the relational-constructivist perspectives. Remember that it is not presented as an addition to Freud's legacy—the significance of an individual mind in producing its own suffering—but as a complete paradigm shift. What follows is one version of what this perspective can lead to.

A patient has been associating for some time about sadomasochistic interactions, sexual fantasies of anal penetration, and feelings of abuse, dominance, and submission. The analyst reports that he "interprets the patient's idea that I am dominating him, controlling him, and expecting him to submit to me" (Aron, 1996, p. 128). The patient agrees—not with the interpretation, though, but with the idea that the analyst wants to do these things to him.[2]

What we have here is a conflict regarding ownership of an idea. The analyst says that it's the patient's ideas that lead him to see the analyst in this way. The patient believes it is the analyst's ideas or actions that lead him to feel so. Put another way, the question is: "Is the patient defending against his own thoughts, is he taking a realistic view of the analyst's unconscious, or are both true to some degree?" Let's see how this analyst deals with the question.

In a tone meant to convey musing or thinking out loud, the analyst says to the patient, "The entire analysis is a sexual conquest for me, in which I become excited by your submission." He goes on to explain to the reader, "I leave ambiguous whether I mean that this is his belief or fantasy or my own experience. As I say this to the patient, I may very well be unclear in whose voice I am speaking. The interpretation is not necessarily directed at him or me; it is not clear whose idea it is, and it may just as well lead to insight in me as to insight in him" (p. 128).

What is the analyst's rationale for these statements? He thinks it is helpful for the patient for him to phrase his interpretations in a less challenging manner, but "more important," he says, "it can have a greater emotional impact on me, at least at times when I am not overly defensive" (p. 129). What often occurs, he goes on to say, "is that the patient will cue me in to some conflictual area I do know about but was not sufficiently aware of at the moment in the present analytic context. The patient serves as my analyst by helping me to work through a conflict" (p. 129).

Three points are striking in this approach. First, it is not clear how the analyst goes from first believing that it is the patient's idea that needs to be interpreted, to believing that it is his own feelings that need interpretation. My guess is that for this analyst it doesn't matter what gets dealt with first in what he believes to be a co-created moment. Second, the patient's mind is completely left out of the process in an example of what some critics, discussing the increasing tendency of biographers to insert themselves into the lives of their subjects, call a *moi* interpretation. What it means for the patient that he has been associating about sadomasochistic fantasies for some time is not considered. Is the ongoing expression of these fantasies a defense against more frightening feelings toward the analyst (e.g., wishes to be loved or cared for)? Is the patient trying to excite or frighten the analyst? Is he repeating an early object relationship? Is he providing what the analyst unconsciously wants? Is it useful for the analyst to have some clue as to whether the patient's associations are a defense, an enactment, an actualization, or an accurate description of the analyst before engaging the patient in an exploration of what is happening? By ignoring this question and a whole slew of other ones about what is going on in the patient's mind, and interpreting the patient's experience primarily for himself, this relational analyst creates his own co-created transference. I have no doubt that we can affect the transference, but to come to the conclusion that there is no individual mind, only a co-created one, shifts the focus to the analyst's importance to a degree that seems to me suspect.

The third issue that strikes me in this example is that the analyst emphasizes actions as the main form of interpretation. His primary method of helping the patient accept an interpretation is to do something (i.e., make his comments less confrontational). The many things that may be going on in the patient's mind that lead him not to take in an interpretation (if it is correct enough) are ignored. From this analyst's perspective, we help by doing something, rather than by analyzing what makes ownership dangerous. This way of thinking about the analytic change process is consistent with current perspectives that champion the analyst's actions over the analyst's thoughts. However, it is a view that comes at the cost of not taking into consideration the patient's mind. Without a careful evaluation of the clinical and theoretical consequences, it repudiates the model of a mind with deep structures. Further, even if the analyst is correct that it is his conflicts that are interfering with the progress of the treatment, his method of finding out what these are again involves doing something (that is, the analyst saying what is coming to his mind).

Schafer (1999), while acknowledging the need to pay attention to a variety of feelings as potential projective identifications or intrusions of the analyst's conflicts, has recently questioned the assumption of the emotionally labile analyst as the model we should accept. Does this apply, he asks, to a "trained, analyzed, experienced analyst, that is to say a prepared analyst, an analyst with a reasonably intact work ego? That analyst—and I claim to be one of them—would usually be thinking about the context, manifestations, and momentary analytic usefulness of that patient's material. I see keeping that much distance as an essential part of the work of analysis" (p. 523).

While I get the gist of their philosophical view of treatment, I have not been able to get clear about what the advocates of co-creationism see as the psychoanalytic goals of treatment. What I see in a successful analysis is a freeing of the patient's mind. The inevitability of action is replaced by the possibility of reflection. This deceptively simple phrase captures an extraordinarily powerful concept: that the repetitions in action of unconscious conflict may be replaced by a newly developed capacity to sense the readiness to act before taking action. It seems to me that to know primarily through action is what psychoanalysis is attempting to cure, not promote, and that the capacity to reflect before taking action is one of the most important contributions a personal analysis makes in the formation of an analyst.

A model for psychoanalytic technique: an introduction

Having participated in many discussions around the country, I have come to the conclusion that we are experts in understanding the most subtle dynamics of our patients, but that we often confuse this with our capacity to help them. In short, knowledge of the unconscious is not particularly useful to the patient unless it is accompanied by the capacity in the patient to become knowledgeable about the unconscious. The complex issue of how the patient gains access to his or her unconscious is given short shrift in our techniques. If a conductor picks a piece of music that is in line with the strength and skill of the orchestra that will be playing it, the music is beautiful, and the orchestra feels satisfied with its efforts. As the orchestra's talent increases, the range of playable music widens. Not to take this into account leads to little music and unhappy feelings. The capacity to gain access to one's mind, and the structure-building that this brings, is what psychoanalysis can offer.

Unconscious fears

Psychoanalysts have always been gifted in their understanding of the human condition. Freud's insights forever changed how humanity looks at itself. Our knowledge base of how to understand behavior continues to grow. However, where I feel we haven't advanced is in our ability to communicate understanding so that it becomes usable by the patient. It is my belief this has occurred because we consistently overlook one key concept and its sequelae. To grasp it leads to different methods and goals for analytic treatment. The key concept I have in mind is that the basis of neurotic and character symptoms is *unconscious fears*. I cannot think of a symptom not explainable by unconscious fears, and this view is inherent in every major theoretical persuasion, although the causative factors may be understood differently. For some reason its importance is consistently overlooked. Before going further, I must note that I am using the term "unconscious fears" as shorthand for many disturbing affects and thoughts. In most of the psychoanalytic work I have observed and read, unconscious fears are either ignored or treated as if they are conscious.

Psychoanalytic objectives

A key aspect of psychoanalytic treatment is to make unconscious fears not so fearsome, and in so doing to alleviate a central factor in the formation of symptoms. I believe we do this, in large part, through psychoanalytic methods that result in changes in thought processes. My technique is guided by changes not in what patients think about, but in how they think about what they think about. Core conflicts do not change. What changes is the capacity to think about them.

What comes about in psychoanalysis, and no other type of treatment can make this claim, is a new ability to bring more highly developed thought processes to bear on conflict. In areas of conflict a patient's mind works like that of a three-year-old waking from a bad dream. The child is totally immersed in the belief of the dream, as the neurotic is immersed in perceptions based on unconscious conflict. The feelings from the dream are his reality. The child cannot separate out that these are thoughts, and he cannot look back upon his thoughts to see the sequence of events that has led to his present fearful state. This is a type of thinking that Piaget called pre-structural, and it has striking similarities to Freud's description of primary process thinking. Pre-structural thinking is the dominant form of thinking throughout childhood, when conflicts are formed, and I believe that conflict solutions have been worked out in the terms of pre-structural thinking. In areas of core conflicts, a patient's thinking is, for the most part, pre-structural.

The use of certain psychoanalytic methods results in structure building, and helps patients change the tools with which they think about conflicts from pre-structural ones to what Loewald (1971) called the "higher-level ego functions." This is seen in the following: A patient comes into treatment believing in the reality of his or her fears and feelings. By the end of treatment, we hope that he or she is able to consider the possibility that in well-known areas of conflict, internal factors may play a role.

This brings me to another psychoanalytic shibboleth that I believe is misguided. We have been told that patients primarily need to regress in treatment. However, it is my experience that in areas of conflict patients are already highly regressed in their thinking. We have mistakenly seen the incapacitating inhibitions patients demonstrate in treatment as something they need to regress from, rather than the result of regressive responses to unconscious fears. To become able to express fruitfully a wide range of feelings requires higher levels of thinking, not more regression.

Psychoanalytic technique

How do unconscious fears become less fearsome, given that analyzing a patient's unconscious fears is like reaching toward an open wound? There are two main ways that patients protect themselves from this danger, and each method of protection demands a different approach.

There are those patients who pull away from the open wound. We would describe them as suffering from inhibitions. As they unconsciously sense a danger, they immediately restrict what they can think, feel, or say. The first step in analyzing the inhibiting defenses is to help the analysand observe the inhibition in action. Here, closely following the patient's associations is invaluable in helping the patient to notice how, for example, talking about some infuriating characteristics of a roommate is immediately followed by a description of how nice the roommate is. Bringing this sudden switch in emotional valence to the patient's attention in a very concrete, un-jargon-like manner shows them the unconscious processes at work—that is, an objection to an expressed feeling is silently working. I am not speculating on underlying processes or causes at this time. The patient first has to grasp that a process is occurring before he or she can be ready to understand this process. One of biggest dangers of the analyst's remaining primarily the interpreter of the patient's experience is that more mature levels of thinking are bypassed. In the example of the infuriated roommate, for instance, when the analyst interprets, "I think you're afraid of your anger," the patient is asked to respond to the analyst's observational and reflective capacities, rather than to use his or her own. With the techniques I have suggested in my writings, we help patients view the most regressive parts of their minds with the most mature parts of their minds. While the analyst needs to be comfortable with patients' regressive states, it is nearly impossible for a patient to analyze regression while within a regressed state of mind.

Analysands who deal with unconscious fears by what I call action defenses—that is, striking the hand that moves toward the "open wound"—require a different technique. To these patients the fears are even more fearful, and they have less room for any awareness of uncomfortable feeling states. Their words are more like actions, designed to do something. The patient's associations may become an invitation to an attack, an attempt to control or seduce the other, and so on. It is at such times that we find ourselves bored, excited, irritated, amused, etc., when the patient seems to be associating. When action defenses are in play, every utterance by the analyst is taken as a frustration or gratification of what the patient is defending against. The patient does not feel safe from his or her unconscious fears unless the analyst is doing what the patient wants. There is also greater unconscious gratification in the defensive behavior of the action defenses than there is with the inhibiting defenses. As there is no working analytic ego to speak to at these times, methods that rely on an observing ego are fruitless. However, it is my belief that it is only by the inclusion of the ego, especially that part of it responsible for thinking, perception, and so on, that the analyst is led to an appreciation of the technical complications in interpreting split-off action defenses. Without this inclusion, the analyst is like a business consultant who holds a company meeting to identify some problems without taking into account whether or not the head of the company is present.

It is with this type of action defense that the method of confrontation is most applicable (bearing in mind that the "method of confrontation" doesn't have to be "confrontational"). The technique requires arousing acceptable limits of anxiety around the split-off defensive behavior by emphasizing the disowned action. As long as the defense remains ego-syntonic it can't be analyzed. Thus, I start the analysis of the action defenses with a description of what the patient is *doing* when he or she is saying what comes to mind. By clear, empathic statements on what the patient is doing with his or her actions, we hope to bring back into operation what Greenson (1967) labeled a reasonable ego.

Focusing on the patient's use of the method of free association provides such a link to the ego, whereas pointing out absent feelings or content (e.g., "I think you still must be having feelings about our canceled appointment last week") requires a way of thinking of which patients are most often not capable during phases of action thought. Thus, I start with concrete examples directly observable to both of us as an indication that something is going on before us. For example, once I determine that a series of thoughts (a recitation of everyday events, for example) over a period of time is an attempt to obscure rather than reveal something, I will highlight it as something going on before us. I invite the patient to consider my impression that "You used to seem able to roam over many ideas and feelings, but recently you're sticking mainly to everyday events. It's as if you are afraid to let your thoughts go wherever they may go." In this I am interested in what is causing the restriction, and not urging the patient to let their mind roam.

The technique I have just described requires a more directive manner of working than is necessary with the defenses of inhibition, where the patient's inhibitions are more clearly displayed. In past writings I have criticized Raphling's (1992) description of aggressive work by the analyst as a method of dealing with resistances, but in the phases of analysis when action defenses are prominent I do sometimes find this way of working apt. Action defenses are often first observable to us through a disturbing feeling that doesn't seem, at first, to fit what the patient is saying. If I believe that the feeling is primarily coming from the patient, I look for what the patient may be doing with his or her associations that have led me to feel this way, and I try to articulate this as clearly as possible to the patient. This technique requires that the analyst go beyond knowing what he or she is feeling to engage the patient's mind, rather than just inviting the patient to tell us why we are feeling what we feel. It is the difference between feeling deadened by a patient and saying, "I think you're trying to make me feel deadened, just as you felt etc. "and articulating what the patient is doing in his or her use of the method of free association that has led one to feel deadened. (A patient after a few years of treatment may start to leave out connecting links, for example, or talk of mundane external events with no psychological interest, or in myriad other ways of associating create this feeling in the analyst.) Only once the patient grasps what he or she is *doing* can the work of uncovering its causes begin.

In summary, there are two different ways of analyzing unconscious fears as they emerge as resistances in a psychoanalytic treatment. Close process monitoring of the associations is most effective when the patient is using inhibiting resistances. Confrontation is most useful when analyzing action resistances. These designations of resistances are not behavioral categories, but descriptions of an underlying unconscious process.

Interpreting unconscious dynamics

Psychoanalytic work is more than just helping patients see that they are showing signs of unconscious fears. The nature of the unconscious fears needs to be explored and explicated, and the dynamics that emerge from them identified—along with their multiple sources (including gratifications), and the expression of all of these within the aliveness of the transference, enclosed in an atmosphere of empathy, respect, and safety. The three basic principles I work within when interpreting unconscious dynamics are:

1. Every interpretation of unconscious dynamics is a balancing act, where the analyst tries to help the patient see in his or her thoughts or behavior something that is an expression of the unconscious dynamic, while trying not to arouse such unacceptable levels of unpleasant feeling that the patient will not keep working with the interpretation.
2. Interpretations should be based, as much as possible, on something actively knowable by the patient; they should not have to rely on the authority of the analyst. This means including the patient's own associations, as well as consciously perceivable actions, as part of the interpretive process. In this way we invite the patient's own mind to be an active part of the analytic process throughout the treatment. We cannot expect a patient to find his or her own mind in treatment if we do not invite it to be part of the process.
3. It is important to keep in mind that an analytic session is a linked process. When we describe an unconscious dynamic, we want to show the patient how his or her mind works in dealing with this conflict. We can do this mainly in the context of an entire process through the use of free association. How can patients see the significance of the associative process if we do not try to demonstrate the powers of their own minds through the use of this same method? Working in the way I suggest invites the patient's ego to do what it cannot do in the midst of conflict: to see a chain of associations, return back to them, and reflect on them. The decline in the analytic use of the method of free association (Lichtenberg & Galler, 1987) is an uncomfortable reminder of how hard it is for us to understand how essential it is if analysis is to take place.

A third of a second

Data from the cognitive neurosciences support the view I've been championing in this paper. Independent studies from Germany (Kornhuber and Decke, as reported in Norretranders, 1998) and the United States (Libet, as reported in Norretranders, 1998) demonstrate that there is an incredibly long period (in brain time) between the moment of readiness to take an action, and the moment that an action takes place. Libet's findings, since replicated, suggest that the readiness to start an act begins .55 seconds before the act.

There is a period of .35 seconds during which a decision is made in the mind as to whether this readiness to act comes into consciousness, and .20 seconds when a potential action enters consciousness for further deliberation. Remember, this occurs in a mind that sorts through millions of bits of information per second. Based on the speed of the mind at work, there is an incredibly long time (1) for us to consider whether a stimulus to act comes into consciousness; and (2) for the mind to consider an action once the idea of it becomes conscious.

In the model I've been describing, I have focused on those methods that reflect the view that a key period of time for psychoanalysis is the third of a second between the first readiness to react to a stimulus, and the time when this stimulus does or does not reach consciousness. From the time a stimulus is received, there is a third of a second during which a decision is made, outside of awareness, as to whether the stimulus or a derivative of it becomes conscious. This is the time in which we can imagine the vital unconscious monitoring for danger going on in the patient's mind. Much of the work of psychoanalysis must revolve around, and take cognizance of, what goes on in this one-third of a second. Here is where we have the opportunity to turn what I described earlier as the *inevitability of action into the possibility for reflection.* That is, only when a thought has reached consciousness is it available for more developmentally advanced thought processes to work on. The potential for change in any analytic hour is heralded by such words as "I noticed," and "I wonder." In the third of a second I've been talking about, the patient has been able to discover, or rediscover, a part of his or her mind. It is not necessarily content that is discovered, but a part of the mind that was working outside of awareness. We have this relatively long period of time to help patients find their own minds at work, and thus not be forced into inevitable actions.

Finally, fascinating data (Blakeslee, 2000) from preliminary studies using functional magnetic resonance imaging (FMRI) also suggest support for the model I've been writing about. From these studies it appears that precise brain locations can be determined for a variety of human traits. There are indications that there are two centers in the brain for the anticipation of pain. The first is deep in the limbic system, the part of the brain associated with primal feeling states. Another center that anticipates pain exists in the frontal lobe, which is associated with higher-level mental functions. If this is correct, it follows that a primary function of psychoanalysis is to build up structures that increase the awareness, in areas of conflict, of these anticipatory processes of pain in the frontal lobes. In this way, the fears that lead to defenses could go from primarily irrational (as in a feeling of catastrophic danger) to the more rational (as in, I'm feeling uneasy, I wonder what it is about). Increased awareness of anticipation of pain in the frontal lobes over time is a hypothesis that could be validated by FMRI studies before and after psychoanalysis.

Conclusion

There's a term that I've pretty much avoided so far because of its negative connotation for many current analysts. It's from a course (ego psychology) that is part of the curricula of most institutes, but few people refer to the concepts from this course in any clinical seminars. What I've been presenting is a clinical ego psychology that never quite was. It's about a structure in the mind that is pivotal for change in psychoanalytic treatment, and that fits what we know of how the mind works in conflict. It is this view of the mind that we are in danger of losing—with unfortunate consequences—and that still provides our best tool for those who seek analysis and dare to know more about their own minds.

Notes

1 When using another's work to make a point, one inevitably simplifies. I found Aron's (1996) book to be very informative, especially his chapters clarifying the differences among schools of thought that are often lumped together, and the history of how these schools came about. I also appreciated his searching criticism of drive theory. I agree entirely with his point that some correction in analytic theory is needed that better includes the relationships between the individual and his social internal objects, and external interpersonal relations.

2 This is not a particularly relational interpretation, but it is unfortunately typical of many interpretations of the transference. I have devoted quite a bit of time to this issue in a recent work (Busch 1999), and thus will not go further into it here, except to raise Schafer's (1983) observation that if it were simply a matter of bringing such issues to consciousness, why hasn't the patient brought it up himself? In such cases it is the hesitation, the reluctance, that counts.

References

Aron, L. (1996). *A meeting of minds*. Hillsdale, NJ: Analytic Press.

Blakeslee, S. (2000). Just what's going on in that head of yours? *New York Times*, March 14, 2000.

Busch, F. (1999). *Rethinking clinical technique*. Northvale, NJ: Aronson.

Dunn, J. (1995). Intersubjectivity in psychoanalysis. *Int. J. Psycho-Anal.*, 76:723–738.

Friedman, L. (1999). Why is reality a troubling concept? *J. Am. Psychoanal. Assoc.*, 47:401–426.

Greenson, R. R. (1967). *The technique and practice of psychoanalysis*. New York: International Universities Press.

Hanley, C. (1999). On subjectivity and objectivity in psychoanalysis. *J. Am. Psychoanal. Assoc.*, 47:427–444.

Katz, G. (1998). Where the action is: The enacted dimension of the analytic process. *J. Am. Psychoanal. Assoc.*, 46:1129–1168.

Lichtenberg, J. D., & Galler, F. (1987). The fundamental rule: A study of current usage. *J. Am. Psychoanal. Assoc.*, 35:47–76.

Loewald, H. (1971). Some considerations on repetition and repetition compulsion. *Int. J. Psycho-Anal.*, 52:59–66.

Norretranders, T. (1998). *The user illusion*. New York: Penguin Books.

Raphling, D. (1992). Some vicissitudes of aggression in the interpretive process. *Psychoanal. Q.*, 61:352–369.

Schafer, R. (1983). *The analytic attitude*. New York: Basic Books.

Schafer, R. (1999). Response to Owen Renik. *Psychoanal. Psychol.*, 16:522–527.

Smith, H. (1999). Subjectivity and objectivity in analytic listening. *J. Am. Psychoanal. Assoc.*, 47:465–484.

8   Conflict theory/trauma theory

I have never seen a patient in psychoanalysis in whom there has not been some form of interference in healthy narcissistic development that has led to unconscious fantasies of causation and solution, resulting in intrapsychic conflict. For example, a child's egocentric view of the world leads him to experience his depressed mother's inability to nurture and mirror his healthy demands as due to his excessive needs. Thus, the ongoing trauma of a lack of mirroring leads to his needs becoming associated with unconscious fears of deadness, abandonment, and guilt. In analysis, when he begins to feel needful toward the analyst, these internal dangers pull him back to an inhibited emotional stance.

In short, it is not only the trauma itself that remains traumatic. Inevitably, the feelings and fantasies the trauma stimulates become part of a dangerous intrapsychic field. In this way, a trauma also becomes part of an intrapsychic conflict. Thus, it seems to me that analytic work has to be informed by attunement to empathic breakdowns, past and present, and their effects on the patient's psychic life both in- and outside of the analysis, while we also listen for the resultant unconscious fantasies and intrapsychic conflict.

However, I still hear many analysts singularly emphasize trauma interpretations in clinical work (based on interferences in development or countertransference enactments), without at some point addressing its intrapsychic meanings. Working with trauma alone helps patients understand that they have split-off feelings due to current or past empathic breakdowns, but without their being helped to understand the intrapsychic conflicts that lead to keeping such feelings unknown. The patient is told he must have felt this or that, while the reasons for his not being able to feel his feelings, especially currently, remain untouched, or primarily viewed as a fear of being re-traumatized. The role of ongoing intrapsychic conflicts in keeping feelings hidden tends to be ignored.

In this paper, I will present some historical reasons that I think are responsible for this way of working and its clinical implications, as well as two clinical examples in which a trauma occurs (i.e., a countertransference enactment), and two different ways it is dealt with in analysis. However, first I will briefly muse about some ways I have come to think of trauma and conflict in the clinical situation.

Conflict and trauma: clinical manifestations

In my work with a spectrum of patients from neurotic to those with moderately severe personality disorders, I have noticed (without any preconceived plan) that I tend to work first with the implications of interferences in narcissistic development. These include such reactions in the analyst as empathy with the patient's feelings induced by having a self-indulgent mother, or having a father whom the child cannot idealize, and the sense of danger to which such feelings lead. A typical interpretation for me at this time is evident in the following interaction:

Early in treatment, a patient whose mother suffered from intermittent depressive rages described one such incident, and his response of going outside to the street to wait for his father to come home. He brought a ball with him and kept trying to throw the ball higher and higher. At this time, I suggested that throwing the ball might have been a type of "smoke signal," representing the patient's hope that his father would get the message and hurry home to intervene by calming the mother's anger.

I have come to realize that these types of interpretations generally speak to important preconscious feelings that are acceptable to most patients (those who do not engage in excessive splitting), as such interpretations do not arouse intense guilt. It is especially important in the beginning of treatment to help our patients understand these behaviors as adaptive strategies, as we begin the analytic process of meaning making in an atmosphere of safety. In theoretical terms, we are speaking to what is most acceptable to the ego at this point in the treatment. Such a strategy serves as an important buffer to those times when areas dominated by an unconscious sense of guilt are explored. Further, since our patients generally suffer, in part, from a feeling of not being heard, the analyst's capacity to hear and to understand the patient's preconscious perspective is crucial as part of the curative process. In working through developmental interferences, this way of working is necessary but not sufficient in itself. Thus, with the patient just described, the father's seeming inability to control the mother's outbursts left the patient with a sense of the father as weak, which both emboldened and frightened him. He marched confidently through life, while simultaneously keeping a low profile. In the treatment, whenever his confident or competitive side came into view, he quickly became deferential. Whatever the initial causative factors, the problem had become an internal conflict between the wish and the fear to "show his stuff." Empathy with his trauma (i.e., mother's rages and his feeling unprotected by the father), or the analyst's way of being, could not resolve this internal conflict.

While the analyst's kindness and tact are essential for analyzing the patient's sense of danger, behavioral methods are not enough in themselves.[1] However, before discussing the benefits of working with both narcissistic trauma and intrapsychic conflicts, I will turn briefly to some of our historical roots for their separation.

The seeds for radical discontent with the role of intrapsychic conflict lie, in part, within our own history. Freud's (1897) move from the seduction hypothesis, to the theory of unconscious fantasies based on intrapsychic conflict as causative in psychopathology, sealed over the role of early object relations for some time. Furthermore, Richards (2003) noted that politics may have played a role in the rejection of the ideas of British object relations theorists in the United States by those associated with the American Psychoanalytic Association, as these theories were embraced by analysts outside the organization. However, within the United States, from the time of Spitz's (1945, 1946) work onward, "mainstream" analysts, showing the centrality of environmental circumstances on mental and physical development, seemed to have little overt effect on clinical thinking.

Ambivalence over Kohut's (1971, 1977, 1984) attempt to integrate intrapsychic conflicts (e.g., the vertical split) with the traumas of childhood, followed by intolerance, seemed to be in part the result of this same threat, at a time when many American analysts were faced with the significance of events from infancy, childhood, and adolescence. Thus, conflict as the result of internal processes only was promulgated in awkward ways through the 1980s (see Busch, 1999, pp. 19–50). As far as I can tell from the literature of the time, it was only in a little-known article by Sachs (1967) that the traumatic effect of treating an external trauma as a purely intrapsychic event was highlighted.

My most painful analytic memory from the early '80s occurred with a stolid, taciturn patient in her fifties, Mrs. S, who came to treatment reluctantly after her daughter's analyst strongly recommended treatment for herself, pointing out the benefit to her daughter. The daughter had been seriously self-destructive, and the analyst felt that the mother's ongoing withholding and denigrating attitude was interfering with the daughter's moving forward.

It did not take long to discover how barren Mrs. S's life was, in part because of her sadistic superego, which was also directed outward. In her controlled, schizoid existence, Mrs. S believed that she needed little, but always felt underappreciated. She found it difficult to take in what I had to offer and had little to give. However, it seemed that enough progress was made on all sides to enable Mrs. S's daughter to take up a profession and marry. The wedding itself was part of the healing process for mother and daughter, as they slowly attempted to build a mutually satisfying relationship.

At the first session after the wedding, the patient came in with a piece of wedding cake. I was touched but having been taught to analyze gifts rather than accept them, I immediately put the wedding cake under the analytic microscope for much of the week. If Mrs. S did not bring it up, I would. It was only when I realized that Mrs. S was becoming increasingly blanked out that I realized this method was not working. Gradually, I came to understand that I had inflicted a mini-trauma on her by ignoring the trust she felt in herself and me in presenting this gift. Luckily, I consulted a colleague, who helped me understand the gift as a sign of both her appreciation and her newfound capacity to give. It dawned on me that I had inadvertently enacted a childhood trauma with Mrs. S, wherein she, at age five, had prepared breakfast for herself and her two-year-old sister so that her parents could sleep late on a Saturday; but all she had heard from her mother afterward was a bitter complaint that she had made a mess in the kitchen.

While unconscious fantasies played an important role in Mrs. S's gift to me and in my response, these could only be taken up when each of us was ready to approach them. However, what I think many of us did not recognize at the time was how the exclusive focus on unconscious fantasies could be traumatic in itself.

Trauma theory

The application of trauma theory in the clinical situation, extant separately from conflict theory, is exemplified in a paper by Lichtenberg and Kindler (1994). Using a self-psychological perspective, the authors describe how they organize clinical material based on the following factors: significant past or present life experiences; the analyst's knowledge of life experiences as organizers of fantasy and transference; and unconscious fantasy and beliefs as based on past and present life experiences. unconscious fantasies also play a role in how the event is experienced. Thus, these authors' clinical lens is focused on past and present traumas. The view expressed in the paper cited seems to be that mental forces—ones that in analysis are based on spontaneously formed structures, such as compromise formations or other intrapsychic structures— do not appear to be significant causative factors. Let us see how this plays out in Kindler's clinical example in the same paper.

Before discussing this case, I wish to point out that I am sympathetic to the authors' highlighting of the importance of empathic attunement and its calming effect on our patients, as well as the significance of understanding split-off feelings as adaptations; however, in my discussion, I will focus primarily on a problematic position to which this approach can lead. Further, I am not suggesting that a trauma-based treatment method is the wrong way to work with the case described; after all, with any case, we are presented with small pieces of an ongoing process. Rather, I hope that the reader will view my comments as musings on a particular approach.

Kindler's patient, Jill, frantically calls him a few minutes before her appointment, saying that there is a power failure and no trains are running. As she is speaking to him, the power is restored, and she abruptly ends the phone call. Kindler takes a nap while waiting for Jill, who shows up halfway through the scheduled session in an agitated state. She curses the transit system, describes the haughty behavior of a ticket collector, and eventually runs out of steam, ending by insisting that Kindler is angry with her.

As Jill demands that her analyst come clean about his feelings, he starts to feel irritated. Musing about his nap, he is aware of feeling quite relaxed and alert in listening to Jill. Yet Jill is positive that he had hurt feelings when she abruptly stopped the phone call. She confesses that it is the type of thing that would make her really angry. Kindler's response is to tell her that he was calm, and in fact fell asleep while waiting for her. Jill then comments, more calmly now, that she has noticed a change in his level of activity in the session. It is not clear how the ensuing material unfolds, but what emerges is Jill's feeling that her analyst has been energetically with her in the past few days, and she views his decreased activity as a sign of his anger in response to her cutting him off on the phone. Kindler understands Jill's reaction as based on the loss of his calming function when he was less vigorously responsive, which often led to her perception that he was being punitive. In a situation like this, where the weekend loomed and the transportation system had let her down so cruelly, she was in need of a welcome that included a degree of attunement to her state of agitation to be able to maintain her sense of connection to me. (Lichtenberg & Kindler, 1994, p. 416). In retrospect, the analyst wonders if, by napping, he was soothing himself in response to the expected onslaught from Jill. However, this point seems to get lost in the latter parts of the discussion.

While I have no doubt of the veracity of Kindler's understanding of Jill's narcissistic vulnerability, we see that his interpretations are geared primarily to past and immediate traumas. The present "trauma" is interpreted as based on the analyst's affective state of calmness not matching Jill's agitated state. The past trauma, as imagined in his model scene, is one of the distress of a child, possibly after an agitating experience such as an unexpected separation, who is attempting to establish a lively intimacy with a disinterested or aversive, possibly depressed, adult. Her efforts go unnoticed, and depletion threatens her fragile sense of self.

Kindler goes on to imagine the child Jill's having become angry, demanding an acknowledgment of her distress, which led to a guilty or shameful response from her parents. This does not convey an authentic understanding of her need for secure attachment, and Jill is left feeling like "an irritable nuisance" (1994, p. 418). Kindler then states: "After my self-revelatory response, contact with my inner affective state, especially the image of me sleeping peacefully waiting for her, served to restore her tie to me and allowed her to return to the self-exploratory dominant mode" (pp. 418–419).

While the analyst struggles with his own inner state (i.e., was he calmly waiting for Jill, or withdrawing into sleep in anticipation of an onslaught?), he seems to bypass the patient's intrapsychic conflict over acknowledging her anger with him. We see indications of her conflict in her insistence that it is the analyst who is angry with her. There seemed to be something in Jill's feeling thwarted in getting to the session that made her angry, but her recognition of this anger as her own seemed to be threatening, thus leading to the projection. Jill could then be angry because the analyst "was upset with her," not because of what was stirred up by being thwarted in getting to the session.

It is clear from the transcript that Jill's thoughts about Kindler's being upset occurred before the session began, when she abruptly stopped listening to him on the phone. In the session, she confessed, "That's just the kind of thing I would get upset over if I were in your situation" (p. 416). Jill calms down only when the analyst asserts his calmness, possibly making it difficult for her to further express her own intrapsychic conflicts over acknowledging angry feelings. Instead, the analyst focuses on the trauma in the session, representing it as a repetition of a previous narcissistic trauma in his model scene.

In one sense, Kindler and I see the challenge of this session in similar ways—i.e., how to help Jill own her split-off feelings. Kindler's answer is to take the blame for her feelings due to his lack of attunement, thus assuaging her unacceptable feelings of anger. However, this leaves Jill's difficulty with owning her angry feelings, and whatever caused them, untouched, at least at this moment. In fact, Jill seems more ready to explore the conflict over owning her feelings than her analyst is, when she acknowledges, in regard to her projection, "that's just the kind of thing I would get upset over." By thinking exclusively about trauma, Kindler possibly deprives Jill of learning more about the conflict over owning her angry reaction. She is left with her unconscious fears of something bad happening if she becomes aware of her anger.

Much of the reaction against helping patients own feelings has, I suspect, been due to an underappreciation of the role of defenses. Overzealous analysts have attempted to get patients to admit to feelings, often with an accusatory tone (Busch, 1992, 1995, 1999). We have not been sensitive enough to the disorganizing effects these feelings produce. If this were not the case, there would be no reason to defend against them. For someone like Jill, it would be important to recognize and analyze the terror of acknowledging her angry feelings, and what the anger was about.

The aim is not simply to help patients recognize how angry they are, which would be based, in part, on topographic technique (Paniagua, 2001) and the belief in aggression as a primary instinct. Rather, we hope to help the patient understand what is so frightening about being angry, or why the need that led to the anger is so intolerable it cannot be fully experienced. While Jill's acceptance of her anger will be helped by making it understandable, as Kindler did, the unconscious terror of her anger and the reasons for this remain untouched.

A clinical example using an integrated perspective

I bring the following example because in this case, as with Kindler's patient, an external event led to a temporarily traumatic effect on the patient, causing him to feel angry, which in turn led to a conflict over this feeling. Analyzing this conflict became a crucial part of understanding the traumatic nature of the event. That is, while the event itself (a countertransference enactment) would not be pleasant for any patient, and in fact touched on this patient's narcissistic disturbances from an earlier time, we can see in this session that it was the patient's conflict over his emotional reaction that made the feelings especially traumatic.

My patient, Harold, was in his mid-forties, the director of a postdoctoral fellowship program in the social sciences, and in his fourth year of analysis.

Harold: I'm thinking about this great applicant for the fellowship. When she came for her interviews, I wasn't prepared for her. Her application was just one amongst many, and it was only a few minutes before I was to meet her that I realized what a great applicant she might be. Then, when I interviewed her, she was a perfect "10." So, at the end of the interview, I told her we would really like her to come here and outlined the various opportunities. She was pleased by the offer but noncommittal. She's also looking at Berkeley, and for personal reasons, she might end up there. About a week later, I wrote her an e-mail telling her again that we'd like her to come, and that we have so much to offer her. It's something I've not done before, preferring to have the program sell itself. She wrote back, saying how flattered she was and how appreciative of the note. I was going to leave it at that, but then decided "what the hell?" I wrote her back and said, "Why don't you just come to Boston—it's great here." It was so unlike my usual stance, but it was fun.

(Here I thought I found myself enjoying the patient's freedom to feel playful, spontaneous, and able to enjoy the sexual undertones of the interaction without withdrawing. This had been a major issue in the past. I also thought he was highlighting something I hadn't allowed myself to think about when I used to interview prospective faculty members and trainees in academia: the element of seduction.)

I then said, "It's like a seduction."

(I thought I would say this in the same playful manner in which Harold was speaking. However, in retrospect, what I said came out as defensively authoritative. It was as if I was showing him something new, rather than that he had just helped me understand something. This was conveyed more by the tone of my remark. I did not grasp this at the time. Even more striking was that I said anything; according to my usual technical stance, there was no reason to speak, since I could see that Harold had a newfound freedom to feel, act, and observe all this.)

Harold: (There was a brief pause before Harold started talking again, and when he did, it was as if all the life had been drained out of his voice. His animated account of his interaction with the applicant was replaced by hesitation and a deadened voice.)

FB: I'm not sure if you heard the change, but after my comment, your whole manner changed from animated and lively to hesitant and much less lively.

Harold: I did notice it. (Now more animated.) I was talking with Esther yesterday. (Esther is a postdoctoral fellow in whom he is consistently disappointed; he has given her many projects, but she barely does them. He feels that she does not appreciate how much he has given her.) I laid out a plan for her for the next few years, including a grant proposal, so that she could get an academic position. It was all there on the blackboard. All she did was complain about how much work she has to do, and how she's torn between working in the private sector, teaching, and research. I wanted to say to her, "Listen, just do the work I'm paying you for." In the midst of my discussion with Esther, Sam (another postdoctoral fellow) came in, and commented on the research design. I said to him, in a not very nice way, "Sam, that's obvious." I guess it's another example of how I stay distant from people. (He then starts to describe various ways he feels he distances himself from others and from me. His readiness to take on blame in the face of irritation has been a familiar defense.)

FB: When I point out the change in your voice after my remark, your thoughts go to someone unappreciative of how much you offer, and how irritated you felt with someone who pointed out the obvious. While it seems likely that this is how you felt about my initial comment, something seemed unsettling about these feelings, which led to your inhibiting yourself and then blaming yourself for your distance, rather than blaming me. While I could have interpreted that the patient felt unappreciated and criticized by me, I would have been telling him HOW HE WAS FEELING, rather than helping him understand how these feelings bring about a CONFLICT OVER KNOWING HIS FEELINGS. As I have written about previously (Busch, 1995, 1999), the latter is a crucial part of the self-analytic process.

Harold: What you said was fine. You were just describing what I was talking about. Hmm! Maybe I just said that you said the obvious. But I didn't feel it. Yet, Sheila (a co-worker) has a habit of summing up what I say, and I know I hate it when she does that. So, I guess what you said was really to the point. I realize I'm afraid that if I say something critical to you, then you won't say anything again. I don't know why I'm thinking this, but I'm worried about not finding Jodie (his wife) attractive. When I saw her this morning, she looked so tired and washed out. But she really looked good once she got dressed and put on her makeup. Did I really have to say that? I guess I did. (Brief pause.) I realize there's been something in the back of my mind while I was just talking. It finally came to me. I was taking this English class as an undergraduate and we were reading one of the American classics (which he mentioned). We were supposed to write a paper on this one novel, and I went to the professor and told him about my idea. (The idea had to do with a character's seeing something and never wanting to go back to the way things had been.) The professor's eyes lit up, like I had literally opened his eyes to something he hadn't seen before. He then spent the first five minutes of the next class talking about how you could never tell from whom you might learn something. You know, I wasn't ever really able to admit this at the time, but I felt disappointed that he wasn't able to say it was me. He made it seem like he saw something, rather than that it was me who saw it.

FB: I wonder if you're telling us that you wish I could have acknowledged that you were seeing something very interesting in recruiting this woman, and that my comment made it seem like I was taking ownership of your observation, and I can see how that could be. While you felt disappointed and angered, you could not show me this side of yourself, which felt unattractive and would drive me away.

Harold: (After a pause.) You mean like I felt toward my mother (who had frequent rages). Or do I mean like I felt toward my mother? I feel myself starting to withdraw again. I was really moved by what you said. I felt we're real partners here. I also felt some irritation with you. Then I felt, "Okay, enough."

(At this point, our time was up.)

In this moment, we can see Harold's moving struggle between the acknowledgment of previously split–off feelings and a return to his old solutions. Harold's analytic triumph is that the struggle is now conscious. He projects his thought that the feelings of anger and disappointment with me echo feelings toward his mother, and then is able to own it. He finds himself withdrawing from owning the feeling, and then pulling back from his usual schizoid-like stance via his feeling of connection with me. However, this arouses his feelings of anger toward me again, and once more he wants to withdraw.

This whole sequence captures Harold's conflict over feelings brought about initially by trauma, which led to the distancing from others that brought him into treatment. The inevitable disappointments in any close relationship aroused such frightening feelings that a pleasant, removed stance was the one in which Harold felt safest.

Discussion

Harold, like Kindler's patient (Lichtenberg & Kindler, 1994), was dealing with angry feelings that were disturbing. I think our ways of approaching this feeling, in the way I've brought the examples, demonstrate significant differences in how the analyst defines the therapeutic task in working through these feelings. Kindler searches for the empathic breakdown in the analytic moment and tries to imagine (via his model scenes) the historical antecedents in parental breakdowns in empathy. In short, he is searching for the cause of the patient's anger in a particular area. However, it has been my position (Busch, 1995, 1999) that looking for the cause of a feeling before exploring the patient's conflict over owning the feeling will often prove fruitless. Thus, with my patient, I focused on the pressure to bury feelings and the resulting deadening effect this had on him. Analysts approaching from the standpoint of the trauma of empathic breakdowns often talk about how deadened the patient becomes if this is not recognized. However, the same thing can be said with regard to conflicts over the awareness of feelings.

I am in full sympathy with Lichtenberg's (1998) question about the patient's antagonism and withdrawal in the analytic situation: Are we, through a perceived empathic failure, the source of the aversive response, or are we a listener sensitive to the patient's aversive stance?... Many instances of antagonism and withdrawal that I had been taught to regard as resistance I now consider a patient's trusting response to an ambiance of safety. [p. 26]

However, Lichtenberg writes this in opposition to the concept of defense interpretation as he understands it. He suggests that motivations become evident only when the patient can experience affects, contents, and actions. But for the past two decades, defense interpretation has focused on the patient's conflicts over experiencing affects, contents, and actions (Busch, 1992, 1993; Gray, 1982). Kindler's patient's antagonism seems primarily based on her resistance to owning a particular feeling (i.e., her anger).

Analysts like Kindler have helped us understand that the patient's antagonism and withdrawal in analysis can be an adaptive response to an empathic breakdown. It has been an important addition to our ways of helping patients understand their feelings. I would have no difficulty with this perspective if it did not also include a dismissal of another important way, we help patients understand feelings—i.e., the analysis of conflicts over the awareness of feelings.

With the flourishing of various methods to understand our patients in American psychoanalysis, adhering to a slavish devotion to any one method of understanding is to deprive our patients and ourselves of new insights. After years of pretending that all we needed to know could be obtained from Freud's Standard Edition, we now realize that we have to keep abreast of current thinking. However, as Goldberg (2004) points out every new idea upsets the apple cart and leads to a tendency to move in two directions for a solution, so that it is all much too diverse to encompass in a single uniformity, or it all boils down to this (or that) particular aspect Further, we all have a tendency to pigeonhole someone (as I have probably done with Kindler), but mostly, we are aware of when this occurs with ourselves. - For example, I am surprised by my colleagues' surprise at the variety of methods I use to understand the clinical moment when I discuss clinical material in various places, even though I have consistently emphasized this (Busch, 1995, 1999).

I dislike the term *pluralism*, because in my experience, those who advocate it justify an "anything-goes" attitude to the clinical experience. However, a well-thought-out pluralism in understanding our patients seems the only justifiable position for an analyst to take at this point. With apologies to Tom

Wolfe, the analyst of today might best be known as the "contemporary Freudian, countertransferentially aware, self-psychological, relationally interested, Kleinian-inspired, ego psychologist."

Note

1 The contemporary clinician would find it difficult to understand his patients without a conceptualization of unconscious conflicts between and among object representations, self-representations, self-object representations, and so on. Such an understanding indicates that we have come a long way from the time when true conflict was thought to occur only in the oedipal phase, and only between particular agencies in the mind fueled by energy sources.

References

Busch, F. (1992). Recurring thoughts on unconscious ego resistances. *J. Am. Psychoanal. Assoc.*, 40: 1089–1115.

Busch, F. (1993). In the neighborhood: Aspects of a good interpretation and a developmental lag in ego psychology. *J. Am. Psychoanal. Assoc.*, 41:151–177.

Busch, F. (1995). *The ego at the center of clinical technique.* Northvale, NJ: Aronson.

Busch, F. (1999). *Rethinking clinical technique.* Northvale, NJ: Aronson.

Freud, A. (1951). Observations of childhood. *Psychoanal. St. Child*, 6:18–30.

Freud, S. (1897). *The complete letter of Sigmund Freud to Wilhelm Fliess, 1887–1904.* Cambridge, MA: Harvard Univ. Press.

Goldberg, A. (2004). *Misunderstanding freud.* New York: Other Press.

Gray, P. (1982). A "developmental lag" in the evolution of technique for psychoanalysis of neurotic conflict. *J. Am. Psychoanal. Assoc.*, 30:621–655.

Hartmann, H. (1950). Comments on the psychoanalytic theory of the ego. *Psychoanal. St. Child*, 5:1–27.

Kohut, H. (1971). *The analysis of the self.* New York: International Universities Press.

Kohut, H. (1977). *The restoration of the self.* New York: International Universities Press.

Kohut, H. (1984). *How does analysis cure?* Chicago, IL: Chicago Univ. Press.

Kris, E. (1956). The recovery of childhood memories in psychoanalysis. *Psychoanal. St. Child*, 11:54–88.

Lichtenberg, J. D. (1998). Experience as a guide to theory and practice. *J. Am. Psychoanal. Assoc.*, 46:17–33.

Lichtenberg, J. D. & Kindler, A. R. (1994). A motivational systems approach to the clinical experience. *J. Am. Psychoanal. Assoc.*, 42:405–420.

Lichtenberg, J. D., Lachman, F. M., & Fosshage, J. L. (1996). *The clinical exchange.* Hillsdale, NJ: Analytic Press.

Paniagua, C. (2001). The attraction of topographic technique. *Int. J. Psycho-Anal.*, 82:671–684.

Richards, A. (2003). A plea for a measure of humility. *J. Am. Psychoanal. Assoc.*, Suppl.:73–86.

Sachs, O. (1967). Distinction between fantasy and reality elements in memory and reconstruction. *Int. J. Psycho-Anal.*, 48:416–423.

Schmidt-Hellerau, C. (2002). Why aggression? *Int. J. Psycho-Anal.*, 83:1269–1289.

Smith, H. F. (2003). Conceptions of conflict in psychoanalytic theory and practice. *Psychoanal. Q.*, 72:49–96.

Spitz, R. A. (1945). Hospitalism: An inquiry into the genesis of psychiatric conditions in early childhood. *Psychoanal. St. Child*, 1:53–74.

Spitz, R. A. (1946). Anaclitic depression. *Psychoanal. St. Child*, 2:113–117.

Vermote, R. (2003). Two sessions with Catherine. *Int. J. Psycho-Anal.*, 84:1415–1421.

9   A shadow concept: preconscious thinking

Since Freud's (1900) discovery of the method of free association, generations of psychoanalysts have depended on the analysand's unwitting links between thoughts and feelings that are coming to mind as a primary method of understanding the patient at a deeper level. There are certain characteristics of these associative links that distinguish them from other forms of communication in psychoanalysis (e.g., words as actions designed to seduce, disengage, or attack the analyst). First, we notice there is an organization and coherence to these associative links, no matter how obscure they may initially appear. Two other central characteristics are that language is used in the formation of these links, and the analysand usually has no awareness of making associative links.

What are these links made via the method of free association, and in what part of the mind are they formed? How are they different from other forms of communication in psychoanalysis? I plan to show that, since Freud, unsettling doubts have remained about these links, and how they are formed. I believe these doubts raise important issues for psychoanalytic technique.

Freud likened the ideal state for free association to "the state before falling asleep [when] involuntary ideas emerge" (1900, p. 102) due to the relaxation of critical functioning. Notice that Freud doesn't suggest that free associations are guided by the same mental state as in dreaming. That is, Freud did not see free associations as guided by unconscious thinking characteristic of dream life. Yet, if Freud didn't believe the ideal state for guiding associations was via unconscious mentation, what did he believe? What is this mental state before the state of falling asleep? I have come to believe that what Freud tried to capture, and what is specific for the process of linking in the flow of associations, is the impact of a particular type of thinking called preconscious thinking. As you will see, Freud, and many others who have struggled with a theory of the mind, keep realizing that they need to account for organized associations that have the imprimatur of unconscious elements, and keep returning to a concept of preconscious thinking, different from how we usually think of it.[1]

Out of the shadow

A shadow doesn't exist by itself, but only in relationship to something else. This is the state of preconscious thinking throughout much of the history of psychoanalysis. Freud viewed the preconscious primarily as the shadow to consciousness, first in the topographical model, as in the system Cs/Pcs. The system Pcs, like a shadow, had no function of its own, except as a storage bin for thoughts and feelings waiting for the illuminating light from the system Cs. When Freud (1923) moved to the structural model, there was no longer a system Pcs. Instead, there was preconscious thought, which remained a shadow to consciousness. As one cannot have a shadow without light, preconscious thoughts and feelings remained formless without the spotlight of consciousness. Given how Freud thought of the preconscious, he could have subsumed it under conscious thinking, if consciousness was given more depth. Yet he retained the concept of preconscious thinking. Why? It is to this question I now turn.

A mystery in Freud's view of the preconscious

Throughout Freud's (1915) paper on "The unconscious," he strictly divides the system Ucs from the system Pcs on the basis of word-presentations and thing-presentations. It is fascinating to note, then, that buried in this 1915 text is a statement about preconscious thinking that dissolves this difference. In this diversion from his main thesis Freud points out that, "*A very great part of this preconscious originates in the unconscious, has the characteristics of its derivatives, and is subject to censorship before it can become conscious*" (p. 191, my italics). In an elaboration, he noted the thoughts he referred to had all the earmarks of having been formed unconsciously, "but were highly organized, free from self-contradiction, have made use of every acquisition of the system Cs, and would hardly be distinguished in our judgment from the formations of that system" (p. 190). Freud used daydreams as the prototypical example of this phenomenon. Thus, in contrast to everything else he'd written in this paper, Freud briefly conceives of complex preconscious thinking with infusions of unconscious elements. In these few sentences, Freud, still in his topographical model, presents a view of preconscious thinking that goes from a permeable border of the system Ucs to the permeable border of the system Cs. This remarkable discovery had such a powerful effect on Freud that he was required to suggest a second censorship between the preconscious and consciousness. This became one of many unwieldy revisions necessary to bring the topographical theory in line with clinical data, which then led to the structural model.

Germane to our current discussion is that when Freud (1923) presented the structural model the ego took over the functions of the systems Cs and Pcs. A portion of the ego, of course, went into the id and was not part of the repressed, but represented only unconscious resistances and the unconscious sense of guilt. However, what Freud had brought up in 1915 regarding these highly organized ideas that had the earmarks of the unconscious was left unexplained in this new model.

The mystery of the drawing from 1933

In the new introductory lectures, Freud (1933) produces a new drawing of the structure of the mind, quite different from the drawing in *The Ego and the Id*.[2] The drawing from 1923 is marked (a), while the 1933 drawing is marked (b).

(a)   (b)

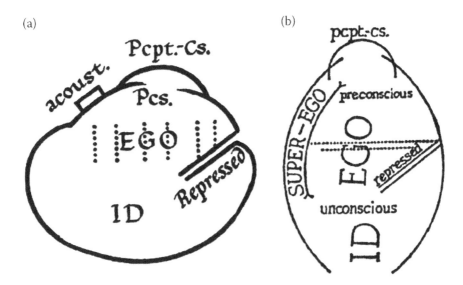

Figure 9.1 In the New introductory lectures, Freud (1933) produces a new drawing of the structure of the mind, quite different from thedrawing in The ego and the id (Figure 1).a) b) Figure 1 Reproduced, by permission of Sigmund Freud Copyrights/Paterson Marsh Ltd, from: a) Freud (1923, SE 19, p. 24); b) Freud (1933, SE 22, p. 78)

I would like to draw your attention to how the shape in the 1933 drawing has changed so that the preconscious is further removed from the Pcpt-Cs, and the area of the ego now extends more deeply into the unconscious, which has been expanded.[3] Further, the boundary between the preconscious and unconscious remains permeable, which would be consistent with Freud's views of 1915, i.e., that what we see in free association are thoughts with the qualities of preconscious and unconscious thinking. What is even more interesting is that Freud mentions nothing in the 1933 paper about these changes. The mystery deepens when Freud states,

It is certainly hard to say today how far the drawing is correct. In one respect it is undoubtedly not. The space occupied by the unconscious id ought to have been incomparably greater than that of the ego or the preconscious. I must ask you to correct it in your thoughts. (1933, p. 79)

What can this statement mean? If Freud didn't think this drawing accurately depicted his views, why didn't he draw it the way he wanted? It's as if Freud hadn't realized he was depicting a very different model from that presented in 1923. It was, as if he was unconsciously compelled to communicate an idea he still hadn't accepted in the conscious part of his ego. I would suggest that he assumed preconscious thinking was more important than he conceptualized it, that there was a permeable barrier between preconscious and unconscious thinking (as he stated in 1915), and *the unconscious ego took a much wider space than he previously thought*, but his ambivalence towards this idea kept him from consciously articulating such a position.[4]

In his last published paper, Freud (1940) returns again to define the concepts of conscious, preconscious, and unconscious, with the same confusing results. He boldly states that everything that isn't conscious, in the everyday use of this term, is (descriptively) unconscious. Preconscious thoughts are those that are capable of becoming conscious. However, Freud is once again not happy with these distinctions and wavers:

> The theory of the three qualities of what is psychical, as described in this generalized and simplified manner, seems likely to be a source of limitless confusion rather than help towards clarification. But it should not be forgotten that in fact it is not a theory at all but a first stocktaking of the facts of our observations. (p. 160)

At various places in this paper, Freud equates the ego with the preconscious thinking and the id with the unconscious thought, e.g., "Id and unconscious are as intimately linked as ego and preconscious" (p. 163). Yet, he keeps running up against his own observation that large parts of the ego are unconscious. Freud believes he came upon a satisfactory solution to the dilemma of the psychical qualities of the unconscious and preconscious, by positing that the unconscious is governed by primary-process thinking, and the preconscious by secondary- process thinking. However, this formulation still didn't solve the problem of organized, consistent fantasies in the preconscious, with the imprimatur of the unconscious as Freud pointed out in 1915.

After Freud, few psychoanalytic writers strayed from the Freud who equated the preconscious with what is readily available to consciousness. What Kris (1950) already noted over half a century ago, i.e., the preconscious mental processes are rarely mentioned, is certainly true today. In this same paper, Kris noted the cogent observations that mental processes in the preconscious are very different from each other in terms of types of thought processes; that preconscious processes reach consciousness with varying degrees of ease; and the reaction to preconscious material emerging into consciousness varies greatly. It may not be noticed or might bring about a strong emotional reaction. In Green's (1974) seminal paper on the preconscious, he decries that one hears little about the importance of preconscious functioning in psychoanalytic treatment. He emphasizes that we need to refine our concept of preconscious mental functioning so that the most effective clinical work can take place. He describes the preconscious as being in a "privileged space" (p. 420), between the unconscious and conscious, and between the ego and id, where patient and analyst can meet. One naturally also thinks of the Sandlers (1983, 1984, 1994a, 1994b) in considering preconscious thinking. However, their focus has been on why certain material in the system Pcs is not available to the system Cs. It is a different question than what I'm drawing attention to, which is the ready availability to awareness of preconscious thinking, heavily infused with what seems like derivatives of unconscious fantasies.

Preconscious thinking and unconscious fantasies

I would agree with Inderbitzen and Levy's statement that the concept of unconscious fantasy "has not been developed and refined as psychoanalytic theory evolved over time. Instead, its usage in psychoanalytic dialogue has grown increasingly imprecise" (1990, p. 113). *I find many of the examples of unconscious fantasies cited in the literature are more accurately described as preconscious thinking infused with unconscious elements.* I would suggest the proposition that, for patients who aren't psychotic, and for those patients who aren't using words to actualize something (e.g., an unconscious wish, defense, object relationship, or self-state), much of what analysands express to their analysts are examples of just the type of preconscious thinking Freud alluded to in 1915, and has been struggled with since then. That is much of our work is based upon a certain logic and coherence to patient's associations that are infused with unconscious elements. If we conceptualize the unconscious as without words (Beres, 1962; Freud, 1915), what we often hear in our clinical work are derivatives from the unconscious that have been deemed safe enough for admittance into a part of the mind where they are expressed in preconscious thinking. To call this type of association an "unconscious fantasy" is technically incorrect.

Clinical examples

In his last session before a weekend rafting trip which he felt anxious about, Mr. A began the session by recounting a daydream he had while in the waiting room. He arrived at the landing where everyone on the rafting trip was waiting for him. The landing was on the top of a steep embankment. He went running up the embankment, and everyone was amazed he could do that. Then the whole group decided to go swimming, and, when Mr. A attempted to dive over the rafts into the water, his head smashed into a raft. He kept replaying the last part of his fantasy to make it different, but each time he would smash his head into a raft.

I would consider this daydream a prototypical example of preconscious thinking, where the derivatives of the unconscious (i.e., phallic narcissism, self-castration for object-love and destructive wishes to the same object) have been allowed into Mr. A's awareness, while his thinking itself is organized and coherent. He is struck by the daydream but befuddled by the content. That is, he is aware these thoughts have meaning, but they cannot yet become meaningful. At these times, what is available to analysands are the derivatives of unconscious thinking presented in preconscious terms. In contrast, unconscious thinking is driven by intensely felt urges and feelings that, no matter how unrealistic and/or disorganized, seem justified to the patient. At these times derivatives from the unconscious cannot be translated into preconscious thinking because of the danger they pose. An example of the latter is Mrs. C.

After my three-week summer vacation, Mrs. C came to her first appointment demanding that I had to change three of her five appointments times. Mrs. C then became silent, apparently waiting for me to offer the three new times, thus indicating there would be no more thoughts forthcoming, and I was supposed to offer the new times immediately. As background, we had difficulty rescheduling even a single appointment in the past. I wondered if she could help me understand more about the urgency of this request. In an angry tone, Mrs. C told me that, since treatment had helped her become more social and more interested in her physical wellbeing, she decided to play more tennis in the fall and the time of our appointments were the only time she could fit with others' schedules. This turned out not to be the case. When I wondered about the anger in her voice, Mrs. C "explained" that she knew I'd ask her about what was going on and she just wanted to make the change.

In this example, we see the driven nature of Mrs. C's feelings. Her needs have to be met, while she defends against any meaning associated with them. Inconsistencies are explained away. While feelings of anger can be expressed, these feelings must remain split off from thoughts and feelings about being left. This is in contrast to the previous example where the derivatives of unconscious derivatives are available to Mr. A. With Mrs. C, no unconscious derivatives can be allowed into awareness. Action-driven "meaningless" thoughts are one way we see unconscious thinking in analytic sessions. Green has likened this to "thoughts without a thinker" (1998, p. 652), and distinguished it from "thinking, which has to be thought by a thinker and therefore can be communicated to another thinker" (p. 652, original italics).

Preconscious thinking runs the gamut from (more or less) coherent, logical thought, the meaning of which is understandable to both speaker and listener, to thoughts and feelings more organized than primary-process thinking but filled with derivatives of the unconscious ego and id. There are no sharp demarcations in the space of the preconscious. Rather one part fuses into another based upon the variables of:

1. degree of organization of thoughts and feelings;
2. fusion of unconscious elements; and
3. the ability of the individual to recognize and bring to consciousness these thoughts and feelings (i.e., degree of resistance)

Mr. B is an example of a patient who falls towards the more primitive of these three criteria. In general, his thinking is concrete, and he is reluctant to see meaning in what comes to his mind. Mr. B came into a Monday session describing how, over the weekend he felt increasingly passive. He kept using the phrase "pooped out"[5] to describe his tiredness. Mr. B then described the various ways his tiredness showed, and then elaborated a number of possible concrete reasons for why he may have been tired (e.g., worked out hard at the gym, didn't sleep so well, drank too much, etc.).

As I was waiting to see if he picked up on this phrase "pooped out," I was reminded of how we recently talked about the importance of a particular childhood experience, remembered in the analysis, where for a number of years his mother would wait outside the bathroom door while he had a bowel movement. When Mr. B was finished, he would call to her, and she would come in and wipe him. It was the one time he brought a memory of his mother waiting to be responsive to him. Most of his memories were of her being in a narcissistic stew. Seeing Mr. B's concreteness as a form of defensiveness, I began my interpretation slowly by saying, "I wondered if we can go back to your use of the phrase 'pooped out.'" Mr. B immediately "explained" why that was an "appropriate" term (i.e., it was a common expression, his wife had used it over the weekend to describe how she felt, etc.).

I see Mr. B's thinking existing somewhere between Mr. A's preconsciously organized daydream, and Mrs. C's more unconsciously driven feelings. Mr. B is able to allow a phrase into awareness that conveys meaning about his experience over the weekend (i.e., a call to the analyst to wipe him now that he is "pooped out," so that he will feel narcissistically valued). The phrase remains in the realm of thought, and he is not demanding that the analyst do something for him. However, the phrase is too closely associated with its unconscious derivatives. In contrast to Mr. A, Mr. B cannot allow himself to feel that this phrase might mean something. We immediately see his resistance to the understanding of "pooped out," more typically associated with unconscious content. Thus, we can see that the phrase, while allowed into thinking, is closer to its unconscious meaning, and Mr. B reacts accordingly.

In short, the understanding of preconscious thinking requires the appreciation of multiple variables and allows for greater clarity in technique. Understanding Mr. B's thinking as a pre-stage of full preconscious thinking helps us realize the need for further work with his unconscious defenses before interpretation of the content. It is as if Green's thinker has stepped up to the front door, but still cannot find a way to gain entry.

Ambiguities in our understanding of unconscious fantasies

I would like to briefly focus on unconscious fantasies as viewed through the lens of a group of American ego-psychologists and the Kleinians, as a demonstration of the semantic confusion and technical problems we run into without a clearer distinction between the type of preconscious thinking I've described and unconscious fantasies. In his classic paper on unconscious fantasies Arlow, after citing Beres's (1962) observation that there are no words in unconscious mentation, states, "it would appear unconscious fantasy embarrasses our methodology" (1969, p. 3). He suggests "unconscious fantasy has been hindered greatly by drawing too sharply the line of distinction between unconscious and conscious" (p. 3). Arlow then makes it clear that he is using the term unconscious fantasy as "it is used in the sense of the daydream" (p. 3). However, the daydream is the prime example of what Freud (1915) used to describe preconscious thinking infused with elements of unconscious fantasies. In short, what Arlow calls an unconscious fantasy seems more to be a preconscious fantasy derived, in part, from unconscious derivatives. Thus, while Arlow was aware of the theoretical problems involved in using the term *unconscious fantasy* to describe the phenomena he focused on, he continued to use it.

Bott-Spillius (2001) points out that little had been written about unconscious phantasies by Kleinians since Isaacs's (1948) defining paper. Klein, according to Bott-Spillius (2001), didn't pay much attention to the distinctions between the systems Ucs and Pcs, or the differences between primary and secondary processes. Hayman (1994) observed this in reviewing the "Controversial Discussions." The problems this lack of differentiation in levels of thinking brings about is evident in their methods of interpretation, even if those like Betty Joseph describe a way of working that might indicate the necessity to distinguish between preconscious and unconscious thinking (Busch, 2004). Eschewing preconscious thinking can be seen in Joseph's statement: "interpretations dealing only with the individual associations would touch only the more adult part of the personality, while the part that is really needing to be understood is communicated through the pressures brought on the analyst" (1985, p. 448). What most Kleinians have focused on is the significance of unconscious meanings in the patient's verbalizations as actions in the transference/countertransference, rather than the unconscious derivatives in the preconscious thinking of free associations, one factor in helping us determine the patient's availability for understanding. This important difference is the subject of the next section.

Some preliminary thoughts on differentiating preconscious thinking from unconsciously driven

From clinical experience, my impression is that one important distinction between the analysand's unconscious communications and a preconscious communication is that in unconscious communication:

1. The patient is driven to actualize a wish, defense, compromise formation, object relationship, self-object relationship, or repair a self-state. J. Sandler (1974) captured the quality of this way of being as preemptory.
2. There is an implicit insistence that, whatever the analysand is attempting to actualize, the analyst must enact it with him. Most often this isn't a

verbalized insistence, but rather *the patient's words are used to bring about something rather than communicate something.* I have described this as *language* action.[6] McLaughlin described it succinctly as words "become acts, things—sticks and stones, hugs and holdings" (1991, p. 598). What he captures is how patients attempt to love, tease, dominate, seduce, and bore us with words an outsider might judge as neutral. Until the analyst understands the attempt to actualize, there is little he can do to stop the enactment.

3. As the press to actualize is an unconsciously driven communication, it is usually registered first in the analyst's unconscious. We first respond to this more primitive level of communication via our more primitive form of reception. Thus, we learn first of what is going on via a feeling-state. It is only with the analyst's beginning awareness of his engagement in an enactment that he can begin, via the use of his countertransference, to understand what he is unconsciously being directed to actualize.

Implications for treatment based on two levels of preconscious thinking

Using the schema above, I think we have not always been so good at making the distinction between working psychoanalytically when the patient is communicating via unconscious communications versus communicating via preconscious thinking (Busch, 2000). However, as we are dealing with two different modes of communication, two different levels for potential awareness, and two different methods of thinking that underlie the communication, our methods of helping patients understand their communications are based upon the same principles, but are addressed to two different levels of preconscious thinking. The principle common to both is that we are attempting to raise what is occurring in the psychoanalytic moment to preconscious thinking.[7] As suggested by Green (2005) … *the aim of an interpretation is not to produce insight directly but to facilitate the psychic functioning that is likely to help insight emerge* by creating the links to get round the resistance or overcome it, thereby ensuring that the preconscious structure of the associations serves as a mirror for surmising the network of unconscious associations. (p. 5, my italics)

When associations are dominated by the logic and coherence of preconscious thought, we can speak to the logic of the sequence, while bringing in the missing meaning. From a series of associations, we say something like, "When we don't meet you feel abandoned, but this makes you feel ashamed." In this way, we bring meaning into the preconscious, which creates a new structure. However, when the analysand communicates primarily in action language, we attempt to translate this language into words, in the hopes of forming a new preconscious structure of thoughts (but not yet meaning), while attempting to understand the fears that may keep the patient communicating in action language.

The first step common to both levels of communication is *clarification*. However, what is clarified when preconscious associations are dominant are the associations while what is clarified in unconscious communications is the action language as a way of helping patients associate at a preconscious level. The purpose of a clarification is to ultimately add meaning, not causes. Meaning leads to causes. It is the elaboration of a dynamic process viewed via the analysand's words or language action. This is not a cognitive process, for, without the analyst's empathic involvement with the analysand's emotional shadings and the analyst's psychoanalytic understanding at multiple levels, any communication will detract from a deeper involvement between the analytic pair. However, I believe a frequent mistake we make is to assume agreed-upon meanings before we interpret.

The Kleinians have given us the best examples of patients who communicate unconsciously primarily via action language leading to the analyst's countertransference. However, we all work with patients who show a mixture of preconscious and unconscious communication. The example presented below is one of these cases. In it, a mixture of dynamics is enacted and expressed in thoughts. I focus on the method of working with each type of communication.

Clinical example

Mr. D is one of those patients for whom the phrase "looking at the world through rose-colored glasses" was invented. I puzzled over this for some time, and noted that whenever he became this way, I felt the need to smile back at him (although he was lying on the couch and couldn't see me). I also started to fall into a state of mind characteristic of times when I was glad to be invited to a party (rather than not be invited) but didn't want to go. One makes brief, pleasant conversation with the hosts and a few others, and then makes a hasty exit noting pressing professional matters. In short, I felt like we were supposed to be "nice" and pretend like nothing deeper or more conflicted was going on between us. All of these enacted transference/countertransference reactions are what is typical of unconscious communications via action language. The reader will not be surprised to learn that this was the role Mr. D felt he needed to take with his troubled mother. However, over time, this way of unconsciously enacting an old object relationship via language action became more of a vestigial enactment, expressed at times of stress and separations.

In the following vignette, Mr. D struggles to tell me of his problems, but then is unconsciously drawn to keep his mother/analyst alive by being upbeat. As usual, I react to the press to actualize this reparation in the countertransference by feeling the need to be "nice." However, having experienced this many times before, I am more able to "catch" the countertransference.

It was a Monday, the week before I was to be away for 10 days. Mr. D began the session with parts of two dreams. It was clear that he felt that, because these were only parts of dreams, they weren't worth going into. I had a familiar feeling of being shut out of his inner life. It was a different reaction to the empathy one has to an intrapsychic defense, especially since we'd discussed how even the smallest part of a dream could tell us something important. What kept being repeated throughout the session was that Mr. D would mention some difficulty, and then put a rosy patina on it by telling me how he resolved it in a happy way. For example, he felt frustrated and agitated when he left work on Friday, but he went to the gym and felt much better afterwards. He then had a good time with some friends that evening. He would end each description by saying, "so that was nice." After this type of incident occurred a few more times, I then attempted to clarify what was going on by saying, "It seems like each time you mention a difficulty, you are drawn to put a positive patina on it." I then gave him a few examples.

My purpose in this is to put into words what the patient is expressing in action language. This clarification is the beginning of the interpretive process. It is difficult to interpret more deeply if the patient cannot grasp what is being expressed in action language. We need to be in agreement on what is being observed before we can interpret deeper meanings.

Mr. D: A song started going through my mind from the movie *Saturday Night Fever*; it was called "Staying Alive." I remember seeing the movie with my girlfriend from high school, the one who was demanding and abusive, like my mother.

We can see here the beginning of preconscious thinking, i.e., where Mr. D can now allow in thoughts that which could only be expressed previously in the language of action.

Analyst: So, putting on a rosy patina may have felt like a way to stay alive. (As Mr. D moves from action language into preconscious thinking I can begin to interpret meanings rather than only putting action language into words.)

P: Well, remember, I came into treatment thinking I had this wonderful childhood.

He then described how on Saturday he was feeling frustrated and irritated, and then went on to list a number of actions he took to make him forget about his frustrations. He described these events as doing something good for himself. I suggested that something happened that led him back to warding off a bad feeling with a rosy patina.

As I had already clarified this defense expressed in action language, and Mr. D had responded associatively, I felt I could simply refer to the previous clarification.

After a brief pause Mr. D mentioned that he had a fleeting thought about one of his dreams while talking before, and then told me the dream.

Here again we see a retreat to action language that, when clarified, leads to associative links typical of preconscious thinking. (I'm not suggesting this is all it takes to change unconscious communications into preconscious thinking. What Mr. D is doing is the result of considerable psychoanalytic work.)

Mr. D: In the dream, I was working and talking to you. I was telling you a dream about something that I think really happened. In the dream, the woman from the family who lived next door—I used to like to go over there as everyone seemed so happy—came over to our house and my sister and I were sitting at the table. We were saying, "Take us with you. Please take us with you." In the dream, my mother was standing by the kitchen sink staring out blankly. In reality, one time my little brother was choking on something, and my mother did nothing. My older brother ran over to the woman next door and she was the one who saved him. I don't know if I was there or just heard about it.

Analyst: So, you put on a rosy patina in the hope of making your mother more alive, so that she can keep you alive. My going away brings up these same feelings.

Once again, I am able to give meaning to the associative links. While also hearing the story of the neighbor as his wishing to come away with me, I thought the meaning of the main way he could make a connection with me took precedence.

Mr. D: You know I have this conference to go to next week. There are some articles I should read before the conference, but I can't find the time. I keep on having this thought that I'll start to read these articles on the plane, but my battery will die.

Analyst: You fear making a connection because it could lead to a sudden death, like you probably felt when your mother would suddenly go blank.

For the first time Mr. D cried in our session, and for the first time he said, "I'm going to miss you."

I believe this is the type of case most of us work with, i.e., where we are dealing with a mixture of communication, some more preconsciously determined and others more unconsciously determined in the form of action language. Each type of communication requires different approaches. While the goal is always the same, i.e., translating to the preconscious, we are attempting to create higher order constructs of different types. With preconscious associations, we are attempting to construct meaning in the preconscious, while with unconscious communications we are attempting to put words for things, as Freud put it, into the preconscious. This speaks to the need for a flexible approach to clinical material depending upon the level of communication.

Playing with thoughts

Another important implication of our understanding preconscious thinking is a particular space located by Green within the range of preconscious thinking, that he labels a "transitional space" (1974, p. 417), "between primary creativity and objective perception" (Winnicott, 1953, p. 95). It is here the freedom for self-expression exists. It is in this space where the capacity to play with ideas as a basis for self-exploration exists. It is in this space where play with created ideas can be comfortably explored without the demands to act due to the press of the unconscious, or the demand to concretely conform to reality due to the press of the external world. Neither the press of the unconscious nor the external world allows the individual a comfortable setting for the curious musing necessary for psychoanalytic self-exploration. Ogden has suggested the patient's exclusive focus on reality is "designed to drain the blood out of fantasy" (1985, p. 135). If

I understand him correctly, he also captures the limitation to play with ideas from what I would call the demands to unconsciously actualize something, which leads to perceptions that "must be got rid of, clung to, concealed, hidden from, put into someone else, worshiped, shattered, etc." (p. 134). One might say that all of psychoanalytic work is directed towards capacity to safely exist in a transitional space, via exploring the reasons it has been so difficult. Green (1975, 1986) calls this space where analysis takes place the analytic object, created by both participants and akin to Winnicott's transitional space.

As with the transitional object, psychoanalysis is ultimately about meaning making. It isn't about the patient's meaning when he talks or acts, or the analyst doing the same thing; *it is about the creation of meaning between them.* The patient talks about something he sees as having meaning. The analyst tries to add meaning. The patient then reacts with more meaning, even if it is an act against meaning. This is how meaning is consistently created in the space between analyst and patient. *The analyst derails the process when he moves too far from the potential space which might be created between himself and the patient, which is inevitable, and, while not recommended as a technique, can lead to other meanings.* Green (1975) has stated the method of meaning making as:

> What determines our formulation of interpretations is not our apprecia- tion of what we understand or feel. Whether formulated or withheld, it is always based on the measure of the distance between what the analyst is prepared to communicate, and how much of it the patient can receive in order to form the analytic object (what I call useful distance and efficacious difference). From this point of view the analyst does not only unveil a hidden meaning. He constructs a meaning which has never been created before the analytic relationship began. (p. 12)

The transitional object must be consistently there to be found (Busch, 1974). While psychoanalytic treatment has many components, the consistent focus on meanings, discovered in a way that is meaningful to the analysand, becomes the vehicle for playing with ideas in transitional space. Preconscious thinking is the destination of our interpretations, and the vehicle for playing with meaning making, while always keeping in mind that we will never find the meaning. Gardner (1983), using the language of the preconscious transi- tional space, describes our goal thus:

> It will do, I think, if we agree we are not talking about introspection, nor of the "life examined" in the Socratic sense, nor of the preoccupation with "inner" in the Cartesian sense, but of the full play of experiencing, attention-paying, sense- making, and synthesizing we call self and other. It will do, I think, if we know that even some of what we refer to seems only about "inner" and some only about "outer," all whether avowedly about the one or the other, is about both. (p. 18)

Notes

1 That is, when the term *preconscious* is used we usually think of the structure Pcs. However, what I will be discussing is preconscious *thinking*.
2 Figure 1 Reproduced, by permission of Sigmund Freud Copyrights/Paterson Marsh Ltd, from: (a) Freud (1923, SE 19, p. 24); (b) Freud (1933, SE 22, p. 78).
3 In a footnote to the 1933 paper, Strachey states that the drawing has changed to show the role of the superego. However, this seems not the only reason given that the old drawing could have easily accommodated this change.
4 I have previously presented data to support this last point (see chapters one and two).
5 A phrase associated with going to the bathroom.
6 See the Chapter 12, "Can You Push a Camel through the Eye of a Needle."
7 For expository purposes, I am drawing a firm line between these two types of communications, while recognizing that in actual clinical practicing these two modes often blend in a way that make them difficult to differentiate one from the other. However, unless we have such models in mind it makes it even more difficult to determine which method of communication is primary.

References

Arlow, J. (1969). Unconscious fantasy and disturbances of conscious experience. *Psychoanal. Q.*, 38:1–27.

Beres, D. (1962). The unconscious fantasy. *Psychoanal. Q.*, 31:309–328.

Boesky, D. (1982). Acting out: A reconsideration of the concept. *Int. J. Psycho-Anal.*, 63:39–55.

Bollas, C. (2006). An interview with C. Bollas (V. Bonaminio). *Meeting of the European Federation of Psychoanalysis*, Athens, Greece, April.

Bott-Spillius, E. (2001). Freud and Klein on the concept of fantasy. In: C. Bronstein (ed.), *Kleinian theory: A contemporary perspective*. London: Whurr.

Bram, A. & Gabbard, G. O. (2001). Potential space and reflective functioning. *Int. J. Psycho-Anal.*, 82:685–699.

Busch, F. (1974). Dimensions of the first transitional object. *Psychoanal. St. Child*, 29:215–229.

Busch, F. (1992). Recurring thoughts on unconscious ego resistance. *J. Am. Psychoanal. Assoc.*, 40:1089–1115.

Busch, F. (1993). 'In the neighborhood': Aspects of a good interpretation and a 'developmental lag' in ego psychology. *J. Am. Psychoanal. Assoc.*, 41:151–177.

Busch, F. (1995). Do actions speak louder than words? A query into an enigma in analytic theory and technique. *J. Am. Psychoanal. Assoc.*, 43:61–82.

Busch, F. (1997). Understanding the patient's use of the method of free association: An ego psychological approach. *J. Am. Psychoanal. Assoc.*, 45:407–423.

Busch, F. (2000). What is a deep interpretation? *J. Am. Psychoanal. Assoc.*, 48:237–254.

Busch, F. (2004). A missing link in psychoanalytic technique: Psychoanalytic consciousness. *Int. J. Psycho-Anal.*, 85:567–572.

Busch, F. (2006). Talking with strangers. *Psychoanal. Rev.*, 93:463–476.

Freud, S. (1900). The interpretation of dreams. *SE* 4–5.

Freud, S. (1915). The unconscious. *SE* 14, pp. 159–216.

Freud, S. (1923). The ego and the id. *SE* 19, pp. 3–66.

Freud, S. (1933). The dissection of the psychical personality. *SE* 22, pp. 57–80.

Freud, S. (1940). An outline of psycho-analysis. *SE* 23, pp. 141–207.

Gardner, M. R. (1983). *Self inquiry*. Boston, MA: Little, Brown. 121 pp.

Green, A. (1974). Surface analysis, deep analysis (the role of the preconscious in psychoanalytic technique). *Int. Rev. Psycho-Anal.*, 1:415–423.

Green, A. (1975). The analyst, symbolization and absence in the analytic setting (on changes in analytic practice and analytic experience)-in memory of D. W. Winnicott. *Int. J. Psycho-Anal.*, 56:1–22.

Green, A. (1986). *On private madness*. New York, NY: International Univ. Pess.

Green, A. (1998). The primordial mind and the work of the negative. *Int. J. Psycho-Anal.*, 79:649–665.

Green, A. (2005). Issues of interpretations: Conjectures on constructions. Presented at the *Meeting of the European Federation of Psychoanalysis*, Vilamoor, Portugal, March.

Hayman, A. (1994). Some remarks about the 'Controversial Discussions'. *Int. J. Psycho-Anal.*, 75:343–358.

Inderbitzen, L. & Levy S. (1990). Unconscious fantasy: A reconsideration of the concept. *J. Am. Psychoanal. Assoc.*, 38:113–130.

Issacs, S. (1948). The nature and function of phantasy. *Int. J. Psycho-Anal.*, 29:73–97.

Joseph, B. (1985). Transference: The total situation. *Int. J. Psycho-Anal.*, 66:447–454.

Kantrowitz, J. (1999). The role of the preconscious in psychoanalysis. *J. Am. Psychoanal. Assoc.*, 47:65–89.

Kris, E. (1950). On preconscious mental processes. *Psychoanal. Q.*, 19:540–560.

Levy, S. & Inderbitzen, L. (1990). The analytic surface and the theory of technique. *J. Am. Psychoanal. Assoc.*, 38:371–391.

McLaughlin, J. T. (1991). Clinical and theoretical aspects of enactment. *J. Am. Psychoanal. Assoc.*, 39:596–614.

Ogden, T. H. (1985). On potential space. *Int. J. Psycho-Anal.*, 66:129–141.

Paniagua, C. (1991). Patient's surface, clinical surface, and workable surface. *J. Am. Psychoanal. Assoc.*, 39:669–685.

Piaget, J. (1926). *The language and thought of the child*. New York, NY: Harcourt Brace.

Piaget, J. (1930). *The child's conception of physical causality*. London: Kegan Paul.

Piaget, J. & Inhelder, B. (1969). *The psychology of the child*. New York, NY: Basic Books. 192 pp.

Sandler, J. (1974). Psychological conflict and the structural model: Some clinical and theoretical implications. *Int. J. Psycho-Anal.*, 55:53–62.

Sandler, J. & Sandler, A.-M. (1983). The 'second censorship', the 'three box model' and some technical implications. *Int. J. Psycho-Anal.*, 64:413–425.

Sandler, J. & Sandler, A.-M. (1984). The past unconscious, the present unconscious, and interpretation of the transference. *Psychoanal. Inq.*, 4:367–399.

Sandler, J. & Sandler, A.-M. (1994a). The past unconscious and the present unconscious. *Psychoanal. St. Child*, 49:278–292.

Sandler, J. & Sandler, A.-M. (1994b). Phantasy and its transformations: A contemporary Freudian view. *Int. J. Psycho-Anal.*, 75:387–394.

Winnicott, D. W. (1953). Transitional objects and transitional space: A study of the first not-me possession. *Int. J. Psycho-Anal.*, 34:89–97.

10 Distinguishing psychoanalysis from psychotherapy

A proviso: I work with patients in psychotherapy; I've helped a lot of people via psychotherapy; I enjoy doing psychotherapy and believe, as with psychoanalysis, I keep learning about how to do it better than I did before.

Recently, to celebrate the anniversary of a prestigious psychoanalytic institute, a program was arranged around psychodynamic psychotherapy. Its stated goal was to identify "areas of commonality that bridge every modality from supportive psychotherapy to psychoanalysis." This led to my imagining going to a psychoanalytic conference where I would find pickets carrying signs that said, "Psychoanalysts are elitists," and, when I looked closer, I was surprised to see that it was my psychoanalytic colleagues who carried these signs. As I went inside, I realized there were more psychoanalysts outside carrying signs than attending the meeting. What this image conveys is what I see as a growing attempt to de-emphasize the distinctiveness of psychoanalysis, in order to better sell it. We seem to feel that psychoanalysis-lite will attract more adherents, forgetting what it might do to what is essential to psychoanalysis.

I am concerned that psychoanalysis is in danger of becoming a pale echo of what inspired Freud, excited psychoanalysts for generations afterwards, and is still true in the 21st century. That is, we are in danger of losing contact with the deeper motives for why people seek us out…i.e., the terror with no name, the unconscious murder, mayhem, and sexual fantasies of every sort that drive our patients into "private madness" (Green, 1986) and lead to the pulsating conflicts that cause our patients *to hate what they want, and reject what they have,* all going on outside of awareness. As Green (1995) noted:

> We prefer to give up the profundity and depth of the unobserved and sometimes unobservable psychic world in order to be proud of our discoveries about the most superficial aspects of psychic life, not minding the tribute we have to pay for this choice. (p. 873)

Further, it is as if our appreciation for the more humane ways of understanding our patients' difficulties resulted in "empathism" rather than empathy

(Bolognini, 1997), leading to a forced and controlling niceness. Kernberg (2001), in reviewing various schools of psychoanalysis, pointed out that the French are especially critical of the neglect of early sexuality and the archaic oedipal complex:

> [and] are particularly critical of intersubjectivity as a seduction into a superficial interpersonal relationship, the denial of Freud's theory of drives, and the implicit supportive psychotherapeutic intervention that occurs when the analyst presents him-or herself as an ideal model, with unconscious acting out of countertransference as a major consequence. (p. 542)[1]

At times it seems like the increased understanding of cumulative trauma resulted in an obsession with the patient as victim, rather than a patient also with a mind who develops fantasies about the trauma and enacts these in a variety of ways in the analysis. We seem to have forgotten it is not only the trauma itself that remains traumatic. Inevitably, the feelings and fantasies the trauma stimulates become part of a dangerous intrapsychic field (Busch, 2005).

In short, I believe the depths of the mind explored in psychoanalysis are being neglected in favor of a more general psychotherapeutic culture. In 1919, Freud wrote: "It is very probable, too, that the large-scale application of our therapy will compel us to alloy the pure gold of analysis freely with the copper of direct suggestion" (p. 167). This prescient observation has now come to fruition in an otherwise balanced paper by Eisold (2005), where he reports, without irony:

> It seems unlikely that the learning that has grown out of the clinical experience of psychoanalysts over the years could disappear entirely, but it may be that psychoanalysis as a distinct profession will become increasingly marginal. What it has discovered to be of enduring value might well survive, *absorbed into the practice of psychotherapy; the rest could fade away.* (p. 1191; italics added)

What is distinct about psychoanalysis?

Since the 1950s, when the differences between psychoanalysis and psychotherapy started to be an important issue for discussion (e.g., Gill, 1954; Rangell, 1954; Stone, 1954), the emphasis has been on what the analyst does differently. Thus, it was posited that it was the technique that was different in psychoanalysis and psychotherapy. While I believe there are similarities and differences in technique, I will argue here that it is the goals and treatment outcomes that differentiate the two forms of treatment, and that our methods of working become distinguished based upon these factors. It is my impression that there has been an evolution in our methods of analyzing, based on these goals, which has led to psychoanalysis being different now from what it was 30 years ago, and which makes the distinction between psychoanalysis and psychotherapy easier. Simply put, we have come to realize that the process of knowing is as important as what is known from psychoanalysis. *What is accomplished in a relatively successful psychoanalysis is a way of knowing, and not simply knowing.* The parameters of psychotherapy make it unlikely the psychotherapy patient can reach this goal. Another type of knowledge gained in psychoanalysis is what I would call *state knowledge*. What was not known is now known. The patient has reached a new state of knowledge. This is primarily the kind of knowledge one gains in psychotherapy.

The endpoint for this process of knowing is the capacity for self-analysis. This is what I see as a major distinguishing goal of psychoanalysis. While this goal was suggested by Freud as early as 1900 and has been in the background of analytic thinking ever since, I will suggest that new ways of understanding self-analysis has led to new methods or ways of working more consistent with the goal of self-analysis. In the remainder of this paper, I will define how I think we have now come to see self-analysis, and the emphases on different methods that help reach this goal. In general, it has to do with a wide acceptance of the expansion of the Ego as central to self-analysis and the curative process. It is important for psychoanalysis that, despite remaining differences, one can see a growing coalescence about these methods amongst the Contemporary Kleinians, the French school, Contemporary Ego Psychology, and thinking amongst some current Bionians.

Self-analysis

The most striking result to come out of the Stockholm outcome studies, probably the most comprehensive research on psychoanalysis and psychotherapy (Falkenström et al., 2007), was the significance of self-analysis in treatment gains. That is, psychoanalytic patients develop the capacity for self-analysis while psychotherapy patients tend not to, and this was responsible for the significantly different post-termination gains in the psychoanalytic group. This confirmed the earlier findings of Leuzinger-Bohleber et al. (2003), and Kantrowitz et al. (1990). These powerful research findings confirm what has always been an argument for the benefits of psychoanalysis, in contrast to psychotherapy (i.e., the analysand's ongoing capacity to profit from self-analysis to deal with the exigencies of life).

Self-analysis is made up of several capacities developed in psychoanalysis and is the result of certain ways of analyzing (Busch, 2007). A number of analysts (Curtis, 1979; Goldberg, 1994; Schlesinger & Wolitzky, 2002; Schlessinger & Robbins, 1974) seem to view the path to self-analysis as a by-product of analysis (i.e., an identification with the analyst). However, it is my impression that the majority of patients develop these capacities via analytic attention. The form of this attention, to be discussed in detail below, seems to be agreed upon by a growing consensus of analysts working within very different traditions (Barranger, 1993; Bion, in Brown, 2009; Gray, 1994; Green, 2005; Joseph, 1997, in Feldman, 2004). It revolves around working more closely with what the patient can understand, rather than what the analyst understands. As Green has stated:

> What determines our formulation of interpretations is not our apprecia-tion of what we understand or feel. Whether formulated or withheld, it is always based on the measure of the distance between what the analyst is prepared to communicate, and how much of it the patient can receive in order to form the analytic object (what I call useful distance and efficacious difference). (1975, p. 12)

Self-analysis is the end-stage of a developmental process in psychoanalysis involving self-observation, self-reflection and self-inquiry, leading to self-analysis.[2] A patient most often begins treatment seeing his thoughts as only a description of real events or feelings. He works in what Fonagy and Target (1996, 2000) have called psychic equivalence, "where ideas are not felt to be representations, but rather direct replicas of reality, and consequently always true" (1996, p. 219). Self-observation occurs when the patient is capable of seeing his thoughts as mental events. It can indicate, if only for a moment, a profound change in the analysand's relationship to his own thoughts and feelings (i.e., the patient is not only experiencing his thoughts and feelings, but also reflecting upon them). Ikonen stated it well when he said: "Without self-observation there can be no study of the psyche; investigating the psyche rests precisely on the subject's own self-observation. Psychoanalysis is built upon this foundation" (Ikonen, 2003, p. 12).

Freud first mentioned self-reflection in 1900. He saw it as the development of the capacity to reflect on a series of associations. His description still rings true:

> Looked at in isolation, a thought may seem very trivial or very fantastic; but it may be made important by another thought that comes after it, and, in conjunction with thoughts that may seem equally absurd, it may turn out to form a most effective link. Reason cannot form any opinion upon all this unless it retains the thought long enough to look at it in connection with the others. On the other hand, where there is a creative mind, reason—so it seems to me—relaxes its watch upon the gates, and the ideas rush in pell-mell, and only then does it look them through and examine them in a mass. (Freud, 1900, p. 103)

Self-reflection is thus another developmental step in analysis in that it is not only the recognition of thoughts as mental events, but the analysand's capacity to see a string of associations as related mental events, and to keep them in mind long enough to reflect upon them.

Self-inquiry is a term introduced by Gardner (1983). It is a particular space in the mind where the capacity to play with ideas as a basis for self-expression exists. It is a space where created ideas can be freely explored, a place for curious musings without a particular destination. Many have described this space in other terms. Green (1975) used Winnicott's (1953) term transitional space, and at other times (Green, 1975) he described it as the analytic object. Ogden (1994) described it as the analytic third, while Bram and Gabbard (2001) used the term *potential space*. All these latter authors are describing a joint creative process that occurs between analysand and analyst, much like the transitional object is created in the space between mother and child.

I prefer to keep the term *self-inquiry* because it speaks to a place in the mind, which develops in psychoanalysis. While the capacity to play with ideas requires the analyst's presence to develop, for it ultimately to be useful for the patient, it needs to be carried out in the privacy of one's own mind. Otherwise, the capacity to play with ideas, which leads to the most interesting and startling places, remains moribund after analysis.

Self-analysis necessitates all the above psychological processes. However, it also requires that it result in some effective understanding that is relieving (in the case of psychic discomfort) or surprising (as with understanding a dream) but, probably most importantly, not frightening. We have all come upon patients who seem able to observe, reflect on and play with ideas, but it never leads to anything helpful to them (Frayn, 1996). This is why I think in many analyses working on the resistance to self-analysis becomes an important part of the termination process. Encompassed within the development of a self-analytic capacity is the patient's readiness to leave the analyst, which arouses again a multitude of primitive fears, whether it is seen as murder, loss of love, loss of the object, etc.

In short, the goals of psychoanalysis have evolved so that equal consideration is given to how one knows in addition to what one knows. It is no longer only a matter of making the unconscious conscious, but how we do that in a way that increases the capacity for knowing.

Evolution of psychoanalytic technique

As the goals of psychoanalysis have changed over the last 30 years there have been changes in the way the psychoanalytic method has been understood that, in important ways, have radically changed the way psychoanalysis can be practiced.[3] These changes have only generally been recognized as such. The methods I describe are the ones that I think have the greatest potential for affecting the factors that go into self-analysis. In general, I would characterize these methods as more systematically working through defenses, interpreting to the preconscious ego rather than unconscious, transforming the un-represented rather than only lifting repression, working with the total transference, and using the countertransference to reach deeper layers of the unconscious. Together, these methods lead to a more coherent pattern of analyzing that allows the patient to find his mind rather than it primarily being the analyst who discovers the patient's unconscious. In this way the mind remains a mystery, *but not mysterious in a way that only a brilliant analyst can understand*.

What follows is a brief elaboration of the methods described above.

Resistance analysis

For much of our psychoanalytic history, resistance analysis was a murderous battlefield, with resistances being seen as something to break through, attack, or overcome (Busch, 1992). With the introduction of Gray's (1994) method of resistance analysis, first outlined in 1973 and 1982 (Gray, 1973, 1982), one can find the first consistent method of resistance analysis based upon our understanding of the mind using the structural model and Freud's second theory of anxiety (Busch, 1993). Gray's writing was instrumental in reminding us that resistances are based upon the greatest fears known to human-kind. There is nothing more important to the freedom to think, feel, and reflect than analysis of the resistances.[4]

While others have taken cognizance of this, it was inconsistently applied to technique (Busch, 1992; Gray, 1982). In the absence of a coherent method of analyzing resistance, many analysts fell back into what Paniagua (2008) called "id analysis."

Preconscious ego (in the neighborhood–see chapter one)

By introducing the concept of the analysand needing to be "in the neighborhood" of the analyst's interpretation, Freud (1910) noted the centrality, among the principles of clinical technique, of the preconscious ego and preconscious thinking. The patient must be able to make some connection between what he is aware of thinking and saying, and the analyst's intervention. The analyst's reading of the unconscious may be quick and brilliant; however, it is not useful data until it can be connected to something of which the patient can be preconsciously aware (Busch, 2004). However, Freud himself was ambivalent about the importance of this and so were many who followed (Busch, 1993), even to the present day (Busch, 2000; Paniagua, 2001). Green (1974) was one of the first to highlight the importance of the preconscious in interpreting:

> I support the Freudian concept of the ego in which the patient's freedom is respected and which allows one to proceed according to what the patient is able to understand of what we are saying to him at that point in time of the treatment, i.e. permitting him to elaborate and integrate in a regression-progression process, and so to proceed from the most superficial to the deepest level. (p. 421)

Increasingly, analysts from different schools use descriptive phrases to capture similar methods. For example, Ferro (2003), working from a very different theoretical orientation and using different language, touches on the issue of the preconscious in the following manner:

> Earlier, I mentioned my contribution to a serene atmosphere—but what exactly does that mean? Does the analyst pretend to agree with everything, or does he or she pretend that nothing has happened? I would say absolutely not to either question, nor can the analyst be seen as simply testing the temperature and distance of interpretations. (Meltzer, 1976). *I do believe, however, that it is essential to respect the patient's threshold for tolerating interpretations, and to recognize that a feeling of persecution in the session is a glaring sign of excessive insistence. (pp.189-90), italics. added*

This brief sampling gives an indication of how working with the preconscious ego, captured in the phrase "in the neighborhood" has crept into our ways of working with little overt notice.

Transformations in the "here and now"

There has been a shift in technique from primarily lifting repression to including transformation of what was not represented (e.g., Busch, 2009; Lecours, 2007; Sugarman, 2003). Again, it is something agreed upon, in various forms, by writers from different theoretical perspectives (Basch, 1981; Bass, 1997; Bion, in Brown, 2009; Ferro, 2006; Green, 1974). There is also general agreement that much of this work takes place in the "here and now" of the analytic moment. Thus, we approach the analytic material in terms of what is going on (via associations or enactment) within the session, rather than only looking for what is hidden. We try to illuminate the patient's mind in the present, rather than primarily elucidating the past. Further, working in the transference has shifted to what Joseph (1985) has called transference as the "total situation." Rather than transference being exclusively seen as a repetition of past object relationships, Joseph describes it as living, changing expression in the transference of the patient's fantasies, impulses, defenses, and conflicts. In short, every aspect of psychic phenomena is brought into the room with the analyst, and this is articulated within the here and now of the session. All this fits more consistently with the mind of the patient in analysis.

Countertransference

With the greater appreciation and acceptance of the analyst's countertransference as an inevitable and integral part of analysis, we have been able to reach an understanding of the depths of the unconscious in a way that was previously unimaginable. It has become clear that this is a primary way the unconscious is communicated to the analyst during treatment. Further, we have become more attuned to how our own unconscious affects our work, leading us to pay greater attention to disturbances in our patient's equilibrium after an intervention as an inadvertent enactment on our part (e.g., Schwaber, 1992). Recognition of our part in the atmosphere of the session, in a non-masochistic fashion, can be relieving for many patients and helps free them to look at their own role in the atmosphere.

The total transference

Earlier distinctions between psychoanalysis and psychotherapy pointed to analysis of the transference as a distinguishing feature, which usually meant restoring the past in the present. This meant showing the patient how his present views of the analyst were based on distortions from and repetitions of the past. In this way, technique barely advanced from Freud's original views on the transference. Over time this view has changed, most usefully characterized by Joseph (1985) as the total transference situation. Feldman (2004) characterized this method as the analyst paying:

> Close attention to the way patients are functioning within the session, how they use their own mind and own experience, as well as the analyst's interventions, can enable the analyst to build up a picture of the forces within their patients which lead them to act upon, and thus to perceive their internal and external objects in accordance with archaic objects and needs. (p. 33)

In summary, we see in our contemporary literature new methods that lead psychoanalysis to be *directed towards a way of knowing, and not just knowing*. In this way our psychoanalytic patients are not limited to what they learned in analysis but move from the inevitability of action to the possibility of reflection. It involves:

- Treatment directed towards the expansion of the ego.
- Working more to the surface rather than the depths, which allows for exploration of greater depth.
- Transference is not only about something else; it is something.
- Transference interpretations are now geared toward understanding the patient's mind in the present, leading to the past, rather than focusing primarily on the past in the present. The "here and now" is given equal primacy to the "there and then."
- Countertransference reactions are understood in multiple ways, leading to a greater understanding of the unconscious.

Comparing psychoanalytic psychotherapy and psychoanalysis

In the "good enough" psychotherapy, in areas of specific conflict with neu-rotics and moderately severe character disorders,[5] repetitive destructive and self-destructive actions can be controlled, a modicum of stability can be obtained, and a more coherent self-state can be established. The changes are frequently based on a greater *intellectual control* leading a patient in the midst of an enactment to realize: "I don't have to do this." Understanding is reached primarily around interferences in development of normal narcissism, and how these interferences converge into cumulative traumas that are played out via internalized object relations. The deeper levels of the unconscious, where madness exists within us all, cannot be reached. The therapist's role is one of greater activity, with interventions being more saturated (Ferro, 2009), and of necessity more speculative. The analyst is a more real and supportive figure, helping overcome unconscious guilt more than analyzing it. In general, psychoanalysis leads one to be intrigued by the mind as the ongoing source and answer to fears and motivations, while psychotherapy leads one to look to the past for answers to the present.

Below are listed some characteristics of what I believe can and cannot happen in psychotherapy, in comparison to psychoanalysis. In addition, I will present some of the limitations on psychoanalytic methods that are applicable to psychotherapy. In general, there are quantitative and qualitative modifications in technique that lead to a different ambiance (Kernberg, 1999) *and goals*. In many ways the themes and results of the "good enough" psychotherapy are like the results of the initial phase of psychoanalysis.[6]

Resistance analysis is possible in psychotherapy but limited, in part, by the infrequency of sessions. There is a necessary safety in coming upon a terrifying feeling and knowing one can return the following day for further understanding as in psychoanalysis. It is too much to ask of the human psyche to hold on to such feelings for a week or several days. Psychotherapy most often leads to identifying and overcoming resistances rather than working them through. For example, inquiry into a patient falling silent will most often lead to her telling about the thought she was avoiding, rather than the feeling that led to the thought being avoided, which is the necessary ingredient for working through.

While the preconscious ego remains as the primary vehicle through which we clarify, confront and interpret in psychotherapy, the limitations in resistance analysis minimize what can be brought into awareness. This leads to restrictions in what the patient can re-experience in the transference, leading the therapist to use the transference to explain external dilemmas. Our capacity to effectively use our countertransference for transformations and understanding of deeper levels of the unconscious is limited by the amount of time we are exposed to our countertransferences. This often leads to a tendency for the therapist to enact the countertransferences, and a longer time to understand and use them. Most often our countertransference can best be used in psychotherapy to empathize with the various positions taken by the patient in re-enacting past object relationships.

What develops in psychotherapy is what I would call directed freer thought rather than self-analysis. I would characterize this difference as between thinking more freely about specific problems and *thinking about thinking*. In areas of specific conflict, psychotherapy patients develop a greater capacity for self-observation (as defined above). Self-reflection is limited to what has already been understood in treatment, and the spontaneity, playfulness and surprise evident in self-inquiry are far less. Thus, while there is freer thought, there is not the freedom of thought necessary for self-analysis and evident in "good enough" psychoanalysis. Explanatory associations usually go to past object relations rather than ambivalence and the resulting internalized conflict.

Brief concluding remarks

As early as 1954 Rangell noted a strong resistance amongst a committee of the American Psychoanalytic Association to investigate the difference between psychoanalysis and psychotherapy, with some feeling that the problem was mainly a matter of semantics. This resistance sometimes seems even fiercer and more ideological today. As noted, I see us drifting into psychoanalysis as psychotherapy. We increasingly view our patients as primarily trauma victims rather than also victims of their own mind. We seem to view our primary goal as comfort via understanding rather than freedom from victimization (self and other) based upon a freer mind. We are losing contact with our more primitive side, and thus become less free to deal with these sides of our patients and the methods that might help them get there. In thinking about psychoanalysis, Green (1995) poignantly asks the question about psychoanalysis:

> What is its aim? Overcoming our primitive anxieties, to repair our objects damaged by our sinful evil? To ensure the need for security. To pursue the norms of adaptation. Or to be able to feel alive and to cathect the many possibilities offered by the diversity of life, in spite of its inevitable disappointments, sources of unhappiness and loads of pains? (p. 874)

While I do not see these as either/or issues, and in fact see working through primitive anxieties as central to what Green calls feeling alive, I see it as touching on some of the same issues I have raised in this paper. Newer psychoanalytic methods, as described above, help our patients move more comfortably into the deeper regions of the mind necessary for the freedom to think and feel, the basis for a freer life via self-analysis.

Notes

1 Roiphe (2009), reviewing a book in the *New York Times*, says that for most of us love has become largely a matter of shared mortgage payments, evenings curled up on the couch in front of a video, or maybe a night in a hotel for an anniversary. In a similar vein, psychoanalysis has become about comfort, soothing and safety (none of which, I think, is negligible), while passion, danger, and desire have disappeared.
2 This process is described in greater depth in Busch (2013) and Chapter Eleven.

3 When I describe the psychoanalytic method, I am talking about what Kernberg (2001) described as "the psychoanalytic mainstream—derived from contemporary Kleinian, contemporary Freudian, and British independent sources" (p. 519). I would also include the work of Andre Green and the French analysts in general.

4 For a full elucidation of this method, in addition to the articles cited above, see, for example, Busch (1993, 1997, 2000), Paniagua (2001), and Pray (1994). After this article was published, see Busch, 2013.

5 Kernberg (1976), Kernberg et al. (1989), and Fonagy's (Bateman and Fonagy, 1993) work provide the basis for working with more severe character disorders in psychotherapy.

6 I think of the initial phase in terms of years, not months.

References

Barranger, M. (1993). The mind of the analyst: From listening to interpretation. *Int. J. Psycho-Anal.*, 74:15–24.

Basch, M. F. (1981). Psychoanalytic interpretation and cognitive transformation. *Int. J. Psycho-Anal.*, 62:151–175.

Bass, A. (1997). The problem of 'concreteness'. *Psychoanal. Q.*, 66:642–682.

Bateman, A. & Fonagy, P. (1993). *Mentalization-based treatment for borderline personality disorder: A practical guide.* London: Oxford UP.

Bolognini, S. (1997). Empathy and 'empathism'. *Int. J. Psycho-Anal.*, 78:279–293.

Bram, A. D. & Gabbard, G. O. (2001). Potential space and reflective functioning: Towards conceptual clarification and preliminary clinical implications. *Int. J. Psycho-Anal.*, 82:685–699.

Brown, L. J. (2009). Bion's ego psychology: Implications for an intersubjective view of psychic structure. *Psychoanal. Q.*, 78:27–55.

Busch, F. (1992). Recurring thoughts on the unconscious ego resistances. *J. Am. Psychoanal. Assoc.*, 40:1089–1115.

Busch, F. (1993). In the neighborhood: Aspects of a good interpretation and a 'developmental lag' in ego psychology. *J. Am. Psychoanal. Assoc.*, 41:151–176.

Busch, F. (2000). What is a deep interpretation? *J. Am. Psychoanal. Assoc.*, 48:237–254.

Busch, F. (2005). Conflict theory/trauma theory. *Psychoanal. Q.*, 74:27–45.

Busch, F. (2007). 'I noticed': The emergence of self-observation in relationship to pathological attracter sites. *Int. J. Psycho-Anal.*, 88:423–441.

Busch, F. (2009). 'Can you push a camel through the eye of a needle?' Reflections on how the unconscious speaks to us and its clinical implications. *Int. J. Psycho-Anal.*, 90:53–68.

Curtis, H. C. (1979). The concept of therapeutic alliance: Implications for the 'widening scope'. *J. Am. Psychoanal. Assoc.*, 27:159–192.

Eisold, K. (2005). Psychoanalysis and psychotherapy: A long and troubled relationship. *Int. J. Psycho-Anal.*, 86:1175–1195.

Falkenström, F., Grant J., Broberg B., & Sandell R. (2007). Self-analysis and post-termination improvement after psychoanalysis and long-term therapy. *J. Am. Psychoanal. Assoc.*, 55:529–673.

Feldman, M. (2004). Supporting psychic change: The Betty Joseph workshop. In: E. Hargreaves & A. Varchevker (eds.), *In pursuit of psychic change* (pp. 20–35). Hove: Brunner Routledge.

Ferro, A. (2003). Marcella: The transition from explosive sensoriality to the ability to think. *Psychoanal. Q.*, 72:183–200.

Ferro, A. (2006). *Psychoanalysis as therapy and storytelling.* London: Routledge.

Ferro, A. (2009). Transformations in dreaming and characters in the psychoanalytic field. *Int. J. Psycho-Anal.*, 90:209–230.

Fonagy, P. & Target, M. (1996). Playing with reality: I. Theory of mind and the normal development of psychic reality. *Int. J. Psycho-Anal.*, 77:217–232.

Fonagy, P. & Target, M. (2000). Playing with reality: III. The persistence of dual psychic reality in borderline patients. *Int. J. Psycho-Anal.*, 81:853–873.

Frayn, D. H. (1996). What is effective self-analysis: Is it necessary or even possible? *Canad. J. Psychoanal.*, 4:291–307.

Freud, S. (1900). The interpretation of dreams. *Stand. Edn.* 4:5.

Freud, S. (1919). Lines of advances in psycho-analytic therapy. *Stand. Edn.* 17:157–168.

Gardner, M. R. (1983). *Self-inquiry*. Boston, MA: Little Brown.

Gill, M. M. (1954). Psychoanalysis and exploratory psychotherapy. *J. Am. Psychoanal. Assoc.*, 2:771–797.

Goldberg, S. (1994). The evolution of patients' theories of pathogenesis. *Psychoanal. Q.*, 63:54–83.

Gray, P. (1973). Psychoanalytic technique and the ego's ability to view intrapsychic activity. *J. Am. Psychoanal. Assoc.*, 21:474–494.

Gray, P. (1982). 'Developmental lag' in the evolution of technique for psychoanalysis of neurotic conflict. *J. Am. Psychoanal. Assoc.*, 30:621–655.

Gray, P. (1994). *The ego and analysis of defense*. Northvale, NJ: Aronson.

Green, A. (1974). Surface analysis, deep analysis: The role of the preconscious in psychoanalytical technique. *Int. Rev. Psycho-Anal.*, 1:415–423.

Green, A. (1975). The analyst, symbolization and absence in the analytic setting (on changes in analytic practice and analytic experience)—in memory of D.W. Winnicott. *Int. J. Psycho-Anal.*, 56:1–22.

Green, A. (1986). *On private madness*. London: Hogarth.

Green A. (1995). Has sexuality anything to do with psychoanalysis? *Int. J. Psycho-Anal.*, 76:871–883.

Green, A. (2005). The illusion of common ground and mythical pluralism. *Int. J. Psycho-Anal.*, 86:627–632.

Ikonen, P. (2003). A few reflections on how we may approach the unconscious. *Scand. Psychoanal. Rev.*, 26:3–10.

Joseph, B. (1985). Transference: The total situation. *Int. J. Psycho-Anal.*, 66:447–454.

Joseph, B. (1997). The pursuit of insight and psychic change. Paper given at *Conference at University College London*.

Kantrowitz J., Katz A. L., & Paolitto F. (1990). Follow-up of psychoanalysis five to the years after termination: II. Development of the self-analytic function. *J. Am. Psychoanal. Assoc.*, 38:637–654.

Kernberg, O. F. (1976). Technical considerations in the treatment of borderline personality organization. *J. Am. Psychoanal. Assoc.*, 24:795–829.

Kernberg, O. F. (1999). Psychoanalysis, psychoanalytic psychotherapy and supportive psychotherapy: Contemporary controversies. *Int. J. Psycho-Anal.*, 80:1075–1091.

Kernberg, O. F. (2001). Recent developments in the technical approaches of English-language psychoanalytic schools. *Psychoanal. Q.*, 70:519–547.

Kernberg, O. F., Selzer M. F., Koenigsberg H., Carr A. C., & Applebaum A. A. (1989). *Psychodynamic psychotherapy of borderline patients*. New York, NY: Perseus.

Lecours, S. (2007). Supportive interventions and non-symbolic mental functioning. *Int. J. Psycho-Anal.*, 88:895–916.

Levenson, L. N. (2007). Paul Gray's innovations in psychoanalytic technique. *Psychoanal. Q.*, 76:257–273.

Leuzinger-Bohleber M., Stuhr U., Rueger B., & Beutel M. (2003). How to study the 'quality of psychoanalytic treatments' and their long-term effect on patients' well-being. *Int. J. Psycho-Anal.*, 84:263–290.

Ogden, T. H. (1994). The analytic third: Working with intersubjective clinical facts. *Int. J. Psycho-Anal.*, 75:3–19.

Paniagua, C. (2001). The attraction of topographical technique. *Int. J. Psycho-Anal.*, 82:671–684.

Paniagua, C. (2008). Id analysis and technical approaches. *Psychoanal. Q.*, 77:219–225.

Pray, M. (1994). Analyzing defenses: Two different models. *J. Clin. Psychoanal. Q.*, 3:87–126.

Rangell, L. (1954). Similarities and differences between psychoanalysis and dynamic psychotherapy. *J. Am. Psychoanal. Assoc.*, 2:734–744.

Roiphe, K. (2009). Feverish liaisons. *New York Times*, 19 July.

Schlesinger, G. & Wolitzky D. L. (2002). The effects of a self-analytic exercise on clinical judgment. *Psychoanal. Psychol.*, 19:651–685.

Schlessinger, N. & Robbins, F. (1974). Assessment and follow-up in psychoanalysis. *J. Am. Psychoanal. Assoc.*, 22:542–567.

Schwaber, E. A. (1992). Countertransference: The analyst's retreat from the patient's vantage point. *Int. J. Psycho-Anal.*, 73:349–361.

Stone, L. (1954). The widening scope of indications for psychoanalysis. *J. Am. Psychoanal. Assoc.*, 2:567–594.

Sugarman, A. (2003). A new model for conceptualizing insightfulness in the psychoanalysis of young children. *Psychoanal. Q.*, 72:325–355.

Winnicott, D. W. (1953). Transitional objects and transitional phenomena: A study of the first not-me possession. *Int. J. Psycho-Anal.*, 34:89–97.

11 "I noticed": the emergence of self-observation in relationship to pathological attractor sites

Self-observation is one of those familiar terms in psychoanalysis that, when we hear it mentioned, we generally believe we know what it means. However, a perusal of the literature leads one to realize that, from its inception, there is little agreed-upon meaning. Starting with discussions of the concept in the 1920s, various meanings have been ascribed to it. Wilhelm Reich's (1924) view of self-observation has a modern feel to it, equating it with a capacity to observe one's own thoughts. However, writing contemporaneously, Theodore Reik ascribed it to a superego function:

> The monologues which many people carry on with themselves are also partly recognizable as a materialization of the censoring or critical faculty in the ego, for the reason that such monologues frequently contain a more or less pronounced element of self-criticism, self-observation, warning and heart-searching. (1924, p. 444)

Freud doesn't mention the concept until 1933, and also places it as part of the superego. Fenichel (1934) described self-observation as both a function of the ego and superego, while Deutsch (1939) viewed it as a form of resistance. In short, from its very beginnings, the term *self-observation* has had multiple meanings.

Contemporary views of self-observation were guided by Sterba's (1934) classic paper "The fate of the ego in analytic therapy." In it, Sterba describes how dissociation between the experiencing and observing components of the ego takes place, as a necessary condition for the patient's ability to contemplate behavior. Sterba, speaking to contradictions in the literature at the time, distinguishes between self-observation as an ego function and a superego injunction in the following manner:

> Thus, whilst the super-ego demands that the subject shall adopt a particular attitude towards a particular tendency in the id, the demand made upon him when therapeutic dissociation takes place is a demand for a balancing contemplation, kept steadily free of affect. (p. 121)

After this clarification, self-observation as a superego function became less prominent. However, over the years, the term *self-observation* became increasingly imprecise. The term is frequently conflated with self-analysis (Horowitz, quoted in Orgel & Gombert, 1994), self-reflection (Gilmore, 2000; Josephs, 2003), and self-inquiry (Weinshel, 1992). I have been a contributor to this confusion in the past (Busch, 1994). Spacal (1990) sees free association as a method of self-observation, while Burland (1997) views it as similar to insight.

Weinshel (1984) staked out the importance of self-observation early on. He felt that a reliable indicator of psychoanalytic work is *"reflected most immediately and most tangibly in the operation of a more effective and more 'objective' capacity for self-observation"* (p. 82, italics added). Yet the two contemporary psychoanalytic writers who consistently championed self-observation (Gray, 1994; Ikonen, 2002, 2003) define it differently. Gray used the term to denote the patient's ability to view mental processes as thoughts, while Ikonen equates it with the capacity for free association.

In summary, a major problem in understanding self-observation has been our lack of conceptual clarity. Inconsistencies in the literature abound, so that we still don't have an agreed-upon meaning as to what a self-observation is. Difficulties arise in using a therapeutic concept without a clear definition. It is to this I now turn.

A definition of self-observation

There are two primary ways patients beginning psychoanalysis express their thoughts. The first is as a description of a real event or feeling. A male patient saying he was "screwed again by his boss" is, in his mind, simply describing his mistreatment by an older male. For him, it is a real event that happened. A second way is when patients enact their thoughts. That is, thoughts are designed to seduce, invite pity, draw the analyst close or shove him away. The statement "I really messed up today" could be an invitation to be helped or rejected.

Since the introduction of the structural model (Freud, 1923), a cornerstone of the psychoanalytic method has been to help patients consider thoughts that come to mind during an analytic hour as mental events. The capacity to consider a thought as a mental event is what I would call a self-observation. It is a capacity that results from the psychoanalytic process.

In the following example, one can see the waxing and waning of this capacity, which is typical.

"I had an odd experience. For the first time ever, as I was coming in from outside, I noticed that I started to reach for the glove in my pocket. It was like I was going to put it on to protect myself from any germs that might be on the door. Well, of course, this being wintertime and so many people having colds, it's a good idea to be careful where you touch. But I've never done that before. I was even careful when I went into the waiting room not to touch the

doorknob. Of course, you may be glad that I don't touch the doorknob because of all the women I've been screwing around with recently. So, I guess
I'm just concerned about a disease."

In this example, we first see the patient noticing his "odd experience." He
then makes an observation of a potential action (reaching for his gloves), and
the thought that accompanied it (avoiding germs on the door). In this, we see
how a potential action was transformed into a mental event. There is then a
defensive retreat from this being his thought to it being the result of realistic
thinking (wintertime and colds). However, the patient returns to the idea this
was not simply a "realistic" thought, but an idea in his mind at that moment
and also when entering the waiting room. As the sexual nature of the thought
emerges, it became my thought ("you may be glad"), and then a generic
"disease." In short, we see the patient moving towards and away from the idea
that what is occurring in his mind is a mental event. It takes considerable
analytic work before the patient can, for the most part, consistently view his
thoughts as mental events.

Before going on to describe the significance of self-observation in psychoanalytic treatment, I would like to try to briefly distinguish it from the
other forms of thinking it has been conflated with.

A definition of self-reflection, self-inquiry, and self-analysis

Freud first mentioned self-reflection in 1900. He saw it as the development of
the capacity to reflect on a series of associations. It would seem useful to
maintain this definition. It is a process whereby the analysand steps back from
his experience of the analysis (i.e., his thoughts and feelings) and reflects
upon it.

> Looked at in isolation, a thought may seem very trivial or very fantastic;
> but it may be made important by another thought that comes after it, and,
> in conjunction with thoughts that may seem equally absurd, it may turn
> out to form a most effective link. Reason cannot form any opinion upon
> all this unless it retains the thought long enough to look at it in connection
> with the others. On the other hand, where there is a creative mind,
> reason—so it seems to me—relaxes its watch upon the gates, and the ideas
> rush in pell-mell, and only then does it look them through and examine
> them in a mass. (Freud, 1900, p. 103)

In this description, Freud differentiates free association from self-reflection.
Self-reflection requires the ability to both associate and mentally hold on to
these associations, in order to look at them at a later time. It is another developmental step in analysis in that it is not only the recognition of thoughts as
mental events (i.e., self-observation), but the capacity to see a string of associations as related mental events, and to keep them in mind long enough to
reflect upon them.

In his usual pithy manner, Friedman (1992) summed it up "as a variant of the normal, characteristically human capacity of reflection, the sort of thing a Piagetian might describe as operating upon one's operations, or a philosopher might refer to as abstracting from one's abstractions, or a man in the street might say amounts to looking hard at oneself" (p. 3).

Self-inquiry is a term introduced by Gardner (1983) who resists defining it while insisting on playing with it. He is one of the few analytic writers offering an experience of his definition in the playfulness of his writing. It is a particular space in the mind where the capacity to play with ideas as a basis for self-expression exists. It is a space where created ideas can be freely explored, a place for curious musings without a particular destination. Many have described this space in other terms. Green (1974) used Winnicott's (1953) term transitional space, and at other times (e.g., Green, 1975) he described it as the analytic object. Ogden (1994) described it as the analytic third, while Bram and Gabbard (2001) used the term *potential space*. All of these latter authors are describing a joint creative process that occurs between analysand and analyst, much like the transitional object is created in the space between mother and child.

I prefer to keep the term *self-inquiry* because it speaks to a place in the mind, which develops in psychoanalysis. While the capacity to play with ideas may develop as a co-creation, for it to ultimately be useful for the patient, it needs to be carried out in the privacy of one's own mind. Otherwise, the capacity to play with ideas, which leads to the most interesting and startling places, remains moribund after analysis.

Self-analysis necessitates all of the above psychological processes. However, it also requires that it result in some effective understanding that is relieving (in the case of psychic discomfort) or surprising (as with understanding a dream). We are all aware of patients who can observe, reflect on and play with ideas, but it never leads to anything helpful to them (Frayn, 1996). This is why in many analyses resistance to self-analysis becomes an important part of the termination process. Over the years I have become convinced that new and useful insights do not come to us in a flash, but as the result of the processes described above.

The significance of self-observation

I consider the analysand's words "I noticed," along with its many variants and elaborations (e.g. "I found myself thinking," "I wonder") *as some of the most important moments in psychoanalytic treatment.* It can indicate, if only for a moment, a profound change in the analysand's relationship to his own thoughts and feelings (i.e., the patient is not only experiencing his thoughts and feelings, but also reflecting upon them). Two major changes are heralded by this development of the capacity for self-observation. At this instant, the patient is no longer the passive recipient of experiences (internal and external), but the active observer, potentially capable of making choices. Pally and Olds (1998) have likened this change to the difference in a video recorder with and without a tape in it. Without a tape, the individual is left with only fleeting images as they occur. With a tape, the individual can study, review, and go back to the beginning of a sequence of any one response. In psychoanalytic treatment, we see this difference in an analysand's relationship to his own thoughts when entering and ending a successful treatment. In the beginning of treatment, most patients experience their thoughts and feelings as momentary real events (e.g., I was sad yesterday: saying it immerses oneself in the totality of this feeling). At a later time in treatment, the patient can experience such a statement as *an experience that can be viewed through various lenses*. It can be thought about, talked about, and played with in a variety of ways to understand what this feeling is about, and what telling it to the analyst might mean. Via the development of a self-observational capacity, an immutable feeling potentially becomes the entry point into multiple possibilities, and its freeing effects that are a crucial ingredient in psychoanalysis.

Clinical vignette

Eric, a patient near the end of his analysis, began a session in a convoluted manner. References to people and places were absent, associations appeared to spin off in many directions, prepositions were left out, and sentences weren't finished. After a while, Eric was able to observe that his way of talking was reminiscent of the beginning of treatment. At that time, we understood Eric's manner of talking as a wish to have me clean up his messes, with the meaning of this symptom revolving around narcissistic gratification and hostility. After *his observation*, Eric's associations went to the previous day at work. Upon returning from getting a cup of coffee, Eric noticed the spilled, unused content from his previous cup of coffee along a trail leading from his desk to the coffee machine. He briefly wondered about leaving the mess for the cleaning woman, but, as the telltale signs immediately identified him as the perpetrator, he decided to clean it up himself. He felt irritated at having to clean up the mess, but while doing so he became amused at "this long trail of brown mess tracing my movements." Eric found himself thinking of his mood before departing on his coffee sojourn and realized he had been irritated. He wondered why and laughed when the thought came to him, "I've spent the last hour cleaning up other people's messes." His mood brightened after this. His thoughts then turned toward an interpretation I made the previous day. He thought about it a lot but couldn't quite get it. I said, "It felt like you had to clean up my messy interpretation." Eric went on to say he hadn't realized until now how irritated he was at my comment, which he felt was "convoluted."

While there is much that could be explored in this rich analytic interaction, what I would like to highlight is Eric's capacity to view his way of talking as a mental event. Once he does this, he has access to an abundance of memories, feelings, and thoughts, while his whole mood changes. His associations lead us to see how the initial transference in the session ("I want you to clean up my messes") was stimulated by his reaction to my interpretation the previous day, which he felt was a real mess that he had to clean up. Another patient, without this capacity, may have spent the session irritated by how much he has to do for others. I see this as a typical example of a patient once he has developed the capacity for self- observation. It is not the core unconscious fantasies of the patient that change. These remain intact ready to be stimulated (although less highly cathected). What does change is the patient's capacity to consider his thoughts and feelings as mental events. In this way, he can gain access to his thoughts as unconsciously motivated. However, I want to make clear that the capacity to observe oneself is the result of considerable analytic work. Further, it is a capacity that is always subject to regression so that, once developed, we can never be sure it will always be available.

As the time between when an individual first receives a stimulus and then responds to it is enormous, in brain time (Libet et al., 1983), the implications of the development of a self-observational capacity are stunning when considering progress in analysis. Pre-analytically, in areas of conflict, this period of time is used for establishing defenses, while the pressure mounts to take action in the form of compromise formations. With the development of a self-observational capacity, this time allows for bringing more developmentally advanced thinking to a conflict, and thus the patient is not forced into action (Busch, 2001). In short, these two words "I noticed" can foreshadow one of the major changes that can take place in psychoanalysis, the change in how our patients can think about what they think about.

The second change inherent in the patient's capacity for self-observation is, as noted above, the patient's ability to modulate the tendency toward action. Patients come to us caught up in longstanding unconscious, repetitive enactments (Freud, 1914). This tendency is one of the most destructive of the neurosis. Thus, the second major change inherent in the words "I noticed" is the movement from the *inevitability of action to the possibility of reflection* (Busch, 1999). A patient noticing that his words and tone seem harsh is potentially the beginning exploration for why he feels this way, rather than an escalation of the feelings.[1] The unexamined is the harbinger of symptomatic action.

I hope to show that this important requirement of psychoanalytic change, the development of a self-observational capacity, is imbedded in our understanding of how the mind works as seen in psychoanalytic and non-psychoanalytic data. Converging data from a wide range of sources, to be explored here, gives added weight to the importance of a self-observational capacity. It is my impression that, at times, it takes different forms of the analyst's attention to bring about this capacity, as it is not simply a by-product of unearthing unconscious fantasies. Using data from various sources, and clinical examples, I will demonstrate how I understand this method of working, where the capacity for self-observation is kept in the forefront of technique.

Attractor sites

Intriguing data emerging from sources outside psychoanalysis add a dimension to the importance of self-observation, and the psychoanalytic methods that might best aid in bringing this about. I bring this data to give further support to the importance of self-observation as an important component of psycho-analytic treatment. While I am not one of those analysts who believe findings from fields outside of psychoanalysis will lead to breakthroughs in our own field, I do think it is important to study this data to see if judicious consideration of it will help us in sifting through the pluralistic hypotheses advanced for the effectiveness of psychoanalytic treatment.

My understanding[1] of how a cognitive neuroscientist would explain the repetitive nature of key conflicts throughout life is the following. Information processing occurs along neural networks that are activated together. Knowledge occurs in connections between nodes in a network (see also Reiser, 1991). Frequently used networks create attractor sites. From this perspective, we can view the repetitive nature with which patients interpret experience, in part, as the result of attractor sites remaining at a high level of activation. We can understand this activation level as due to the experience of trauma, and the resulting vigilance for similar situations, along with the on-going pressure from unconscious fantasy and gratification. The pain, and/or guilt, and/or fear keep these attractors out of consciousness, while they continue to maintain their strong pull on how the individual experiences psychological events. According to Westen and Gabbard,

> The salience of traumatic memories keeps them at a high state of cognitive activation. This makes sense from an evolutionary perspective, because events related to survival and reproduction should be readily and chronically activated. Once traumatized, we should remain vigilant toward situations that resemble the traumatic one. At the same time, however, the intense painful affect associated with traumatic memories activates inhibitory mechanisms defenses–aimed at keeping them out of awareness. This means they can never be worked through, and hence, paradoxically, the cognitive-affective network remains outside awareness even while being readily triggered. (2002, p. 84)

One can think of these attractor sites as black holes in psychological space, sucking everything in that comes near its orbit, remaining outside of awareness and thus unable to be modified by other structures.[2] It gives one an appreciation for the enormous difficulty a patient has in considering attractor sites as mental events.

Chaos theory and attractor sites

The term *attractor* had its modern scientific birth in chaos theory, which revealed constancy in what appears to be random, especially in non-linear systems. Nonlinear systems are those that can only be understood by looking at the interactions of the different components within the system, and not simply by the addition of the system's qualities. Using this criterion, Moran (1991)[3] describes psychoanalysis as a non-linear system in the following manner:

The interaction of various mental features is taken for granted in most psychoanalytic models and is given formal importance in the structural model. From a phenomenological standpoint, the psychoanalyst takes this view of the mind (as interacting with itself, or intra-acting) into account when he considers, for example, the interdependence of the patient's affect, verbal associations, and sensations of physical posture on the couch (and this would only be three of many variables). These three variables, and, of course, many more, must be considered not only additively, but as to how they relate to each other, in order to understand the nature of the psychoanalytic process at any moment (p. 213).

Moran goes on to explain that there are simple and complex attractors. Simple attractors, which may be linked to a limited number of neuronal pathways involved in a response, are most affected by disturbances in the system. Conversely, complex attractors, due to their greater number of neuronal pathways, give stability to the system. Thus, a chaos theorist might explain the persistence and intensity of response in pathological reactions as based on the workings of simple attractors. Simple attractors, like pathological systems, guide a system in a rigid manner, and are profoundly affected by minor external factors. As analysts, we could understand the simplicity of pathological attractors as due, in part, to the defense process, which keeps these attractors unconscious, and thus unmodified by further developments.

Pathological attractor sites[4]

From the perspective of cognitive neuroscience and chaos theory, the first clinical problem we face in psychoanalysis is the same. How do we modify pathological attractor states? That is, how do we modify them in a way that the rigid, stereotypic responses typical of pathological attractor states lead to the potential for a more complex, nuanced, attractor state? The first challenge we face is that pathological attractor states are kept intact, in part, by primitive, unconscious fears of modification. This is due to the fact that their very existence is based on a developmentally adaptational (at the time of formation) response to perceived trauma that circumvents re-traumatization.

The above data supports the importance in psychoanalytic treatment of analyzing unconscious resistances. We cannot approach pathological attractor sites psychoanalytically except through the unconscious threats that keep them in place. While other methods of working might lead toward alternate attractor states, pathological attractor states remain unmodified unless approached through the primitive fears that keep them in place as demonstrated in unconscious resistances in psychoanalytic treatment. Creation of a feeling of safety via the analyst's empathic attunement may alleviate fears, but the specific working through process of primitive fears available only in psychoanalysis requires more than just empathy.

One problem for the psychoanalytic clinician in approaching unconscious resistances is that they are like invisible laser beams connected to an alarm system protecting what seems to be a valuable piece of antiquity in a museum. Another problem is that the patient doesn't even know about this elaborate alarm system, as it is occurring unconsciously.

LeDoux, in mapping the "emotional brain," presents the following example, which gives us insight into the problems in, the necessity of, and pathway toward, analyzing unconscious resistances:

> Imagine walking in the woods. A crackling sound occurs. It goes straight to the amygdala through the thalmic pathway. The sound also goes from the thalmus to the cortex, which recognizes the sound to be a dry twig that snapped under the weight of your boot, or that of a rattlesnake shaking its tail. But by the time the cortex has figured this out, the amygdala is already starting to defend against the snake. (1996, pp. 163–164)

Thus, while the direct thalmo-amygdala response is very beneficial in situations of extreme danger, this pathway can only give a crude representation of the stimulus. It is limited by lack of involvement of cortical processing. Thus, while walking through the woods under these conditions there are snakes everywhere. This is analogous to the state of the neurotic where potential dangers are always there. Finer discriminations amongst stimuli are not available. Thus, the problem in approaching pathological attractor sites is that the patient unconsciously perceives any approach to it as a vague but unmistakable danger. Approaching them from the side of higher-level cortical functions can help patients feel it is not a snake approaching, but their boot snapping a stick. Building up more cortical involvement in responding to dangers becomes a key component in the movement from fear to interest.

Blakeslee (2000), reporting on recent research, also indicates there may be two centers in the brain for the anticipation of pain. One is deep in the limbic system; the other is in the frontal lobe. It follows that a primary function of psychoanalysis is to build up structures that increase the awareness of these anticipatory functions in the frontal lobes. In this way the fears that lead to defenses could go from primarily irrational (as in a feeling of catastrophic danger) to the more rational (as in a feeling of uneasiness). However, in proposing this, we immediately come upon another significant problem, which leads us to take a detour into some more recent findings. That is, the language and thinking of pathological attractor sites, and the defenses that guard them, are not the language of symbols, or the logic of well- functioning adult thought. It is not so well recognized in psychoanalysis (Busch, 1995b) that thought is under the domination of action for a long time.[5] Piaget and Inhelder (1959) believe it is not until a child is around seven years old that one can talk of his having the beginning of an integrated cognitive system to organize the world around him without heavy influence from action referents. Our patients, who may be bold and creative in their profession, become concrete in the area of their conflicts and are bound by immediate impressions.

They cannot easily contemplate that there is meaning to what is on their mind beyond its initial knowable quality. Most analysts would agree that this is how analysands are throughout periods of analysis. They think, but they cannot think about their thinking. Thoughts and feelings are not so much expressions of psychic reality; they just are.

The problem we face is daunting. Bringing to the attention of a patient a powerful force in his mind that is causing him major problems, that he is terrified of seeing, and gratified by not noticing. Further, the force, the fear, and the gratification are coded in a way of thinking not easily reflected upon. Fonagy (1999) and Fonagy and Target's (1996a, 1996b, 2000) work has been central in bringing this to our attention.[6] To go back to the description from Pally and Olds (1998), it is like asking someone to watch a videotape of themselves, when there is no videotape in the video recorder. How do we deal with this fundamental dilemma?[7]

Clinical implications

In a nutshell, psychoanalytic treatment revolves around working with the patient's pathological attractor sites (neurotic conflicts) that are in a heightened state of responsiveness, guarded by invisible lasers (resistances) ready to sense shadowy dangers everywhere, all of which are conceptualized by the patient in a way that doesn't easily allow for reflection. How does this information modify technique in a way that helps the patient move from action to self-observation? This has been written about extensively by the various authors, and I have discussed my own perspective on this (Busch, 1995a, 1999, 2000, 2001). It is based on what have been some fundamental principles of psychoanalytic technique and our theory of the mind: resistance analysis; use of the method of free association; and the concept of analytic surfaces. It is these methods that converge with what we have recently learned from sources outside of psychoanalysis.

Resistance analysis

Freud's (1923) recognition that resistances were unconscious, and his introduction of the second theory of anxiety (Freud, 1926), laid the groundwork for a technique of resistance analysis that never quite was (Busch, 1995a; Gray, 1994). While the importance of resistance analysis is accepted by analysts from all theoretical perspectives in the abstract, and is bolstered by the data from cognitive neuroscience and chaos theory noted above, there is little agreement about technique. It has been our position that many techniques ignore the fact that resistances are unconscious. Therefore, their very existence needs to be brought into consciousness before they can be analyzed. Freud understood this when he stated, "All knowledge is invariably bound up with consciousness" (1923, p. 19), and "Our investigations too must take this perceiving surface as a starting point" (p. 19). Yet this very basic point keeps getting lost (Busch, 1999; Paniagua, 2001).

As unconscious resistances are, in part, the guardians of pathological attractor sites, preventing them from becoming more complex structures, *their importance in analysis cannot be overemphasized.* The technique based on the principles outlined above is a two-step process. The first step involves bringing the resistance to conscious awareness so that it becomes available to higher-level mental processes. The second step involves understanding the fears leading to the resistance, rather than the feelings leading to the fear (this second part occurs more easily after the fears are understood) (Busch, 1999, pp. 33–50).

A number of analysts (Curtis, 1979; Goldberg, 1994; Schlesinger & Wolitzky, 2002; Schlessinger & Robbins, 1974) seem to view the path from self-observation to self-analysis as a by-product of analysis (i.e. an identification with the analyst). However, it is my impression that the majority of patients develop these capacities via analytic attention, especially resistances to these ways of thinking. Below is an example of how this works.

This is a Monday session, in the fourth year of analysis, a week before I'm away for a week. My comments will be in italics.

Patient: I had a dream last night. In the dream I was going on a business trip. I got on the plane and there was this game going on. People would take different seats. I sat down next to—well actually it was across from—this older woman.

While I notice that in the dream Alex is taking a trip, rather than the other way around, I find myself wondering about how, in describing the dream, he changes where he was sitting from "next to" to "across" from this older woman. As I have, over time, focused with Alex on moments when we can observe, before us, a psychological shift like this (i.e., in the dream he was further away from the woman, but at the moment in the session he brought himself next to her), I wonder if he will comment on it. He doesn't. As one can see, in listening to Alex I have one component of my analytic ear attuned to his capacity for self-observation. In this way, we have the possibility of analyzing what can become "as if" analyses, where the patient associates freely, has dreams and transference feelings, and the analyst keeps interpreting their meaning. In such analyses, we implicitly expect the analysand to identify with our analyzing function, rather than analyzing the patient's reaction to his own thoughts, a crucial part of the path toward self-analysis. However, in this particular situation, since it is early in the session and the telling of the dream, I wait to see if there are further associations that allow us to understand more.

Patient: (continues): Linda (his wife) has been angry recently, and maybe that's why I thought of going away.

He then goes over familiar territory of how she feels the relationship isn't going anywhere. In his telling of it there is his familiar feeling of him being the injured one, i.e. people are continually mistreating him, although his way of being seems to be off-putting to others. Although we've been working on this issue and its meaning for several sessions, he seems to be telling me this without realizing he's recently talked about it a great deal.

I find myself increasingly emotionally distant from what he's saying, and I feel put off, like so many others in his life. I wonder, "Why hasn't he noticed what we've talked about?" At this point, there seems to be congruence between his lack of self-observational capacities, and my countertransference reaction of feeling distant from him. My feelings were similar to Linda's whereby I was feeling that the relationship was going nowhere.

Here we can see an important point. The capacity for self-observation is not an isolated variable, but is part of the fabric of the analysis, enmeshed with the patient's conflicts. The advantage of analyzing the patient's relationship to self-observation is that it is occurring right before us in the session. Thus, one doesn't have to hypothesize about Alex's conflicts over being close, as it has a concrete, "before the eye" reality (i.e., in his relationship to self-observation). As I have noted (1995b), a patient's thinking in the midst of conflict is concrete, and therefore patients understand us most easily the further we are from abstractions.

Patient (continues): In the dream, we all were supposed to get up and move to another seat to get to know different people. I saw Bill Hargrove, my history of European literature professor, but didn't talk to him. When I had him as a teacher, I liked him. There were a bunch of us in this class, smart guys, and we formed this group to frustrate him. We would decide that on a certain day we would act like we didn't know what he was talking about. So, after a class when we were particularly active, we all agreed that at the next class we would shrug with indifference whenever he asked a question. It really freaked him out. Some years later, I was talking with a friend who did a research project with him who said, "Hargrove was a real jerk." My immediate fantasy was that Hargrove had tried to molest him.

Analyst: Pretending like you don't know something with some guy is associated with a fantasy that this guy is gay. I wonder if this is related to how, during the session, I've had the impression a few times that there were things you might have noticed at other times but didn't today.

Patient: I had the same feeling. I don't know why I didn't say anything. This reminds me of something else I noticed. For the first time ever, as I was coming in from outside, I noticed that I started to reach for the glove in my pocket. It was like I was going to put it on to protect myself from any germs that might be on the door. Well, of course, this being wintertime and so many people having colds, it's a good idea to be careful where you touch. But I've never done that before. I was even careful when I went into the waiting room not to touch the doorknob. Of course, you may be glad that I don't touch the doorknob because of all the women I've been screwing around with recently. So, I guess I'm just concerned about a disease. (The rest of the session was taken up with elaborating his anxiety and how it affected his relationships with men.)

Once again, we can see how Alex's self-observational capacities are intimately connected to a central conflict resulting in homosexual anxiety. Analyzing the resistance to self-observation using his associations as a guide to what he is most readily able to hear, leads to an elaboration of his homosexual conflict and its manifestation in other forms in the session. Of course, the resistance at this point is very thin, and Alex's observation of his non-observing self has silently happened already. It is my impression that, by successfully analyzing this capacity, the resistances to it, and the conflicts it arouses, we allow the patient greater freedom toward the path of self-analysis rather than relying on a vague identificatory process.

Free associations

Looking back to the time when he switched from hypnotism to the method of free association, in part because of the copious associations from his un-hypnotized patients, Freud stated, "It was to be expected—though this was still unproved and not till later confirmed by wide experience—that every-thing that occurred to a patient setting out from a particular starting point must also stand in an internal connection with that starting point" (1923, p. 236).

This perspective, which became the essential component of the talking cure, receives support from a variety of non-analytic data. As reported by Westen and Gabbard,

> Pieces of information are associatively connected to one another, so that activating one node (or unit of information) on a network spreads activation to other related nodes. Another way researchers have described the organization of memories is in terms of schemas, patterns of thought that guide perception and memory, such as patients' enduring view of the analyst. (2002, p. 63)

In short, if we go back to the concept of "pathological attractor sites," existing in a state of high excitation, with neuronal networks connected along multiple memory stores, we see the importance of the method of free association in un-derstanding the full depth of the "neurotic core" (Rangell, 1990). Its power in understanding the depths of the human psyche was demonstrated first in the in-terpretation of dreams (Freud, 1900), and was the foundation upon which psy-choanalysis was built. Thus, it is striking that, with very little notice of its implications, the "talking cure" has become the "feeling cure." In the thinking and writing of many analysts throughout the world, the importance of the analyst listening to his own thoughts and feelings is not presented as an additional com-ponent of psychoanalytic technique, but the essence of technique itself. By taking such a position, the analyst not only loses the richness of what he can learn from the patient's associations, but, as I will show, also gives up a method of interpretation that, for much of analysis, is closer to the patient's capacity to hear and understand.

The second component of the method of free association that needs to be emphasized is its use as primary data in the analyst's interpretations. Remember, as noted above, when we work with patients in the midst of conflict, their thinking is often at a concrete "what is, is" level, with little capacity to reflect back on a chain of associations. At these times, we have to work more concretely and less symbolically, and working with the patient's use of the method of free association is ideal for this. I have described this method of working previously (Busch, 1999, 2000), and thus will only present a short example.

Charles, a business executive, came to treatment two years after having been elected to the managing board of his company. It was what he had dreamed of from the time he joined the firm, but since this happened, he had continuously shot himself in the foot so that he was on the verge of being asked to leave the company. Approximately a year into the analysis, we had a session where our understanding of the material seemed to have particular significance. Near the end of the session, Charles fell silent for a few minutes. This was an unusual event, and I noted it as such with Charles. He told me he was trying to make sure he remembered what we had talked about during the session, out of fear that he would forget it shortly after walking out of the session (he often had a feeling that he forgot what we talked about). His thoughts then turned to a situation he was going to have to deal with when he returned to work. He had given up an important assignment, from which he would have obtained national recognition, to a junior female executive. Her male boss, who had an international reputation for his expertise in this area, was very angry with him. Charles had felt very competitive with this man, and a similar situation had arisen previously.

I said to Charles, "In response to a familiar feeling of depriving yourself of what you've found valuable in what we've discovered, your thoughts go to a situation where you gave away something valuable to a woman, while keeping it from another man."

What I focus on in this vignette is a moment when there is an action (i.e., in this case a silence), in which Charles is both defending against and actualizing a fantasy. Based on our understanding of forms of thinking in analysis noted earlier in this paper, an "action thought" (Busch, 1995b) represents a more regressed type of thinking. It is associated with thinking that is more concrete and thinking that cannot turn back on itself and see where it's been. This is why, in my interpretation, I return Charles to the moment when the action started, and present a concrete, condensed, dynamic version of his associations, before bringing it back to the transference. In short, in approaching this pathological attractor site, I am taking into account that we are dealing with a way of thinking from an earlier time. Thus, I first present the evidence to him (i.e., his own thinking) in a concrete fashion, of something going on outside his awareness. I am appealing to a part of Charles that may not be immediately enmeshed in the core conflict, implicitly asking him, "Can you see this?" and "Does this make sense to you?" In presenting the data in this way, I am taking into account that Charles is approaching something very frightening for the first time in the treatment, and its frightening aspects need to be appreciated. Every interpretation is an attempt to bring something to a patient's awareness in a way that doesn't arouse undue anxiety. I believe we must not underestimate the degree of threat the ego is under in the midst of conflict, or else we risk interpretations that, if accepted, are on the basis of compliance or intellectualization. On the other end of the spectrum, I believe we may frequently cause pathological regressions if we consistently interpret at deeper, more symbolic levels than the patient can understand or integrate. What we are trying to help the patient engage in is a controlled regression, where thoughts and feelings previously unacceptable are tolerated and able to be explored.

The question might be asked, "Since Charles already associated to what is going on, isn't this already an indication that he's ready for a deeper interpretation?" I don't think we should confuse a patient's associations with manifest content. The fact that Charles is making these associations simply tells us that a preconscious connection has been made, but this is very far from his awareness of needing to castrate himself and give his penis to a woman, and then castrate a man. I'm afraid we too often confuse our understanding with the patient's intention.

Analytic surfaces

I start from the premise that knowledge of the unconscious is not useful unless it is capable of being acknowledged by the patient, and that technique has suffered because of a preoccupation with deep interpretations (Busch, 2000; Paniagua, 2001). We have not paid enough attention to the degree to which a patient is open to thoughts and feelings that come to his or her mind as a potential statement of a psychological state, and how we help patients get to this state. A man beginning a session talking of his preoccupation with a beautiful woman he just passed on the street can be the start of a monologue on how this woman would be so perfect for him instead of his wife, or the beginning of associations as to why he came into the session so preoccupied with this woman. Each is a psychological statement, but the patient's availability to see each as a psychological statement will vary. The approach I advocate adds to our perspective by highlighting the patient's capacity to understand and utilize an intervention in an emotionally and cognitively meaningful manner. The ways the analyst functions may foster or hinder this essential component of treatment. The patient's increasing freedom to use his mind in a self-observational manner becomes both a beacon for interventions, and a necessary part of the change process. Yet, in listening to discussions of the clinical process, I am impressed with how many interpretations seem based less on what the patient is capable of hearing, and more on what the analyst is capable of understanding. We are frequently not clear enough on the distinction between an unconscious communication and our capacity to communicate with the patient's unconscious. What the patient can hear, understand, and effectively utilize are rarely in the foreground of our clinical discussions.

Using my own terminology for Paniagua's (1991) guidelines for analytic surfaces suggests a way of conceptualizing the interpretive process that co-ordinates well with the type of thinking associated with pathological attractor sites. Looked at broadly, there are three surfaces at any one time in an analytic session. There is how the patient is thinking about what he is talking about. This is the patient's surface. There are the thoughts and feelings the analyst is having in reaction to what the patient is talking about. This is the analyst's surface. For an interpretation to be successful, there needs to be a blending between the patient and analyst's surface. How much the interpretation is tilted toward one versus another depends on the stage of treatment, but there is always an amalgam of these two surfaces. This is called the workable surface. What the analyst ends up interpreting to the patient must in some way touch upon what the patient thinks he is talking about.

Why is this approach crucial in approaching the pathological attractor sites? This becomes evident if we return to the type of thinking associated with pathological attractor states. Thinking associated with these states is concrete, dominated by a "before the eye" reality, and an inability to keep in mind a series of thoughts so they can be reviewed. Earlier I likened it to a video recorder with no tape. The individual is only aware of the fleeting images as they briefly appear and disappear. Thus, for long periods of time in analysis the analyst must serve as the recorder of these fleeting thoughts, to play back to the patient at the time of interpretation.

Consider the following example. A patient comes into a session 15 minutes late, saying he doesn't know what happened, "the time just seemed to get away from me." His thoughts then drift to a series of interactions where he feels he is not being treated well. It would not be an uncommon interpretation for an analyst to ask, "I wonder if you're feeling not treated well by me?" While the intent of the intervention is one that could be agreed upon by many analysts, it is likely that the patient would be quite surprised by the analyst's question. The patient is oblivious or resistant to the idea there is anything going on with the analyst. His feeling is: "time got away from me." At this point, it is something that the patient feels happened to him, not something he did. Further, at this point in the treatment the patient does not have the benefit of his series of associations in the same manner the analyst does. For the patient there is no recording, while for the analyst there is. How might we connect the analyst's surface to the patient's? If I felt it was important to interpret here, I might say, "In coming in late, it seemed unclear to you why this might have occurred. Your thoughts then went to a number of occasions where the theme was your feeling not treated well by others. I wonder if this suggests a difficult topic to approach, the possibility of your feeling not treated well by me recently?" In this, I am playing back the tape to the patient before making my interpretation. I am saying, "If we follow your actions and thoughts, we can see a possible understanding of what just happened." This is one important factor in approaching a patient who is in the midst of thinking that cannot think back upon itself.

The question at every point is how much we rely on the mature parts of the ego to understand the less mature parts of the personality. Every interpretation needs to appeal to that part of the patient's mind that needs to step aside, evaluate, and integrate what it is we have just interpreted. Thus, our interpretations need to appear like there is some understandable reasoning behind them. At these times, we see the necessity for the patient to keep thoughts in mind in order to understand them, and the importance of the appeal to reason in this process. As noted above, thinking in the midst of conflict has neither. Therefore, we sometimes need to serve the role as the retainer of the patient's many associations, while offering it back as part of the interpretive process in a way that appeals to the more mature sides of the ego.

A final thought

In this paper, I explored the significance of self-observation as an essential part of the analytic process, and its congruence with data from the cognitive neurosciences and developmental data. Ikonen stated it well when he said, "Without self-observation there can be no study of the psyche; investigating the psyche rests precisely on the subject's own self-observation. Psychoanalysis is built upon this foundation" (2003, p. 12). As a profession we have struggled with the place of self-observation in psychoanalytic treatment, with some viewing it as too intellectual and others objecting to its one-person focus. However, I see it as a precondition on the path toward self-analysis. It leads to a process that defines the goal of psychoanalysis as "best understood not as a decision to terminate the analytic process but as a judgment that the analyst's input is no longer required to adequately maintain the analytic process" (Weinshel, 1992, p. 339).

Notes

1 Based on the comprehensive review of the literature by Westen and Gabbard (2002), but my own interpretation of it.
2 Schmidt-Hellerau (2001) notes that Freud (1895) had already conceptualized similar processes in "Project for a scientific psychology," in particular what he would later call the cathexis of structures that function like attractors for subsequent excitations.
3 For a general view of chaos theory and its relationship to psychoanalysis, see Spruiell (1993) and Quinodoz (1997).
4 I will be using this term, as it seems to fit best with what we are dealing with in psychoanalytic treatment. In short, the remarkable stability and volatility of neurosis can be viewed as the result of pathological attractor states which are simple in nature (and thus limits the number of responses available), and in a high state of activation.
5 Child analysts have recognized this for some time (A. Freud, 1945).
6 Although Fonagy's (1999; Fonagy et al., 2004) technical approach is quite different.
7 For a fascinating description of the role of children's thinking leading to a reconceptualization of the goals of child analysis, see Sugarman (2003).

References

Blakeslee, S. (2000). Just what's going on in that head of yours? *New York Times*, March 14.
Bram, A. D. & Gabbard, G. O. (2001). Potential space and reflective functioning: Towards conceptual clarification and preliminary clinical implications. *Int. J. Psycho-Anal.*, 82:685–699.
Burland, J. A. (1997). The role of working through in bringing about psychoanalytic change. *Int. J. Psycho-Anal.*, 78:469–484.
Busch, F. (1994). Some ambiguities in the method of free association and their implications for technique. *J. Am. Psychoanal. Assoc.*, 42:363–384.
Busch, F. (1995a). *The ego at the center of clinical technique.* Northvale, NJ: Aronson. 257 pp.
Busch, F. (1995b). Do actions speak louder than words? A query into an enigma in analytic theory and technique. *J. Am. Psychoanal. Assoc.*, 43:61–82.

Busch, F. (1999). *Rethinking clinical technique.* Northvale, NJ: Aronson.

Busch, F. (2000). What is a deep interpretation? *J. Am. Psychoanal. Assoc.,* 48:237–254.

Busch, F. (2001). Are we losing our mind? *J. Am. Psychoanal. Assoc.,* 49:739–751.

Curtis, H. C. (1979). The concept of therapeutic alliance: Implications for the 'widening scope'. *J. Am. Psychoanal. Assoc.,* 27S:159–192.

Deutsch, H. (1939). A discussion of certain forms of resistance. *Int. J. Psycho-Anal.,* 20:72–83.

Fenichel, O. (1934). Outline of clinical psychoanalysis. *Psychoanal. Q.,* 3:42–127.

Fonagy, P. (1999). Memory and therapeutic action. *Int. J. Psycho-Anal.,* 80:215–223.

Fonagy, P., Denis, P. & Hoffman, I. Z. (2004). Miss A. *Int. J. Psycho-Anal.,* 85:807–814.

Fonagy, P. & Target, M. (1996a). Playing with reality: I. Theory of mind and the normal development of psychic reality. *Int. J. Psycho-Anal.,* 77:217–233.

Fonagy, P. & Target, M. (1996b). Playing with reality: II. The development of psychic reality from a theoretical perspective. *Int. J. Psycho-Anal.,* 77:459–479.

Fonagy, P. & Target, M. (2000). Playing with reality: III. The persistence of dual psychic reality in borderline patients. *Int. J. Psycho-Anal.,* 81:853–873.

Frayn, D. H. (1996). What is effective self-analysis: Is it necessary or even possible? *Can. J. Psychoanal.,* 4:291–307.

Freud, A. (1945). Indications for child analysis. *Psychoanal. St. Child,* 1:127–149.

Freud, S. (1895). Project for a scientific psychology. *Stand. Edn.,* 1:281–293.

Freud, S. (1900). The interpretation of dreams. *Stand. Edn.,* 4–5.

Freud, S. (1914). Remembering, repeating, and working-through (Further recommendations on the technique of psycho-analysis, II). *Stand. Edn.,* 12:145–156.

Freud, S. (1923). The ego and the id. *Stand. Edn.,* 19:3–68.

Freud, S. (1926). Inhibitions, symptoms and anxiety. *Stand. Edn.,* 20:77–178.

Freud, S. (1933). Lecture XXXI: The dissection of the psychical personality. *Stand. Edn.,* 22:57–80.

Friedman, L. (1992). How and why do patients become more objective? Sterba compared with Strachey. *Psychoanal. Q.,* 61:1–17.

Gardner, M. R. (1983). *Self-inquiry.* Boston, MA: Little Brown. 121 pp.

Gilmore, K. (2000). A psychoanalytic perspective on attention-deficit/hyperactivity disorder. *J. Am. Psychoanal. Assoc.,* 48:1259–1293.

Goldberg, S. (1994). The evolution of patients' theories of pathogenesis. *Psychoanal. Q.,* 63:54–83.

Gray, P. (1994). *The ego and analysis of defense.* Northvale, NJ: Aronson. 254 pp.

Green, A. (1974). Surface analysis, deep analysis (The role of the preconscious in psychoanalytical technique). *Int. Rev. Psycho-Anal.,* 1:415–423.

Green, A. (1975). The analyst, symbolization and absence in the analytic setting (On changes in analytic practice and analytic experience)—in memory of D. W. Winnicott. *Int. J. Psycho-Anal.,* 56:1–22.

Ikonen, P. (2002). The basic tools of psychoanalysis. *Scand. Psychoanal. Rev.,* 25:12–19.

Ikonen, P. (2003). A few reflections on how we may approach the unconscious. *Scand. Psychoanal. Rev.,* 26:3–10.

Josephs, L. (2003). The observing ego as voyeur. *Int. J. Psycho-Anal.,* 84:879–890.

LeDoux, J. E. (1996). *The emotional brain: The mysterious underpinnings of emotional life.* New York, NY: Touchstone Press. 384 pp.

Libet, B., Gleason, C. A., Wright, E. W., & Pearl, D. K. (1983). Time of conscious intention to act in relation to onset of cerebral activity (readiness-potential): The unconscious initiation of a freely voluntary act. *Brain,* 106:623–642.

Moran, M. G. (1991). Chaos theory and psychoanalysis: The fluidic nature of the mind. *Int. Rev. Psycho-Anal.*, 18:211–221.

Ogden, T. H. (1994). The analytic third: Working with intersubjective clinical facts. *Int. J. Psycho-Anal.*, 75:3–19.

Orgel, S. & Gombert, H. L. (1994). Self-observation, self-analysis, and reanalysis. *J. Am. Psychoanal. Assoc.*, 42:1237–1250.

Pally, P. & Olds, D. (1998). Consciousness: A neuroscience perspective. *Int. J. Psycho-Anal.*, 79:971–989.

Paniagua, C. (1991). Patient's surface, clinical surface, and workable surface. *J. Am. Psychoanal. Assoc.*, 39:669–685.

Paniagua, C. (2001). The attraction of topographical technique. *Int. J. Psycho-Anal.*, 82:671–684.

Piaget J. & Inhelder B. (1959). *The psychology of the child*. H. Weaver (trans.). New York, NY: Basic Books. 173 pp.

Quinodoz, J.-M. (1997). Transitions in psychic structures in the light of deterministic chaos theory. *Int. J. Psycho-Anal.*, 78:699–718.

Rangell, L. (1990). *The human core: The intrapsychic base of behavior*. Madison, CT: International University Press.

Reich, W. (1924). General. *Int. J. Psycho-Anal.*, 5:471–474.

Reik, T. (1924). Psycho-analysis of the unconscious sense of guilt. *Int. J. Psycho-Anal.*, 5:439–450.

Reiser, M. F. (1991). *Memory in mind and brain: What dream imagery reveals*. New York, NY: Basic Books. 218 pp.

Schlesinger, G. & Wolitzky, D. L. (2002). The effects of a self-analytic exercise on clinical judgment. *Psychoanal. Psychol.*, 19:651–685.

Schlessinger, N. & Robbins, F. (1974). Assessment and follow-up in psychoanalysis. *J. Am. Psychoanal. Assoc.*, 22:542–567.

Schmidt-Hellerau, C. (2001). *Life drive & death drive, libido & lethe: A formalized consistent model of psychoanalytic drive and structure theory*. New York, NY: Other Press. 312 pp.

Spacal, S. (1990). Free association as a method of self-observation in relation to other methodological principles of psychoanalysis. *Psychoanal. Q.*, 59:420–436.

Spruiell, V. (1993). Deterministic chaos and the sciences of complexity: Psychoanalysis in the midst of a general scientific revolution. *J. Am. Psychoanal. Assoc.*, 41:3–44.

Sterba, R. (1934). The fate of the ego in analytic therapy. *Int. J. Psycho-Anal.*, 15:117–126.

Sugarman, A. (2003). A new model for conceptualizing insightfulness in the psychoanalysis of young children. *Psychoanal. Q.*, 72:325–355.

Weinshel, E. M. (1984). Some observations on the psychoanalytic process. *Psychoanal. Q.*, 53:63–92.

Weinshel, E. M. (1992). Therapeutic technique in psychoanalysis and psychoanalytic psychotherapy. *J. Am. Psychoanal. Assoc.*, 40:327–347.

Westen, D. & Gabbard, G. O. (2002). Developments in cognitive neuroscience: I. Conflict, compromise, and connectionism. *J. Am. Psychoanal. Assoc.*, 50:53–98.

Winnicott, D. W. (1953). Transitional objects and transitional phenomena: A study of the first not-me possession. *Int. J. Psycho-Anal.*, 34:89–97.

12 Can you push a camel through the eye of a needle?

A patient was recently talking about a conversation with his father. It was a type of conversation he told me about many times. As he was talking, I realized he wasn't telling me about the conversation, rather he was repeating his part of the conversation. His words and tone were apologetic, as if he had to explain why his very existence was a bother to him and those around him. We had seen many times how his sad, repentant feelings were often nostalgically revived with a bittersweet longing. In this he was creating a mood with his words, a mood of sadness, of regret, of self-abasement, a mood designed to have me love him ... or hate him ... it was all the same to him. During the analysis I often had one feeling or the other, without a deeper grasp on it at the time.

Listening to the patient talk, I had questions I have had many times before: Why was this conversation being repeated in action? Why, at this moment, could the patient not tell me about the conversation, and his multiple thoughts and feelings about it? From what part of the mind was this current form of expression coming? It seemed different from an understanding of feelings we learn about via the patient's associations.

In this paper I will explore the proposition that the closer we get to unconscious content, the more likely it will be expressed in a particular form of action called action-language.[1] This is where words become more like concrete acts, evocatively captured by McLaughlin (1991) when he stated that words "become acts, things—sticks and stones, hugs and holdings" (p. 598). While it seems like the patient is describing a dream, an upsetting event, or complaining about his wife, the analyst feels mocked for his interest in dreams, blamed for the patient's bad luck, or a demand for unconditional love.

Certainly, the regressive nature of action has been well known by psychoanalysts for some time. Unfortunately, its exploration as an important psychic phenomenon became bogged down by pejorative judgments of what was called "acting out." As Roughton (1993) noted, there was a strong tendency to exclude action as worthy of study. Over the past two decades this critical stance has been corrected, as many explored the role of action in psychoanalysis, bringing new understanding to its highly complex role for both patient and analyst alike.[2] However, it is my impression that our thinking of action—language specifically in relationship to unconscious phenomena, as well as the clinical implications of this formulation, has not been fully considered. This is the particular focus of this paper. Further, there is a worrisome trend amongst contemporary theorists to critique the distinction between words as communications and words as actions (Vivona, 2003)[3], leading to the blurring of methods of interpreting when specific approaches may be necessary for each. As I have noted earlier (Busch, 2006), distinct methods for listening to and interpreting preconscious and unconscious thinking are necessary.

When Freud (1914) introduced the repetition compulsion, he used the phrase "the compulsion to repeat in action." Why did he need this addition, "in action"? If he were primarily trying to describe how certain mental events recur, the "compulsion to repeat" would have been sufficient. Since Freud did not use words injudiciously, we have to assume this term "in action" had particular significance for him. As so often happened, Freud left it open to us to think about this repeating "in action." In his 1914 paper we see Freud explaining the in action part of the compulsion to repeat as "a resistance to remembering, and the patient's only way of remembering." It is puzzling that Freud does not elaborate this seeming paradox, which has been a source of confusion for analysts ever since (Busch, 1995). Whole schools of psychoanalytic thought have been built upon one side, while the other side has been conveniently ignored.

Freud (1914) described actions in the following manner:

> For instance, the patient does not say that he remembers that he used to be defiant and critical towards his parents' authority; instead, he behaves in that way to the doctor. He does not remember how he came to a helpless and hopeless deadlock in his infantile sexual researches; but he produces a mass of confused dreams and associations, complains that he cannot succeed in anything and asserts that he is fated never to carry through what he undertaken. (p. 149)

As one can see this is a very modern description of what Loewald (1971, 1975, 1980) also labeled action in speech. He was one of the first in the modern era to suggest that words have a special power primarily because of their roots in the sensory-motor elements in the development of speech. In addition, we have learned, primarily from the Kleinians, of the times when the patient's verbalizations are meant to do something or bring about something, rather than communicate something. This occurs and remains at an unconscious level (for the most part). As we have gradually learned, the whole range of psychic states and dynamics can be expressed via action—language. Action—language is used to ward off anxiety, to repair a self-state, to bring about a response from the analyst that is gratifying, traumatizing, or reinforces a resistance, and to express every other human emotion or fantasy. Loewald (1975) captured the ubiquitousness of action—language in psychoanalytic treatment when he stated that: "We take the patient less and less as speaking merely about himself, about his experiences and memories, and more and more as symbolizing action in speech" (p. 366).

I do not think there would be much disagreement with the statement that, within the neurotic to severe character disorder range, the more regressed the patient the more likely it is that he will communicate via action—language. When this happens, we can no longer listen to the words as associations. Instead, we turn our attention to a feeling state conveyed by the words, usually captured best via our countertransference.[4] The Kleinians, who seem to seem to see more regressed patients (Hinshelwood, personal communication), have been writing about this type of communication for years, focusing on projective identification. Ferro (2006), writing from a Bionian perspective, describes disturbances in the "apparatus for thinking thoughts" (p. 97), which leads to thinking dominated by action. In this, and in subsequent citations, you will see how seemingly widely different schools of thought have come to similar conclusions regarding action—thoughts.

The development of action language

What does this tell us about action—language? Why would it be that the closer one comes to expressions of the unconscious in psychoanalytic treatment, the more likely it is to occur as action—language? As I have indicated elsewhere (Busch, 1989, 1995), thought is under the domination of action for a much longer period of time than has generally been recognized in psychoanalysis. The reason for this "action" type of thinking has to do, in part, with the way thought processes develop (Piaget, 1930; Piaget & Inhelder, 1959) One of the major characteristics of all intelligence is that it is a matter of action. As Basch (1981) demonstrated, imaging is not the foundation for thought; action encoded in sensori-motor schema is that foundation. The main distinction between different stages of intellectual development is the degree to which actions become internalized and behavior is based upon representations rather than a motoric underpinning. It is important to note that the process of internalization is a very lengthy one. It is not until a child is around age seven that one can talk of his having an integrated cognitive system with which he can organize the world relatively free from action referents.[5] Before that time, the child's thinking is heavily influenced by its motoric underpinnings. For example, a five-year-old can successfully walk to school and negotiate a number of school corridors to find his kindergarten class, but he is unable to reproduce this in representational form, as his thinking is of a "doing" type. The younger the child, the more his thinking will be dominated by action. For children capable of higher-level functioning, conflict and regression will heighten the tendency toward thinking based on action.

Thus, what has not been sufficiently emphasized is that actions become increasingly woven into the fabric of the psychoanalytic process, in part, because of the long period of time the child's thinking remains under the influence of action determinants. Central conflicts and the adaptations to them are first experienced, organized, and worked out at an action level. Whatever the danger, the original defensive adaptations and compromise formations were undertaken in action terms, and thus may remain unavailable to higher-level ego functioning or remain in waiting as regressive flash points. Up until the oedipal phase and its crucial importance in shaping psychic development, action—tendencies remain as a primary mode of the child's thought processes.

So, what is earliest and most primitive in the unconscious is stored in action—thoughts. That is why so many characteristics Freud identified as "primary process" thinking is similar to the way Piaget described the action determinants of children's thoughts.[10] Thus, the closer we come to what is unconscious, the more likely patients will express themselves via action. The deeper we go into the unconscious, and it is useful to think of gradients in the unconscious, the more thought is equated with action. What is most unconscious is always enacted. Think of our most disturbed patients where, in areas of their disturbance, thoughts are closer to reflex actions. In English a term has been coined for these repetitive reactions that captures its reflexive nature… a knee-jerk response.

Implications for treatment

What does all this tell us about technique when analyzing the compulsion to repeat in action? How can we access the compulsion to repeat in action, and how do we introduce it to our patients in a therapeutically effective manner? Three main issues will be elaborated on in this section:

i.   The use of countertransference in understanding action—language ii. The importance of changing actions into representations
ii. The emphasis on the process rather than the content

Action—language stirs up the analyst's countertransference, eliciting a reaction like being taken aback, wanting to reach out, or turning away from the patient. Once we recognize this countertransference reaction and reflect upon it, the action has already begun to be translated, i.e., represented within the mind of the analyst. From here the analyst can formulate the action—language into words as a necessary step in helping patients find increasing degrees of freedom to think and feel. That is, we try to understand what a patient is doing with us in their words, tone, phrasing of sentences, and ideas expressed. "Good morning," said cheerily to the analyst, can be uplifting, depressing, distancing, discouraging, and a multitude of other meanings, depending on subtleties in tone, phrasing, intonation, and its context within the transference, all occurring outside awareness. It is the understanding with the patient of how this doing takes place that is the first important step in freeing the patients from these repetitions in action by making them representable. It takes a different form of attention than the "free-floating attention," which has been the staple of psychoanalytic technique in the midst of preconscious verbal associations (Busch, 2006).

Put another way, our primary focus at these times changes from the content of the associations to the process by which they are delivered, and the transference/countertransference meta-communication beyond the meaning of individual words. Thus, the content of a dream becomes secondary to such things as: the form in which the dream is told; whether or not there are associations to the dream; how dreams are used in the analysis, etc. We hear one patient tell a dream at the beginning of each session, and we see it as a sign of a new-found capacity for regression as a result of the analytic work. We hear another patient do the same thing and we inwardly groan as we anticipate the patient dutifully telling a dream that will last several sessions with an absent narrator. With the first dreamer we are more likely to pay attention to the content, and with the second the process. With the first dreamer the process emphasizes the content, while with the second the process contradicts the content; the process then tells a different story from the content. This is what I take Bion (1967), quoted in Feldman (2007), to have meant when he said: "Psychoanalytic "observation" is concerned neither with what has happened nor with what is going to happen but with what is happening" (p. 18). It seems clear, in Feldman's (2007) recent explorations into the importance of history in psychoanalysis, that he sees us as having moved to how history is enacted in the psychoanalytic moment by focusing on the process. Feldman's own emphasis on the process can be seen in his statements: "If we are now able to recognize, understand, and address these processes as they manifest themselves in the transference—the way the patient's impulses, anxieties, and needs construct and change their experiences within the session, we may be able to engage the patient's ego in recognizing and understanding" (p. 623). Feiner (1997) notes that Sullivan expressed an early interest in the importance of the how as well as the what of interpretation.

When working with action—language we first need to address the doing because of the analysand's pre-symbolic thinking, governed by the rules of preoperational thought.[6] Thinking is dominated by a "before the eye" reality. Therefore, we must start with what can concretely be brought to the patient's attention, i.e., what he is doing. We are attempting to help the patient move from doing into thinking. Working in this way there is a theoretical shift, as noted by Lecours (2007), from a paradigm of repression to a paradigm of transformation, i.e., transformation of the non-symbolic into the symbolic.

Ogden (2007) provides an excellent example of what I am describing. A patient in her second year of analysis had lost all hope that her analyst could be any help to her. Most of what Ogden describes then is the analytic process and what the patient is doing. "She spoke spasmodically, blurting out clumps of words, as if trying to get as many words as she could into each breath of air" (Ogden, 2007, p. 578). "She barely paused after I spoke before continuing the line of thought that I had momentarily interrupted" (p. 578). The patient flooded "the sessions with clump after clump of words" (p. 578). Ogden's interpretation is of this process not the content. He next tells us that over several months the patient's speech became less pressured. I bring this as an example of how the intuitive clinician senses the need to work with the process without labeling it as such. Ogden's goal in working with the patient is to increase the mental space for what he calls, "talking-as-dreaming" (p. 575), which I would see as akin to creating the capacity for free association, the bedrock for self-analysis (Busch, 2007).

Building representations

Our treatment goal, then, is to try to change *the inevitability of action to the possibility of reflection* via representing what was previously un-representable, and thus expressed in action—language. This is the basis for insightfulness. That is, increasing freedom of mind is what leads to insight, and not pre-formulated knowledge gained from the analyst or a sudden burst of intuitive understanding. Our method relies on trying to engage the patient's higher-level ego functions to deal with the most regressive parts of the personality. Put another way, at these times of action—language there is no thinker thinking (Green, 1975) and we try to wake up the thinker. We do this by putting words to actions and building up representations. Until this basic step is accomplished, it is difficult to see how analysis of action—language can occur.

We attempt to build representations, also, as a way of helping the patient contain previously threatening thoughts and feelings so that he can move toward deeper levels of meanings. As noted by Lecours (2007), what is represented can build structure and enhance the ability to contain. This leads to what Green (1975) called "binding the inchoate" (p. 9) and containing it, thus giving a container to the patient's content and "content to his container" (p. 7).

As a first step we need to identify the occurrence and nature of the action—language and communicate this to the patient. This basic step is often bypassed in favor of deeper interpretations. We too often assume agreement upon meanings before we interpret. It is my experience that, unless the patient is in some agreement on what is being talked about, interpretations become authoritative directives. We cannot meaningfully interpret the patient's provocative behavior until he can get a glimpse of this behavior.

In one of his few clinical examples, Brenner (1976) reports the following vignette. A patient returns from holiday saying she found romance with an old lover, and waxes rhapsodically about the encounter. She goes on at length about this. The analyst feels pressure from the patient to agree with her view. This moment of felt pressure (i.e., the countertransference) is what might lead us to consider the emergence of action—language, and to begin exploring how this pressure is being communicated. This is best explored via analytic observation, rather than asking the patient to explain our feelings. However, the analyst does what many of us do in such a situation, which is to react against the countertransference via an interpretation. Thus, the analyst feels highly suspicious of this old lover and, detecting an edge in the patient's voice, says: "Aren't you really angry at him?" The patient gets furious with the analyst, which the analyst sees as confirmation of her anger.

The problem with this intervention, looked at from the perspective I am presenting here, is that the analyst was pointing out exactly what the patient was defending against via her use of action—language. Her resultant anger seemed to be the result of a threat to a bypassed defense. The main way I would see of bringing the patient's attempt to have me side with her defense (the action—language), would be to see if I could help her begin to explore the defensive nature of her commentary on the week-end, i.e., her need to go over the same material with no room for thought. I would begin the exploration of this dynamic with the observation/question: "Have you noticed that in describing the weekend you've frequently emphasized how great it was?" In this I am exploring, in a very concrete fashion, the patient's capacity to view the defense. Thus, I start with what I think is most observable by the patient, i.e., something she has repeatedly done. As I have noted elsewhere (Busch, 1999, 2004), the patient's ability to think in the midst of conflict is dominated by concrete thought. Further, I put my observation in the form of an invitation to consider the question, rather than my view of what is happening. As the patient is pressing for her perspective, presenting an alternative view as a fact could easily be interpreted by the patient as a battle of wills.

If the patient can see this, we have a chance to explore the press to have us both agree to her view of the weekend. If the patient cannot see this, we have to accept that the patient needs to hold on to her defense for the moment and wait for another time.

Another way to understand our goal when the analysand communicates primarily in action—language is that we attempt to translate this language into words (i.e., making observable what is unconsciously enacted, and thus accessible to the ego) leading to the formation of new preconscious structures of thoughts (but not yet meaning). This helps to contain and modulate the fears that may keep the patient communicating in action—language. The first step is clarification. What is clarified is the action—language as a way of helping patients associate at a preconscious level. For example, the analyst finds his mind drifting to mundane matters halfway through a session. We then look for what is specifically happening in the patient's manner of talking that leads us to this drifting away (e.g., a shift from lively to robotic talking), and try to characterize what just happened in the session to the patient in a concrete fashion that does not arouse undue anxiety.

The purpose of a clarification is ultimately to add meaning, not causes. Meaning leads to causes. It is the elaboration of a dynamic process viewed via the analysand's action—language. This is not a cognitive process, for without the analyst's empathic involvement with the analysand's emotional shadings and the analyst's psychoanalytic understanding at multiple levels, any communication will detract from a deeper involvement between the analytic pair.

As I have indicated elsewhere (Busch, 2006), part of what we are attempting to do is to build bridges to preconscious thinking. Pally (2007) has shown recently how, as we move toward conscious awareness, thinking involves more fine-grained perceptual distinctions and choice, while unconscious thinking is automatic and imprecise. From this we can see the importance of preconscious thinking in understanding threats and meanings.

Clinical example

In order to exemplify what I am concerned with here, I will present a case where the patient moves from action—language to communicative language, from preconceptual thinking to symbolic thinking. It is my impression that this is characteristic of what happens in analysis of the neurotic to moderately severe character disorder, within and between sessions, when the patient has been in analysis for some time.[7] I will primarily focus on the form of the interpretation rather than its content, as this is what I am trying to demonstrate.

Alex is a 30-year-old international relations lawyer, whose good feeling in life is interfered with by an omnipresent feeling that people are slighting him. He is in the fifth year of a four-times-weekly analysis (lying on the couch).

In the session previous to the one I will describe, Alex and I had talked of how his feelings of not being appreciated were, in part, a projection. Neither of us could recall anyone he truly valued. In our work together he idealized me, in the abstract, but it often felt like his response to an intervention of mine was: "Yes, but…" At an earlier time, he realized he silently responded to an interpretation with the feeling, "That's all well and good, but what about…" I could sense this in that I felt my interpretations were accepted, as far as they went, but rarely taken up and worked with. I often found myself feeling slightly discouraged as if I had nothing worthwhile to offer. These feelings became clearer only over time, as the overt atmosphere in the sessions seemed congenial. However, this is how action—language often gets expressed in the cases I am describing. That is, the patient's words themselves do not quite register as having any underlying message until we realize we have been feeling a particular way for some time. It is only by listening more carefully for the action—thoughts that we are then able to specify what is occurring that leads to this feeling.[8]

At the end of the previous session I told Alex that his insurance company requested that I give them my office address,[9] and I had sent it in. He responded that they requested the same information from him, and said: "I sent it in," with the emphasis on the "I." This statement led me to feel taken aback, and then surprised by my reaction, I mused on it after the session. I realized I felt rejected by his reaction, as if I had offered him something, which was refused. There did not seem to be anything in Alex's words that caused me to be taken aback, as his response seemed reasonable. However, I recalled his emphasis on the "I," and wondered if I experienced it as being told I hadn't sent in the same information. While reactions to subtle language cues are typical in the patient's use of action-language, I did not feel fully confident about these feelings, nor could I rule out that there was something within me that led to a susceptibility to these feelings that day. Therefore, I did what I think is best in these situations, and that is wait. What happens in the next session should be our guide.

Upon greeting Alex for the next session, I found myself musing on our work together, and surprisingly wondered whether I had served as a "good enough" father-introject for him. It was a point brought up in the affirmative by a colleague in discussing this case. I was not accustomed to musing on this issue with Alex, or my other patients. I was then reminded of a meeting with a patient the previous day, where she had criticized a paper of mine for what she perceived as a dismissive attitude toward the role of benign introjects in treatment. As I remembered the paper, I didn't dismiss the role of benign introjects, rather I saw psychoanalysis as offering that plus much more. These countertransference musings, which revolve around whether I am giving Alex enough, and a patient rejecting what I offer in the article while rejecting what is offered in it, mirrored my feelings at the end of the previous session of my offering being rejected. This is what I believed, at the time, was being conveyed unconsciously via Alex's action—language and picked up in my countertransference reaction. These are the complex feelings stirred up when the patient is communicating unconsciously via action—language, and what leads to mutual enactments unless we can "catch" the thoughts. While I believe enactments are inevitable (Renik, 1993), I also believe we can observe the type of thoughts I have described which can lead to analysis of potential enactments rather than their inevitability.

Session

Alex: So, I'll start with what happened at the end of last session. When I said I sent in the information to the insurance company you looked surprised, like I didn't appreciate what you did. But I was feeling badly that you had to do all that work, and I wanted to explain that I had done this work so that you wouldn't have to. I imagined you were thinking that I should have taken care of all this, and I wanted to tell you I had.

Analyst: So, you thought I thought that you didn't appreciate what I did, but you were actually thinking something else?
Here we see the defenses *of projection and negation in operation. These are usually not easy defenses to bring to the patient's attention, as they involve questioning a belief rather than demonstrating a mechanism. However, in the work with Alex at this point in treatment, we had seen many times how his thoughts about my thoughts could reside in him and pointing out this possible dynamic was often enough to gain some distance from the projection. In this way we temporarily serve as an auxiliary ego to help the patient gain some space from the immediacy of his thoughts. There is nothing particular to action—language in this exchange. However, in this, as in all my interventions, I am focused on the immediacy of what is going on in the process.*[10]

Alex: I can see how this goes on all the time.

Alex then went on to tell a lengthy story about how one of the senior partners rejected him again yesterday. It is a familiar story. As he is telling me this, I feel discouraged by his response before I realize why. It then dawns on me that, while it appeared at first that Alex agreed with me, in his example he is back in a familiar stance of feeling primarily not being appreciated. That is, it isn't his feeling of not appreciating that causes him problems, but rather people aren't appreciating him.

Analyst: I wonder what just happened? After you seemingly owned that you might find it difficult to appreciate what I did, you go back to an example where the problem is you aren't appreciated. In this way you end up rejecting what I said to you.

*Here my countertransference of feeling discouraged clues me into the possibility of a complex use of action—*language. *By overtly agreeing with me, but subtly disagreeing, Alex leads me to feel slightly discouraged with our work without quite knowing why. However, I "catch" the countertransference feeling and put into words what seemed to happen, and in this way put the action—language into a conceptual framework. Further, as you can see, I am primarily focusing on the developing process occurring before us. If I was focused on the content, I might have wondered about the particular senior partner to whom he was referring. In this way I might have been looking for something in that particular relationship that would help us understand the current transference. However, in this way I might have bypassed what was happening in the transference, and the chance to put it into words. Finally, I use the word "rejecting" to describe the feeling, rather than the possible deeper thoughts and wishes behind it, as we are venturing into territory that is still defended against.*

Added 2020: Again, in retrospect, I can see Alex's association to the rejecting senior partner as a reaction to my response to him which he experienced as disappointing.

Alex: When I heard what you said before I felt like I was being given a softball[11] and thought, "OK, I've been given this softball, but somehow I can't play. It's like I have it, so now what." When I say that I think of the fight for the baseball after Barry Bonds broke Hank Aaron's[12] record, and that the Internal Revenue Service said they would tax whatever profit the owner of the ball made on its sale, and that he would be taxed even if he didn't sell it based on estimated value.

(Here we see Alex moving from action—language to symbols.)

Analyst:	So even if you feel I give you something valuable, you anticipate a huge fight over it, and having to pay a steep price for this gift.

As you can see, I'm continually attempting to define what is happening in the patient's action—language or words. As Alex's thoughts were more symbolic in nature, I can interpret in a language of concepts (i.e., giving, valuable, fighting). Of course, Alex's saying, "I gave him a softball" is also filled with potential meaning. However, following this content-oriented word would, I believe, have taken us away from the context of the entire associational flow, and thus could have been experienced as dismissive. I think this is a point not emphasized enough. That is, the value of using as much as we can of what the patient is able to tell us, rather than us leading the analysis in an investigative manner.

Alex: It's surprising that I would say I didn't know what to do with a softball, as I really like playing the game. Then again, maybe it isn't so surprising. I was taking a run last night with Elaine [his wife], and I saw some people playing softball. I really miss the game. When I think of it, it was a beautiful night and the weather was just the right temperature for a run, but all I could think about was Elaine running too slow for an aerobic effect.

As Alex's associations led him to a memory confirmatory of what seemed like the primary theme, I didn't feel it would be prudent to interrupt him. It is our goal to help the patient find his own way through the associative process and interpreting at this point would be an action that undermined what just happened. I had two thoughts here. His experience of my giving him a softball might have been experienced as my saying, "C'mon, let's play." However, he couldn't enjoy it as he couldn't enjoy the run with Elaine. The fighting over getting something, and the price he would have to pay, in his mind, would be too high. It complicates his feeling of being given to, and his need to push the other away.

Alex [continued]: For some reason I'm reminded of what happened walking into the office today. I was thinking that here we are, two adults, and walking in seemed childish and silly. I wonder if this is the same thing we talked about yesterday, my need to ruin a good feeling.

(This is a fascinating response, in terms of action—language. Alex seemed to be remembering something that fits well with the current theme. However, my immediate response was not one of continued engagement, but rather I found my thoughts drifting to other matters. It is a point when I may have withdrawn for the rest of the session. I was puzzled, and then it dawned on me that Alex's portrayal of what we talked about yesterday was not how I remembered it. In fact, we were talking about his feeling dismissed and his dismissiveness of others, without attribution of particular causes. In this way I felt like Alex has thrown a wet blanket over the session. When I "caught" my thoughts I wondered about the expression "wet blanket." I then remembered an incident Alex told me about when he was about seven. Waking up one night he had to go to the bathroom. The house was cold and rather than go to the bathroom he urinated in his bed, which he had never done before. His mother was furious with him, which was the desired effect. It seemed to be an excellent example of how a potential enactment could have occurred in response to the use of action—language.)

Analyst: I wonder about something. As I remember it, we were talking about your being dismissive yesterday. I feel like you've just thrown a wet blanket over the session.

(While I'm using the term "wet blanket" descriptively, I'm also alluding to its historical meaning. It can be taken either way by Alex. While I am confronting Alex on his use of memory as an action, I am leaving it to him to see if he can grasp it, by saying, "I wonder," and "As I remember it." In this way we hope to re-stimulate the capacity for thinking. Confronting the patient with our reality can have the effect of deadening thinking.)[23]

[Alex starts to argue. However, at some point he realized that he had an inkling that his description of the previous session wasn't central to the session.]

Alex (continued):   For some reason the dreams I had last night come to mind. In the first dream Elaine and I were in a hotel room, and a maid came in with a young child who soiled himself. The maid used our room to clean the child off. Elaine got very mad. In the other dream I was concerned about terrorists coming into my room. Last night Elaine and I had a fight before going to bed. She said something to me that she often does, and I usually take it in a teasing way. Yet last night I got very angry and said some very mean things to her. I was really angry when I went to sleep.

Analyst: So, you come in feeling like a child and later your thoughts go to a dream where there is a child who soils himself and gets Elaine mad, who you were angry at when you went to bed. So, the child terrorist seems to be you. These dreams come to mind when I mention your throwing a "wet blanket" over the session.

(Here I am clarifying the feeling conveyed in the dream. The aggression in his "presentation" comes to the fore. One cannot interpret the further specific meanings (e.g., pissing, defecating on the session) before we determine whether the patient can grasp the affect expressed via the dream images, i.e., he is coming into my office as a urinating terrorist. However, since he associated to the dreams immediately after my bringing up the "wet blanket," it seemed a connection could be made that was concrete. On the other hand, I felt it was possible to move into symbolic thinking, following Alex's movement from action—language into dreams.)

Alex: I can see that, but I'm not aware of feeling angry. Then as soon as I say that I have different thoughts. My first thought is about the insurance discussion. Last week I was talking to a friend about his treatment, and it came out that his therapist bills the insurance company directly for treatment, and I wondered why you don't do that. Then I thought about your recent time away, and how much time it seems like you've been away this year. [Alex goes on to list several other ways he's felt slighted by me.] It sounds like I have a number of things I'm angry at. Sometimes I just feel like a monster [a common feeling for Alex]. Maybe this is why I can't know about these feelings toward you. They don't seem right.

Analyst: And maybe why it's difficult to feel like you deserve to get something from me.

(In this example we see how Alex, deep in his treatment, moves between action—language and communicative, symbolic associations, and the different ways of dealing with each. With action—language we continually try to define the nature of what the patient is "doing" with the process that brings about the analyst's countertransference reaction. With communicative associations the analyst has a greater freedom to play with the associations in symbolic form.

Alex leaves the previous session with a communication in action—language having to do with not appreciating me, which I pick up through my countertransference. Intervening in the way described above, Alex moves between action—language and free associations as communications, ending with the recall of a dream from the previous evening which, in symbolic form, captures what was expressed in the initial use of action—language.)

I agree with Ferro's (2006) description of the importance of "unsaturated interpretation." In both our methods we attempt to not clutter the field with premature direction of the patient into one view or another. Rather we put a verbal form to the transference to see in which direction the patient may be able to take us. It allows us to see just what part of a multi-layered dynamic the patient is able to deal with or defend against at a particular clinical moment. I believe it ultimately leads to a greater specificity of interpretation.

A final thought

Words are not just convenient labels for "things"; rather they are powerful mental tools, as are representations. Once there are these potential symbolic entities, there are many things the mind can do that are not possible when actions remain un-represented. Representations can be played with, observed, turned upside down, or backwards, flipped into other representations, or build into a thought, a novel, or a psychoanalytic paper. So, the answer to the question posed in the title of this paper, "Can you push a camel through the eye of a needle?," is this: "*It's easy if 'camel and 'needle' are words*" (Kenneally, 2007, p. 2, italics added).

Notes

1 This is a descriptive term, not to be confused with Schafer's (1976) work, which was an attempt to build a new language for psychoanalysis. It is closer in meaning to Loewald's (1975) description of language action.
2 See Katz (1998) and Vivona (2003) for excellent discussions of the emerging literature on this issue.
3 While the distinction needs to be maintained, there is a continuum upon which every communication falls, with the distinguishing characteristic being the degree of the analyst's countertransference.
4 Action—language is distinguishable from the patient speaking with feeling in that there may be no particular feeling that the patient is expressing.
5 Anne-Marie Sandler (1975) emphasized the importance of persistent modes of un-conscious childhood cognition still used in the present when she stated: "What persists is not only the content of past memories, fantasies, defences, wishes, object relation-ships, instinctual urges, and so on, but also schemata or structures representing organized modes of functioning, of making connexions, conceptions of causality or temporal sequentiality, of anticipation and justice, of the absence of chance events, the egocentric cognitive viewpoint—all the things which Piaget has investigated and described" (p. 373). [...] "We have tended to neglect, I think to our cost, the information which can be provided by a knowledge of the dominant modes of unconscious childhood cognition which persist in the present and which are still utilized in the pre-sent" (p. 375).
6 Frosch (1995) considered what I am describing as "pre-conceptual thought," while Bass (1997) emphasized certain patients with "concrete thoughts" while offering a number

of important ideas for their causation. Hanna Segal's (1957) work on symbol formation presages most of the current work now done on this topic.
7 While I am presenting thinking in terms of dichotomies for expository purposes, it is useful to think of thinking more heavily weighted in one direction or another.
8 With more primitive patients we feel the pressure of having to be some way or do something almost immediately.
9 It was a peculiar request in that they requested information I had already provided (i.e., address, telephone number, etc.). In general, I let patients know about any dealings I have with their insurance company, which is minimal.
10 *I can see now that I was primed to pick up on Alex' use of projection, rather than following more empathically with what was occurring. Alex accurately picked up on what I was feeling at the end of the session. It wasn't a projection. I'm not sure why I couldn't see that at the time. In retrospect, I think now I would have either kept quiet, or said, 'You're right, I was surprised', to see what developed then.*
11 An expression that means being given something easy to deal with, like a question, that is easily answered.
12 Barry Bonds, a baseball player, broke a record held by Hank Aaron. Baseball memorabilia have become extremely valuable so that the fight for such a baseball must have been ferocious, and the taxes for obtaining it would be enormous.

References

Basch, M. F. (1981). Psychoanalytic interpretation and cognitive transformation. *Int. J. Psycho-Anal.*, 62:51–175.

Bass, A. (1997). The problem of 'concreteness'. *Psychoanal. Q.*, 66:642–682.

Bion, W. R. (1967). Notes on memory and desire. *Psychoanal. Forum*, 2:271–280.

Brenner, C. (1976). *Psychoanalytic technique and psychic conflict*. New York, NY: International UP.

Busch, F. (1989). The compulsion to repeat in action: A developmental perspective. *Int. J. Psycho-Anal.*, 70:535–544.

Busch, F. (1995). Do actions speak louder than words? A query into an enigma in analytic theory and technique. *J. Am. Psychoanal. Assoc.*, 43:61–82.

Busch, F. (1999). *Rethinking clinical technique*. Northvale, NJ: Jason Aronson Press.

Busch, F. (2004). A missing link in psychoanalytic technique: Psychoanalytic consciousness. *Int. J. Psycho-Anal.*, 85:567–572.

Busch, F. (2006). A shadow concept. *Int. J. Psycho-Anal.*, 87:1471–1485.

Busch, F. (2007). I noticed: The emergence of self-observation in relationship to pathological attractor sites. *Int. J. Psycho-Anal.*, 88:423–442.

Feiner, A. H. (1997). The note in Beethoven'ss brain. *Contemp. Psychoanal.*, 33:211–225.

Feldman, M. (2007). The illumination of history. *Int. J. Psycho-Anal.*, 88:609–625.

Ferro, A. (2006). *Psychoanalysis as therapy and storytelling*. London: Routledge.

Flavell, J. H., Miller, P. A., & Miller, S. A. (2002). *Cognitive development*. Upper Saddle River, NJ: Prentice-Hall.

Freud, S. (1914). Remembering, repeating and working through. *Stand. Edn.*, 12:147–156.

Frosch (1995). The preconceptual organization of emotion. *J. Am. Psychoanal. Assoc.*, 43:423–447.

Green, A. (1975). The analyst, symbolization, and absence in the analytic setting. *Int. J. Psycho-Anal.*, 56:1–22.

Katz, G. (1998). Where the action is. *J. Am. Psychoanal. Assoc.*, 46:1129–1167.

Kenneally, C. (2007). *The first word: The search for the origins of language*. New York, NY: Viking.

Lecours, S. (2007). Supportive interventions and non-symbolic mental functioning. *Int. J. Psycho-Anal.*, 88:895–916.

Loewald, H. W. (1971). Some considerations on repetition and repetition compulsion. *Int. J. Psycho-Anal.*, 52:59–66.

Loewald, H. W. (1975). Psychoanalysis as an art and the fantasy character of the psycho-analytic situation. *J. Am. Psychoanal. Assoc.*, 23:277–299.

Loewald, H. W. (1980). *Papers on psychoanalysis* (pp. 178–206). New Haven, CT: Yale UP.

McLaughlin, J. T. (1991). Clinical and theoretical aspects of enactment. *J. Amer. Psychoanal. Assoc.*, 39:595–614.

Ogden, T. H. (2007). On talking-as-dreaming. *Int. J. Psycho-Anal.*, 88:575–589.

Pally, R. (2007). The predicting brain. *Int. J. Psycho-Anal.*, 88:861–888.

Renik, O. (1993). Analytic interaction: Conceptualizing technique in light of the analyst'ss irreducible subjectivity. *Psychoanal. Q.*, 62:553–571.

Rizzuto, A.-M. (2002). Speech events, language development and the clinical situation. *Int. J. Psycho-Anal.*, 83:1325–1343.

Roughton, R. E. (1993). Useful aspects of acting out: Repetition, enactment, and actua-lization. *J. Am. Psychoanal. Assoc.*, 41:443–472.

Sandler, A. (1975). Comments on the significance of Piaget'ss work for psychoanalysis. *Int. Rev. Psycho-Anal.*, 2:365–377.

Sandler, J. (1969). Towards a basic psychoanalytic model. *Int. J. Psycho-Anal.*, 50:79–90.

Sandler, J. (1983). Reflections on some relations between psychoanalytic concepts and psychoanalysis. *Int. J. Psycho-Anal.*, 64:35–45.

Schafer, R. (1976). *A new language for psychoanalysis*. New Haven, CT: Yale UP.

Segal, H. (1957). Notes on symbol formation. *Int. J. Psycho-Anal.*, 38:391–397.

Segel, N. P. (1961). The psychoanalytic theory of the symbolic process. *J. Am. Psychoanal. Assoc.*, 9:146–157.

Sugarman, A. (2006). Mentalization, insightfulness, and therapeutic action: The importance of mental organization. *Int. J. Psycho-Anal.*, 87:965–987.

Tuch, R. H. (2007). Thinking with, and about, patients too scared to think. *Int. J. Psycho-Anal.*, 88:91–111.

Vivona, J. M. (2003). Embracing figures of speech: The transformative potential of spoken language. *Psychoanal. Psychol.*, 20:52–66.

13 Searching for the analyst's reverie

The most erroneous stories are those we think we know best and therefore never scrutinize or question.

—*Stephen Jay Gould*

What happens when a psychoanalyst from one theoretical perspective tries to immerse himself and discuss a concept from another tradition? Does this work? Can it be constructive? Ferro's (2015) criticism of attempts to understand his work from a Freudian perspective, believing the models were not comparable, is a typical reaction. Ogden (2011) offers a different perspective in his discussion of a paper by Susan Isaacs.

> The important thing is what one is able to do with the ideas Isaacs makes explicit in combination with the ideas that her language suggests … In addition, and probably more important, I have a mind of my own, and that allows me to see in her work a good deal that she did not see. The same is true for you the reader, in reading Isaacs and in reading what I write. (p. 4)

Ogden's need to defend his understanding of Isaacs speaks to a larger issue in psychoanalysis of our tendency to dismiss critics from outside our circle, and thus lose whatever contribution they might make to our understanding.

One key finding in my attempt to understand what post-Bionians mean when they describe a reverie is that *there are important differences amongst them*. I'll explore these differences, as it is my belief that in order for a psychoanalytic concept to be generally useful it needs, within a certain degree of elasticity, some clarity and agreement with regard to its meaning. Without such agreement our discussions can become our virtual "Tower of Babel," with support and enthusiasm for a concept that actually means different things.

A further problem in discussing a concept like reverie is that, over time, certain terms become reified. In countering such a view, I believe O'Shaughnessy (2005) said it best when writing about Bion,

Bion's writings are not sacred texts. They are open to criticism and his psychoanalytic writings belong not to any one of us, but to the 'systematic ensemble' that is called psychoanalysis. (ibid., p. 1527)

Introduction

Grotstein (2009) noted, "Of all Bion's new ideas, that of 'reverie' seems to be acquiring the most cachet as an instrument of technique" (p. 69). I believe this is because reverie holds the possibility of being a distinct form of the analyst's mental activity that offers information unavailable through any other source. It is my impression that da Rocha Barros and da Rocha Barros (2016) capture the essence of reverie, which they describe as "a basic tool for building an interpretation of the meaning of the emotional experience that happens between the analyst-analysand" (p. 141). Yet, as Birksted-Breen (2016) indicated, the "notion of reverie needs some discussion, as it is used to mean, in my view, somewhat different things" (p. 29).

Given the outpouring of articles on reverie in the last 20 years that trace their roots to Bion's work, it is fascinating to note two facts: (1) how little Bion actually said about the term; and (2) while Bion is most often referenced for introducing the term *reverie*, it was Breuer (1893) who first coined the term to describe the hysteric's hypnoid state. Breuer also used the term "waking dream" to describe this state, which has come into the Bionian psychoanalytic perspective on technique fairly recently via articles by Ogden (2001) and Ferro (2002a). However, it was Bion who first used the term "reverie" to describe a state of mind in the analyst.

Bion's primary writing about reverie appears in a few pages from his book, *Learning from Experience* (Bion, 1962a, pp. 36–37). Here he focused on the mother–infant relationship, specifically the mother's capacity for reverie as the key element in modulating the storm of feelings the infant is bombarded with from inside and outside his body. This "makes available to the infant what would otherwise remain unavailable for any purpose other than evacuation as beta-elements…" (ibid., p. 36).

Using it in this restricted sense reverie is that state of mind which is open to the reception of any "objects" from the loved object and is therefore capable of reception of the infant's projective identifications whether they are felt by the infant to be good or bad. In short, reverie is a factor of the mother's alpha-function (ibid., p. 36).

As one can see, Bion used the concept of reverie to explain a process between mother and infant where beta elements (primitive mental states of the infant) can be transformed into alpha elements and is a function of her alpha function. While in Learning from Experience Bion explains that what is basic to reverie is the mother's feeling of love for the infant (p. 36), earlier in this same book he describes the analyst's reveries as the result of a more abstract process:

To review the terms I have used so far: (1) the ego is a structure that, as Freud describes it, is a specialized development from the id having the function of establishing contact between psychic and external reality. (2) Alpha-function is the name given to an abstraction used by the analyst to describe a function, of which he does not know the nature, until such time he feels in position to replace it by factors for which he feels he has obtained evidence in the course of the investigation in which he is employing alpha-function. It corresponds to that function of a number of factors, including the function of the ego that transforms sense data into alpha-elements. (pp. 25–26, italics added)

In short, if the function of reverie is to change beta elements into alpha elements as a result of alpha function, and this is an abstract process that can only be determined sometime after it occurred, then the feeling of love as basic to reverie would also have to be an abstract process. This makes sense with regard to the analyst's feelings toward her patient, and the mother's towards her infant. We all know that feelings of love can, in certain circumstances, be still another beta element for the infant or patient to contend with. In summary, it would seem to me that the feeling of love, and the way its expression is received, is a highly complex process, and is revealed as a *reverie or not after some time*.

My reading of Bion is that he left the process of reverie sufficiently abstract so that one couldn't tell from any one interaction whether a mother or analyst's reverie occurred or if it led to a transformation of beta into alpha elements. From this perspective, it is only over a period of time that one could judge if a mother or analyst had been sufficiently engaged in a process of reverie.

As we shall see, the term has shifted so that it now refers to a particular state in the analyst's mind, usually a dream-like state that is supposed lead to a transformation in the patient's mind so she can dream her thoughts. Further, in contrast to Bion who saw reverie as a process that occurred over a period of time, and could only be identified after it happened, current Bionians have attempted to define reverie, and a method of working with it, *within a single analytic session*. It is a bold attempt to elaborate a concept in a new way.

It is interesting that in reviewing the notes of Bion's many clinical seminars (1987, 1990, 2005; Aguayo & Malin, 2013), I could find no evidence of Bion ever referring to his reveries, nor does he ask those presenting clinical material about their reveries. Ferro and Nicoli (2017) pointed out that Bion never overcame his Kleinian training in thinking about working with patients, and one notices that in some of his clinical seminars (especially those in Brazil), Bion could be quite confrontational about the patient's aggression, which may have been typical of early Kleinian methods. Thus, one is left with many questions as to how Bion thought about reverie's role when working clinically. It was up to the post-Bionians to take this concept of reverie and apply it to the immediacy of the clinical situation. In contrast, Taylor (2011) believes

Bion used his terms in a highly provisional way to explore hypothetical notions not yet fully defined. However, out of their original usage—these terms can easily begin to sound like established entities with a real existence. Adopting them then begs many questions concerning the nature of the phenomena to which they were supposed to refer. (pp. 1099–1100, parenthesis added)

The post-Bionians' attempts to define reverie

In looking through the references on reverie in Levine and Civitarese's (2016) excellent book, The W.R. Bion Tradition, one finds multiple views regarding what is happening in the analyst's mind that determines she is having a reverie, in contrast to other mental activities, or what the analyst might do with her reverie that is transformational for the patient. It leads to the conclusion that with regard to reverie *there is a tradition waiting to happen.* That is, there is obviously something important these authors are trying to get at, which may not have been elucidated before, but exactly what that is remains elusive.

There are a vast number of analysts in the post-Bionian group, and I cannot do justice to all of them. Therefore, I have chosen to focus on the work of analysts who represent three distinct views of reverie, and how it might be used in the clinical setting. The analysts I have chosen are: Thomas Ogden; Elias and Elizabeth de Rochas Barros[1,2]; and Antonio Ferro. Briefly, the Barros and Ferro have a very specific view of reverie, which requires a dream-like image. It is a view of reverie similar to that of Cassorla (2013) and Civitarese (2013) as well as many others. Ogden, who is the most widely quoted author of the last 20 years in this area, thinks of reveries as including a wide variety of psychic states. Further, regarding the use of reveries, the Barros have a unique position in that they think it is necessary to transform the analyst's reveries into something that can be symbolized. Influenced by the Barros, this view can be seen in the work of Cassorla (2013, 2016) and de Cortiñas (2013). In contrast, Ferro and Ogden believe the analyst's capacity to have a reverie is transformative in itself (i.e., changing beta to alpha elements).

In reviewing the work of the post-Bionians, I start from two underlying premises:

1. In evaluating the usefulness of any psychoanalytic concept there has to be a certain reliability or consistency of meaning amongst those using the term. This is basic to the development of any construct across fields of study. At its simplest level, it can only lead to confusion if we think the post-Bionian we are reading or listening to has one definition of reverie, but he has his/her own definition of the term.
2. Freud gave us a method, free association, to help us understand not only what is on our mind, but why that may be. The post-Bionians are brilliant in seeing what comes to mind, but those like Ogden seem not to reflect

on *why what comes to mind comes to mind,* as he sees himself in a state of reverie where everything he thinks is a reverie. Self-reflection, with all of its problems as a source of information about what is on our mind, is the analyst's one bulwark against self-deception. Diamond (2014) captured this position when he stated,

> The analyst's reflections upon his/her mental processes often functions like an internal supervisor that disrupts the dyadic fusional patient-analyst connection dominated by imaginary identification. This unique psychic activity on mind use by the analyst in relation to the patient, analyst, and analytic couple-often facilitated by consultants when the capacity for it is lost or blocked-remains a constant, essential factor in the complex process of therapeutic action. (p. 533)

Thus, for those post-Bionians who believe everything in an analytic session is a co-construction, Cassorla (2013) reminds us that "It is important to note that even though the analyst's dream is part of a dream-for two it is a dream of his or her own" (p. 204).

Definitions of reverie

I will start with the work of the Barros and Ferro since they define reverie similarly as a surprising dream-like image that comes to the analyst's mind and contains strong emotional elements. Ferro uses the term *pictograms* and the Barros call these images affective pictograms. Da Rocha Barros (2000) defined the elements of these images most succinctly as "containing powerful expressive-evocative elements" (p. 1094). He goes on:

> I use the concept of pictogram specifically to refer to a very early form of mental representation of emotional experiences, the fruit of alpha function (Bion, 1963), that creates symbols by means of figurations for dream thought, as the foundation for and the first step towards thought processes. (p. 1094)

In short, Barros presents the analyst's affective pictograms as the first step in a transformational process, as one might approach analyzing a dream symbol.

Ferro makes a similar connection between what he calls the analyst's pictograms and their potential for transformation of disturbing affects. Thus, he

> postulates the centrality of the metabolizing activity we carry out on any and all sensorial and psychological impressions (occurs via) ... forming a visual pictograph or ideogram from every stimulus, in other words a poetic image that synchronizes the emotional result of each stimulus or set of stimuli. (Ferro, 2002b, p. 185)

In short, what the Barros and Ferro suggest is that an emotionally charged image comes to the analyst's mind as a way of capturing a patient's un-metabolized affect, and this image has the potential to change a non-verbal symbol into a thought that can be symbolized in words. In this way it has the possibility of fulfilling Bion's concept of a reverie as an image that transforms what is primitive to more integrated mental functioning (i.e., in Bion's terms, beta elements into alpha elements).

Ogden's brilliance as a translator of Bion is unquestioned, along with his capacity for observing his internal states while reporting them unflinchingly. His ability to use what comes to his mind and the feeling states it leads to are models for how an analyst can use his inner world to better understand his patients. However, in reviewing the work of Ogden, I don't think it has been so clear in the literature *just how different his view of reverie is from those of Ferro and the Barros*. In contrast to these two authors, Ogden (1997a, 1997b) suggests that a certain slippage in using reverie is useful, and thus he considers a variety of mental and physical states as a type of umbrella concept, which includes: somatic states; memories; associations; and countertransference reactions. As stated by Ogden (1997b), reveries

> are our ruminations, daydreams, fantasies, bodily sensations, fleeting perceptions, images emerging from states of half-sleep (Frayn, 1987), tunes (Boyer, 1992) and phrases (Flannery, 1979) that run through our minds, and so on. (p. 568)

Recently Ogden (2017) has re-stated his 1997 view:

> Reverie, as I understand it, comes unbidden in mundane forms, such as thoughts about an argument with one's spouse, the lyrics of a song, thoughts and feelings about a fall taken by one's two-year-old child, childhood memories grocery lists and so on (p. 5).

In Freudian terms these thoughts that drift into the analyst's consciousness would have been called his associations, already in a verbal form, and a va-luable tool in understanding the developing transference–countertransference once the analyst was able to center them in the interpsychic field (Bolognini, 2010; Diamond, 2014).

At times, Ogden views reveries as

> a state of mind in which the two are, to a large degree, free to engage in an unimpeded stream of consciousness, a type of consciousness generated by means of a relatively unencumbered interplay of the conscious and unconscious aspects of their two minds working/dreaming separately and together. (Ogden & Ogden, 2012, p. 249)

At other times, Ogden (2007, 2009) sees talking about plays, movies, or books in a particular way as "talking as dreaming" (Ogden, 2007, p. 575).

Ogden sees his reveries coming from his own unconscious, but also the "unconscious experience co-created with the analysand" (Ogden, 2001). Birksted-Breen (2016) has suggested that Ogden's form of mental activity is not consistent with Bion's view of reverie.

One way to conceptualize the differences in technique amongst these authors, within a Bionian context, revolves around whether one follows the views of early or late Bion. As captured by Vermote (2011),

> Bion moved away from focusing on how something becomes represented (the so-called early Bion), and began to consider what happens at an unrepresented, undifferentiated level and how changes at this level can be initiated or at least not be inhibited by the analyst (the so-called late Bion) (p. 1090).

Bion believed these primitive mental states could not be known, only experienced. This has led to different approaches where Ferro and Ogden believe the analyst's capacity for reverie is *transformative by itself, while for the Barros it is necessary to symbolize the meaning of the reverie in the context of the patient's associations, language action, and affects.* Thus, for Ogden and Ferro, the analyst's experience of reverie, which they believe is unconsciously co-created, is indicative of a change in the patient, while for the Barros the analyst's reverie needs to lead to something known that can be transformed into symbolic thinking in order to stimulate psychic change in the patient's mental functioning.

On the technique of working with reverie

Ferro

Ferro theoretically eschews the significance of the role of symbolization in the change process, yet it's my impression that many of his interventions do just that, as we will see in one of his clinical examples below.

In brief, there are two key elements in Ferro's stated approach to reverie. The first seems based on Bion's original view of reverie, i.e., a mind/feeling state in the mother that allows her to change beta elements into alpha elements. In conjunction with this, Ferro sees growth in the patient's capacity to think, feel, and dream in treatment as *based on what is going on in the analyst's mind, rather than interpretive work per se.* In this he is following Bion's late views that one can only experience undifferentiated states, and this is what analysis is about. Thus Ferro (2002c) notes

> What matters is how far the analyst's mind receives and transforms the patient's anxieties in the present; the extent to which the analyst's theory includes this is irrelevant. The essential point is what the analyst does in

reality from the standpoint of the micro-transformations occurring in the session, irrespective of what he thinks he is doing or of the dialect he thinks he is doing it in. (p. 9)

In various clinical examples one gets the impression that Ferro believes that the analyst's ability to transform undigested elements even after a session can affect how the patient responds the following session.

I shall here apply this Bionian principle (the patient as one's best colleague) to a dream, which I shall present as evidence that the α-function is constantly at work. A kind of satellite navigation system dreams in real time what takes place in the analyst's consulting room after an interpretation need not in my view necessarily be interpreted, but it can be used to facilitate the development of the field. (Ferro, 2008, p. 199, italics added)

Certainly, many analysts would agree that having a thought, image, or feeling state could help us understand a patient in a new way, leading to a change in atmosphere in a session. Our understanding doesn't have to lead to an interpretation for this to take place, but rather there may be a change in the timbre of our voice or phrasing that communicates a greater empathy for the patient's difficulties. However, the question remains, as to whether such a state of changed attitude in the analyst leads to the type of psychic change associated with interpretations that changes what has been insufficiently represented into symbolic thinking, and its containing function. I think Ferro would argue that he is working with psychic states that can't be known but can only be experienced. Does he suggest that a pictogram links words and symbolic thinking with what has loosely been called un-mentalized states? My impression is Ferro believes that with more primitive thinking the analyst's capacity for a pictogram is sufficient for metabolizing the beta elements associated with such states.

Ferro has published innumerable clinical vignettes, although rarely do we get a glimpse of the pictograms he sees as basic to reverie. However, in the case of Lisa (Ferro, 2005) he does have a spontaneous image, and it is instructive to see how he works with it. Ferro describes a heroic treatment with Lisa, where she moves from being seriously disturbed, with fragile boundaries, that at times necessitated hospitalization, medications, and broadening of the frame, to finishing her studies, getting married, having a job, and two children by the tenth year of analysis. Ferro's admirably open and detailed presentation of what he did and what he struggled with in four widely spaced sessions raises many interesting questions regarding psychoanalytic technique, but I will focus on the session where he has an image and how he works with it.

In the session before the one reported, Lisa talked about her shame over people finding out that she goes to psychoanalysis. Ferro's attempts to understand more about this leads Lisa to associate to an elementary school teacher who made her read things she didn't know how to read. Ferro, by now familiar, with Lisa's "persecutory" crescendos, leaves off further investigation on this topic. When Lisa described her fear of neighbors seeing the mess in her house, he "interpreted this in the transference" (ibid., p. 1253), but this interpretation isn't reported. She then talked about her husband who, seeing her undressed, commented, "What horrible big legs you have" (ibid., p. 1253). Ferro then reports that the image of "an enormous gorilla appeared to me in reverie" (ibid., p. 1253). The brief summary of the previous session stops there.

(The complex question of what a reverie is can be seen in Ferro labelling his "enormous gorilla" image a reverie. In non-Bionion language this would probably be called an association, possibly helping the analyst understand how the patient experienced her husband's remark. Birksted-Breen (2016) delineated reverie from other forms of thinking in the following manner:

> Reverie is also not the same as an image that might come to mind to represent as a metaphor, what is taking place. The single image I am referring to be closer to dream images than "thoughts," and may seem quite unconnected with anything conscious occurring in the material…. (p. 30)

Within this definition, the closeness of Ferro's image to Lisa's husband's remark would lead to further questions as to whether this was a reverie.

In Ferro's account the next session takes place on a Monday, after Ferro cancelled the previous session. The patient comes in saying she was "bad," reporting panic attacks, wanting to run away, but being unable to move. With prompting the patient indicated this wasn't about analysis, but about her husband and being glad he was away and frightened he wasn't there. Ferro mirrors the patient's ambivalence, staying away from a transference interpretation for the moment. Lisa then talked about two movies she saw the previous evening, King Kong and Krakatoa East of Java, saying one was in black and white.

Ferro: It's as though in certain situations a volcano starts moving, or a gorilla, and you flee or remain paralyzed, in both cases terrorized. I have the impression that the volcano and gorilla correspond to a series of emotions that you haven't been able to "read moment for moment" and that arriving all together they terrified you. I thought this was the meaning of your words in the last session about the elementary teacher who forced you to read things that you didn't know how to read, as I did in insisting on trying to get you to say why it was monstrous that someone knew that you were in analysis.

One may wonder about Ferro's idea that transformations of beta to alpha is that "what matters is how far the analyst's mind receives and transforms the patient's anxieties in the present" (2002c, p. 9), i.e., a silent process in the analyst's mind. Further, it is worth noting that after Ferro has the image of the gorilla the patient has a weekend filled with panic and feeling paralyzed. Unmetabolized beta elements seem to remain prominent. Ferro cancelling the previous session might likely have been complicated Lisa's reaction. However, one might also think that Ferro's gorilla image allowed Lisa to seek out the two movies that expressed her terror. However, this is only my impression, as Ferro doesn't offer an explanation for how the gorilla image was transformative. Most striking to me was how Ferro's response to the movies was primarily an attempt to put the fears embodied in the *movies into words; in essence providing symbols when there were none.* The session then continues:

P: I have the impression now that you haven't spoken to me like this for a long time; I think you've understood me ... that you are close to me.

P: I also had three dreams: in the first I was on the motorway, going from one place, I had to reach another, but there were flyovers, crossroads, junctions; I couldn't understand anything anymore—I was panicking; in the second dream, there was Angela, my maid, who had taken sheets covered in shit to the laundry; I was so ashamed; it wasn't possible; and then the laundry didn't clean them; they sent them back dirty; in the third dream, there was the countryside and they were cutting a tree down; it was the tree of life; it wasn't possible, it was excruciatingly painful and yet they were doing it, I was desperate. (ibid., p. 2005, pp. 1253–1254)

Ferro then asks Lisa what these dreams make her think of, and she replies, "Nothing. Once I knew how to interpret my dreams, lots of ideas came to me, now no longer; I don't know what to say ... it's as though I had got lost in Rwanda;[18] I don't know which way to go" (ibid., p. 1254).

What follows is that Ferro, using the dreams as metaphors, attempts to dream Lisa's dream for her, with varied success. It seems that Ferro felt, at that point, she primarily needed a "teacher" (i.e., the alpha function of the analyst).

Can one see in this example how Ferro's image of the gorilla was transformative? Impressionistically one can see the possibility that the gorilla image might have led Lisa to watch the movies she watched, using them to express her fears. It also may have allowed her to have a dream and remember it. While beta elements infused her experience of the break and the dream, it may have been enough that this very disturbed woman was able to dream. However, ultimately, I find the connection between Ferro's image of the gorilla, and the subsequent session, vague and difficult to pin down. It is my sense that Ferro's use of an image, along with his capacity to put Lisa's fears into words, is what leads to her feeling closer to him, leading to her reporting her dream where she is able to show him what she fears most (i.e., what a mess she can make). Thus, one comes away with questions about Ferro's example. Was his gorilla image a reverie? What does it mean? Is a reverie in the analyst's mind enough for a transformation to take place? Does Ferro attempt to change the under-metabolized into words more than he acknowledges? Reading through the many examples Ferro offers, it is my impression that transformations into words is a key element in his analytic work.

Da Rocha Barros

The Barros' work is more in the tradition of building representations, and it is to their views I will now turn.

The view of the de Rochas Barros of how the analyst might use his reveries is closer to the way many analysts work; i.e., they focus on the development of symbolic thinking via interpretation. They reject the idea that the analyst having a reverie is enough for a transformation to take place. They believe that "those who argue that the experience of dreaming is more important than its interpretation and that, as a result, interpretations can be dispensed with, are confusing two types of problem." In a joint paper, the Barros (2011) highlight the significance of symbol formation for thinking.

> We start by stressing the idea that the process itself of constructing the symbol in its different components and its vicissitudes is centrally important to contemporary psychoanalysis since symbols are essential for thinking and for storing emotional experiences in our memory and for conveying our affects to others and make them explicit for ourselves. (p. 879)

So, in their view, the task for the analyst is to translate his reverie into symbols.

The Barros see a reverie as only the first step towards the ability to think about an experience in that "interpretations that symbolize the meaning of the reverie are essential for storing emotional experiences in our memory and for conveying our affects to others and make them explicit for ourselves" (da Rocha Barros & da Rocha Barros, 2011, p. 879).

One is reminded of the work of Aisenstein, continuing the work of Marty with psychosomatic patients, where there has been an "erosion or erasure of psychic work, or mentalization" (Aisenstein & Smadja, 2010, p. 344). Yet Aisenstein (2006) maintains that "If psychoanalysis is unique, and irreplaceable, in relation to other forms of psychological treatment, it is so, in my view, because it opens up thought processes and enables the subject to reintegrate into the chain of psychic events even something unthinkable" (p. 679). Green (2000), in his paper on The Central Phobic Position, showed how one could understand the pernicious effect of a patient who destroys representations within a classical Freudian position.

A clinical example by Bergstein (2013) provides how I think the Barros might apply their method. He describes his work with Eric, who floods the session with words, leading Bergstein to become numb and uncomprehending. As Eric is talking one day, Bergstein has an image (reverie) from a movie, *Eternal Sunshine of the Spotless Mind,* where erasing memories is a key component. He realizes "the scene foggily fits with the situation I'm in with Eric...." (p. 636). Eric then talks of various people he eradicated from his mind, and while speaking to Bergstein he has various landscapes in mind, which he experienced with others, but when he remembers them there is no one else.

Using his own reverie and Eric's associations, Bergstein eventually interprets,

> You are making a tremendous effort to remain present here with me, and to keep an impression of me and my words within you, and of the feeling invoked in you by my interventions. Yet, the experience seems to slip away, and you don't seem able to capture it. You remember the words, but the feeling dissolves away. (p. 637)

Using his reverie, in conjunction with Eric's associations, Bergstein puts into words what he understands of how Eric's mind works, giving form to Eric's experience and Bergstein's experience of Eric. The wish to be connected and the difficulty in doing so are now put into symbolic form, allowing for further inquiry where previously there was only fog. As stated by the Barros (2016), "*we transmute the evocative language of visual symbols...into a verbal language descriptive of meanings and in this way amplify the capacity to think the experience on attaining meaning to the involved feelings*" (p. 151, italics added).

In summary, I see the Barros' work as part of a Freudian–Kleinian perspective, where the key to working with more primitive states is the transformation into symbols. Bucci (2012) recently reminded us of "the particular role of language in enabling change in emotional schemas; the power of certain forms of verbal expression to evoke autobiographical memory, and to connect memories to one's current state, and the power of other uses of language to reorganize emotional schemas..." (p. 283).

Ogden

As mentioned above, Ogden broadened the definition of reverie to include psychic states that had previously been identified by other names (i.e., countertransference, free associations, somatic states, defenses, etc.). It seems like, for Ogden, it is the analyst's state of mind that determines if a thought is a reverie, regardless of the affective meaning or its context. Ogden's trust in the veracity of all types of thinking as reveries comes close to what Taylor (2011) believed as characteristic of late Bion where he "was proposing that intuitions and acts of faith are the main means of analytic apprehending" (p. 1102). Kernberg (2011) regards the difficulty with such an approach as being due to the fact that

> elements stemming from the analyst's personality and from unconscious reactions to the patient in terms of the analyst's own unconscious conflicts tend to be confused with the overall nature of the intersubjective field,

with the potential risk of loss of the capacity to differentiate clearly what comes from the patient and what from the analyst, and exaggerating the contribution of the patient's projective identification in the subjective experience of the analyst. (p. 651)

In his 1997 paper on Reverie and Interpretation, Ogden begins his description of his work with Ms. B by describing various unpleasant somatic reactions to hearing her racing up the stairs (e.g., tensed stomach muscles, nausea). He then describes how he experiences Ms. B.

> It seemed to me that she was desperate not to miss a second of her session. I had felt for some time that the quantity of minutes she spent with me had to substitute for all of the ways in which she felt unable to be present while with me ... As she led the way from the waiting room into the consulting room, I could feel in my body the patient's drinking in of every detail of the hallway. I noticed several small flecks of paper from my writing pad on the carpet. I knew that the patient was taking them in and hoarding them "inside" of her to silently dissect mentally during and after the session. I felt in a very concrete way that those bits of paper were parts of me that were being taken hostage. (The "fantasies" that I am describing were at this point almost entirely physical sensations as opposed to verbal narratives.) (p. 572)

Ogden considers these reactions (and others he has when Ms. B lays down on the couch and talks) as transference–countertransference reactions and includes them under his umbrella concept of reverie. It leads him to make an interpretation in what he recognizes as a chilling tone. In my mind, questions abound. Where does this chilling tone come from? How is it different as part of a reverie rather than a countertransference? How would it relate to Bion's definition of reverie?

As Ms. B continues to talk and Ogden listens from a critical perspective, he has what seems like a series of associations that he considers reveries. First there is a Mafia boss being shot, followed by Ogden's obsessional preoccupation with the clocks in his room. This is followed by a memory of a phone call about a friend who has emergency bypass surgery, which Ogden then imagines he would have to go through. Following this, there is an association to a friend where her breast cancer had recurred and widely metastasized, and Ogden's shame over his behavior as protecting himself from her painful aloneness. He then relates this to what he's avoided with Ms. B, and is able to empathize with her from a more sympathetic position.

When I read this, I thought this could be the transformation that occurred from these latter reveries, i.e., a change in the way Ogden could listen to Ms. B. As one might expect, Ogden doesn't make an interpretation from his reveries in this session. However, when the patient reports a dream to begin the next session Ogden sees it as a result of the patients "experience of and participation in the unconscious intersubjective movement that I have been describing" (p. 589, italics added). This would fit with Ogden's late Bion view that primitive mental states can only be experienced.

Ogden *expands* the definition of reverie to include almost anything he thinks, introducing the term "talking as dreaming" in 2007 (p. 576). He likens it to free association and views its purpose as akin to Bion's view of reverie, when he describes its theoretical context. "Thinking [dreaming] has to be called into existence to cope with [dream-] thoughts'" (Bion, 1962b, 306).

> In the absence of function (either one's own or that provided by another person), one cannot dream and therefore cannot make use of (do unconscious psychological work with) one's lived emotional experience, past and present. Consequently, a person unable to dream is trapped in an endless, unchanging world of what is… I view talking-as-dreaming as an improvisation in the form of loosely structured conversation (concerning virtually any subject) in which the analyst participates in the patient's dreaming previously undreamt dreams. In so doing, the analyst facilitates the patient's dreaming himself more fully into existence. (Ogden, 2007, p. 577)

He describes talking as dreaming as a "loosely structured form of conversation between patient and analyst that is often marked by primary process thinking and apparent non sequiturs" (p. 575). Ogden finds this technique important for patients who are unable to engage in wakeful dreaming or free association in sessions and claims that it leads them to be able to begin to dream formerly un-dreamable experience.

He then cites the case of Mr. B, where after four years of a "listless" analysis, Mr. B begins to dream. So, before the reported session something had already changed that allowed Mr. B to reach this important step that Ogden sees as the goal of talking as dreaming. In that part of the session where Ogden demonstrates talking as dreaming, Mr. B began the session by saying that at work he had overheard a woman saying to a colleague that she could not bear to watch the Coen brothers' film *Raising Arizona* because she could not see the humor in the kidnapping of a baby. Mr. B then asked me, "Have you seen that movie?" (p. 583).

Ogden reports, "I told Mr. B that I had seen the film a number of times. I was aware only as I was saying these words that in responding in this way, I was saying to the patient more than he had asked of me. I experienced this not as a slip, but as a line that I was adding to a squiggle game." It is interesting that as Ogden realizes that Mr. B's question only required a "yes," "no," or silence, he doesn't reflect on why he said more, *but without explanation as to how he came to his conclusion* he sees his response as part of a Winnicottian squiggle game. From a more classical perspective I might have wondered about a competitive countertransference, as another way of understanding something about the treatment.

After Ogden muses on the possible transferential meaning of the patient bringing up a movie by two brothers, but doesn't say anything, Ogden reports:

> With an intensity of feeling in his voice that was unusual for him, Mr. B said that he thought that the woman whom he had overheard talking about Raising Arizona was treating the film as if it were a documentary: "It seems crazy for me to get worked up about this, but that film is one of my favorites. I have seen it so many times that I know the dialogue by heart, so I hate to hear the film disparaged in a mindless way. (p. 58)

Ogden then says, to the patient, "There's irony in every frame of that film. Sometimes irony can be frightening. You never know when it'll be turned on you." This conveys Ogden's idea that whatever comes to one's mind when the analyst believes he is talking as dreaming is part of a squiggle game. The significance of irony in the film is completely Ogden's, along with the idea that this is what is frightening Mr. B. I am reminded here of De Saussure's (1993) observations,

> I am convinced that the most effective analysts have a capacity to use their whole selves, that is their own past and present experiences, their physical sensations, emotions, intellectual knowledge, etc. in the effort to understand their patients as thoroughly and as profoundly as possible, and to formulate their interpretations clearly and pertinently, using words which have an emotional as well as an intellectual impact. The ability to do this demands a basic minimum of confidence in ourselves, which permits an inner mobility of functioning and allows us to use our own free associations as a means of enlarging our comprehension of what is communicated to us. *This does not mean that we accept the results of our spontaneous thoughts and feelings uncritically.* It does, however, require an effort on our part to avoid repressing awareness of our own desires, phantasies and habitual ways of reacting. I think this implies that in the mind of an analyst who is listening to a patient there is a constant dynamic interaction among innumerable conscious, preconscious and unconscious thoughts and feelings. Perhaps we need to remind ourselves periodically that, in ourselves as well as in analysands, that which is conscious is just a small part of our mental functioning. (p. 1158, original italics)

The patient, in an excited voice, tells Ogden why the movie isn't a documentary, and then apologizes for getting so carried away. Ogden replies, "Why not get carried away?" Ogden then explains,

This was not a rhetorical question. I was saying in a highly condensed way that there had been very good reasons for the patient as a child to feel that it was dangerous to talk with excitement in his voice, but that those reasons were true to another reality, the reality of the past, which for him often eclipsed the reality of the present. (Ogden, 2007, p. 586)

This was not a rhetorical question. I was saying in a highly condensed way that there had been very good reasons for the patient as a child to feel that it was dangerous to talk with excitement in his voice, but that those reasons were true to another reality, the reality of the past, which for him often eclipsed the reality of the present. (Ogden, 2007, p. 586)

As Ogden views Mr. B's restriction of his affective exuberance as an important problem, from my perspective I would see these moments when Mr. B restricts himself within the session as an ideal moment to analyze the inhibitions that suddenly occurred. Wouldn't it be difficult for a patient to get carried away if the inhibitions against getting carried away weren't analyzed? While Ogden might be right that his comment is a construction of what was previously talked about with Mr. B, how might the patient's psychic growth be affected if a persistent defense is not analyzed the moment it occurs?

Later in the analysis, Mr. B spoke about that session:

I think that it doesn't matter what we talk about – movies about—movies or books or cars or baseball, I used to think that there were things that we should be talking about like sex and dreams and my childhood. But it now seems to me that the important thing is the way we talk, not what we talk about. (p. 586)

As with Ferro, we can understand how a particular way of talking with a patient can change the atmosphere in a session, which leads to therapeutic benefits. However, as Stein (1981) showed in his paper on the "unobjectionable transference," that in certain kinds of patients what passes for a benign, positive, and productive transference can serve as a crucial resistance against the emergence of important analytic material.

A search for a model of reverie

Bion's view of reverie, an ineffable state of mind in the mother that transforms beta elements, is likely a necessity for any analysis to be successful. It is my impression that Grinberg (1987) came closest to applying this view of Bion's definition of reverie to psychoanalytic treatment when he stated,

In the course of the analytic process, just as in infancy in the mother-child relationship, the analyst's capacity for "reverie," his ability to contain and metabolize the projections of the patient, returning them through the interpretive activity, gradually becomes assimilated by the ego of the analysand. It is then possible for the patient to continue learning to "dream" his dreams in the same way that he gradually learns to "think" his thoughts. (p. 165, italics added)

The process Grinberg describes is a probably necessary background for any analysis to occur, while the metabolizing process is something that, like in Bion's definition, remains unspecified. What the post-Bionians have been attempting to do is specify how this metabolizing process occurs, and what one does with the result. As I've indicated above, in pursuing this issue it would be useful to clarify what a reverie is, and how it becomes transformative for the analysand. That is, is reverie a particular type of thought process stimulated in the analyst by the patient, and/or is reverie rather a state of mind in the analyst that leads to many types of thoughts as potential reveries? Put another way, is reverie an analytic function or a state? Also, in order to transform un- and under-represented thoughts, is it sufficient for the analyst to just experience his reveries, or does he have to use his reveries as the beginning of a process whereby these early states will be symbolized?

I think most analysts would agree that, at times, we enter a dream-like state during analyses, where many different types of thoughts and feelings occur to us. I also agree with those who view these waking dreams as leading to potential insights that have not yet been put into words. In pioneering the exploration of these states in minute detail, Ogden and others have alerted us to their metabolizing potential. *However, I'm concerned about such an all-encompassing conception.* Not only would it diminish the particular specificity the reverie notion might contribute to our clinical toolbox, but such a broad-tent understanding would take all thoughts and feelings in this dream-like state as metabolizing, thus de-emphasizing a key method of the analyst, i.e., ana-lyzing his inner associative process in order to sort out which of his thoughts and feelings are his own and which are truly arising from the field. In this way, a major barrier against the analyst's omnipotent belief in his own thinking might be lost. That is, if we believe we are always thinking reverie, any thought becomes part of a transformational process. A countertransference feeling doesn't have to be reflected upon by the analyst if it is seen as part of a reverie; it just is. Thus, *an analyst realizing he is saying more than he needs to doesn't need to question why if it is seen as part of a squiggle game.*

It is my view that the Barros' and Ferro's idea of an image that suddenly comes unbidden to the analyst's mind has important potential for contributing towards understanding the metabolizing process. A surprising, spontaneous image, which is the way dreams appear, is something entirely new and created in the analyst's mind in the analytic moment. It seems to be created from the preconscious/unconscious border of the analyst's mind leading to its form (as an image) and encompassing strong emotional feelings as noted by the de Rochas Barros and Ferro. As many have seen it as basic to a psychoanalytic cure, I agree with the de Rochas Barros' position that an image (reverie) allows *for but also requires the development of symbolic thinking via interpretation.* While a change in the atmosphere of a session may well occur with the analyst having an image, as Ferro suggests, it would be mysterious or at least difficult to see how simply having it would lead to the type of structural change that deserves to be called transformative.

Birksted-Breen (2012) has added her thoughts to the importance of images as a pathway toward symbolization. As it is

> closer to dreaming, it enables the mental work of "figuration" (Botella & Botella, 2001), of transformation of elements inhabiting the field between patient and analyst into a condensed evocative image that thus is meaningful to both patient and analyst and hence an important potential meeting ground between them. The more "regressed" expression of drive and affect in the visual image offers the possibility of meeting in the concrete realm and bringing together the two perspectives, concrete and metaphoric. The unfocused state of mind in this way creates the optimal conditions for symbolization. (p. 830)

The one thing I would add to the Barros' view is the necessity for the analyst to enlist his own associative process in understanding the image that comes to mind, like we would do with any dream. Like the manifest content of a dream, the image invites us to work on understanding a reverie. Many analysts find it difficult to understand dream images without the patient's associations. In that same sense, a reverie may not only be co-created in the field but may also need to be elaborated by both the analyst's inner work and the patient's further contributions, when available. I see this as one way we can potentially speak to Kernberg's (2011) suggestion that it is important for the analyst to try and distinguish between his own unconscious conflicts and the inter-subjective field.

Below is an example of how one might work with an affective pictograph in conjunction with an associative and self-reflective process.

Phillip, a senior executive, was describing a committee meeting where he was annoyed that people were saying things he thought he'd already said. He believed the others didn't acknowledge his authorship of these ideas. As he was talking, I was reminded of the times in our sessions when I made an interpretation that he felt he already said. My impression at these times was that he had vaguely touched on the same topic, often with emendations, but that much of what I interpreted was left out of his narrative. I was also reminded how Phillip complained that he thought he was giving clear instructions to people working for him, but they ended up not understanding what he wanted. Phillip then described his conversation with his colleague R, where he was trying to explain his feelings about another colleague S, and R said this colleague was a "real jerk." Phillip realized he couldn't just come out and say the same thing. Here I was reminded of a time when, at the dinner table he was talking about his feelings about a family friend and his son-in-law said, "She's really dense." He was amazed he could say this so clearly. At this point an image came to my mind that looked like a woman with a face without any distinguishing characteristics. It was a white circle with no mouth, eyes, or nose. I was taken aback by the image, it felt threatening, and I found myself wanting to push it out of my mind as unrelated to the patient. My reaction to the image seems typical for an idea or feeling that breaks through from the preconscious–unconscious border, as I am able to create a non-verbal symbol (Bucci, 1997). This is in contrast to an image deeper in the unconscious where thoughts are more primitively organized and may result in a disturbing feeling state without an image. However, I was able to hold on to the image, and I realized the woman had hair that looked like Phillip's (i.e., Phillip has dense, tightly curled hair that he keeps long). As my thoughts drifted, an image of a Japanese geisha came to mind, and the phrase "losing face" came to mind. It then came to me that most often in talking to me, Phillip is self-effacing. After a while I said to Phillip that sometimes when he was telling me something it was hard to follow because of his self-effacing manner of talking. His thoughts then went back to the committee meeting, and he wondered why he had it in the first place. He knew what he had to do, and why didn't he just do it? He then said, "Well I didn't just want to shove my decision down their throats." He caught the negation in that statement, laughed, and began to explore the implication of his sadistically tinged sexual fantasies for one of the first times.

In my understanding, the image that appeared to me was an affective/cognitive symbol that encapsulated a feeling state first picked up by my unconscious and translated into a preconscious image. The feeling I had when it suddenly appeared, and the difficulty I had holding on to the image, speak to its closeness to the unconscious border. At these times, like with a dream, it is only through our own associations that we glean the meaning of the image. In my view the image and the associations need to be symbolized by the analyst before a meaningful interpretation can be given to the patient. My interpretation was to the defensive aspects of Phillip's transferential way of talking, and his associations led me to think it was the sadistic element of his sexual fantasies that led me to want to push it away, and led to the negative hallucination of the facial openings; an image in the form of compromise formation. That is, at its base this fantasy was a wish to shove his penis down my and everyone's throat. However, in my defensively informed image, with no mouth on the face, there was no throat to shove his penis down, and no eyes to see what was happening. Further, my own image of geisha woman is twofold; i.e., a delicate flower and a sexual courtesan. Thus, the fantasy of defiling this sexual delicate flower in this violent act expresses the sadistic quality I felt I was picking up on.

I'd like to explore another aspect of the image that came to my mind in the session with Phillip as a way of demonstrating what I see as the complexity of understanding the analyst's images, and how much they still need to be explored. Here I'd like to focus of my feeling of threat associated with the faceless image. While I've presented a few reasons for this feeling, I realized later there was something more in the content of the image. I was reminded how, at times, when Phillip was talking in his self-effacing manner, I didn't feel I was with someone real, and I would withdraw. This reaction was, in part, based upon my own history, but I couldn't appreciate the depth of feeling associated with this, and what Phillip was protecting against, until having this image. This touches on the belief of many post-Bionians on the co-construction of reverie, which is another topic that needs further exploration.

Some final thoughts

Since reverie was resurrected as a central clinical concept by the post-Bionians, its incorporation into clinical practice and articles over the last two decades around the world has been astounding. It is my impression there is nothing comparable to it. While I believe it captures something new and essential to understanding what is occurring in psychoanalysis, there is much that needs to be clarified and elaborated further. Taylor (2011) has raised an important issue about late Bionian technique that seems very relevant to what has seemed like a *reluctance to engage in critical thinking about reverie.*

> We need to be able to see the "workings" of the analyst's observations and reasoning if we are to be able to assess the warp and weft, the fiber, of the analyst's engagement with the particular psychic reality to which the analyst's hypotheses putatively apply. This is necessary if we are to judge and to dispute, to decide when an act of faith—if we consider it to be such—has proved to be well- founded or misfounded, when there has been too little in the way of leaps of the imagination, or when by contrast there is too much self-indulgence, and finally when the hunches or intuitions actually have those rather important predictive, extrapolative and other qualities which take us closer to what lies behind the surface facts. (p. 1111)

In general, I believe it will be difficult to define reverie, and differentiate it from other forms of messages we may pick up from the patient's unconscious, without considering an unconscious with a layered depth. I think there isn't one unconscious, there are only different levels of unconsciousness. This was captured in Freud's (1933) drawing of the structural model, where the unconscious was shown to go from a permeable border with the preconscious to an endless depth and is validated in everyday clinical experience. This allows us to hypothesize where the analyst's unbidden experiences may come from. A rough topography of the analyst's reactions, depending on what level it may come from in the patient's unconscious, might include the analyst's somatic reactions, feeling states, images, and daydreams, with somatic reactions representing a deeper region of the patient's unconscious. I don't want to get into too many complications at this point, but just want to point out there are varieties of feeling states we have as analysts, from confusion to dislocation to sadness, etc., each of which likely corresponds to different levels of unconscious depth in the patient's unconscious to which the analyst may be responding to. The analyst's affective image, as described by de Rochas Barros and Ferro, potentially adds a new dimension to our understanding as a non-symbolic symbol standing between a feeling state and a thought. Thus, the analyst seems to pick up something from the patient's unconscious that allows for a more developed level of though than pure feeling.

Finally, in thinking about why the post-Bionians themselves have not confronted the differences in approach amongst them, I would suggest that like many pioneer thinkers, it is tempting to rush ahead to see where one's new discoveries can lead. Like with Freud, for most of us it is not always easy to look back upon one's work and correct earlier views, while for those with a great demand for their thinking the temptation is to keep expanding ideas that are popular. Further, and I think we see this often in psychoanalysis, there is a temptation to not look too closely at the work of others on the same theoretical team. It then is left to others to look at these concepts with the advantage of not needing to support others, but with the disadvantage of being outsiders. It is too easy to then condemn these views because they come from an outsider. Hopefully, the advantages of this outsider's approach in this paper have outweighed its disadvantages.

Notes

1 Writing together and separately.
2 In the interest of simplicity, I will refer to de Rochas Barros as Barros.

References

Aguayo, A. & B. Malin. (2013). *Los Angeles seminars and supervision*. London: Karnac.
Aisenstein, M. (2006). The indissociable unity of psyche and soma. *Int. J. Psychoanal.*, 87:667–680.
Aisenstein, M. & C. Smadja. (2010). Conceptual framework from the paris psychosomatic school: a clinical psychoanalytic approach to oncology. *Int. J. Psychoanal.*, 91(3):621–640.
Bergstein, A. (2013). Transcending the Caesura. *Int. J. Psychoanal.*, 94:621–644.
Bion, W. R. (1962a). *Learning from experience*. London: Heinemann.
Bion, W. R. (1962b). The psycho-analytic study of thinking. *Int. J. Psychoanal.*, 43:306–310.
Bion, W. R. (1963). *Elements of psycho-analysis*. London: Heinemann.
Bion, W. R. (1987). *Clinical seminars and other works*. London: Karnac.
Bion, W. R. (1990). *Brazilian lectures*. London: Karnac.
Bion, W. R. (2005). *The Italian lectures*. London: Karnac.
Birksted-Breen, D. (2012). Taking time: The tempo of psychoanalysis. *Int. J. Psychoanal.*, 93:819–835.
Birksted-Breen, D. (2016). Bi-occularity the functioning mind of the analyst. *Int. J. Psychoanal.*, 97:25–40.
Bolognini, S. (2010). *Secret passages: the theory and technique of the interpsychic relationship*. New Library. London: Routledge.
Botella, C. & S. Botella. (2001). *Psychic figurability*. London: Routledge.
Boyer, L. B. (1992). Roles played by music as revealed during countertransference facilitated transference regression. *Int. J. Psychoanal.*, 73:55–70.
Breuer, J. (1893). Fräulein Anna O, case histories from studies on hysteria. *S.E.* II:19–47.
Bucci, W. (1997). *Psychoanalysis and cognitive science*. New York: Guilford Press.

Bucci, W. (2012). Is there language disconnected from sensory/bodily experience in speech or thought? Commentary on Vivona. *J. Am. Psychoanal. Assoc.*, 60:275.

Busch, F. (2009). 'Can you push a camel through the eye of a needle?' Reflections on how the unconscious speaks to us and its clinical implications. *Int. J. Psychoanal.*, 90(1):53–68.

Busch, F. (2014). *Creating a psychoanalytic mind*. London: Routledge.

Busch, F. (2015). Our vital profession. *Int. J. Psychoanal.*, 96:553–568.

Cassorla, R. S. (2013). In search of symbolization. In: H. Levine, G. S. Reed, & D. Scarfone (eds.), *Unrepresented states and the construction of meaning* (pp. 202–219). London: Karnac.

Cassorola, R. (2016). Commentary on supervision A34. In: H. Levine & G. Civatarese (eds.), *The Bion tradition* (pp. 69–72). London: Karnac.

Civitarese, G. (2013). The inaccessible unconscious and reverie as a path of figurability. In: H. Levine, G. S. Reed, & D. Scarfone (eds.), *Unrepresented states and the construction of meaning* (pp. 220–239). London: Karnac.

da Rocha Barros, E. M. (2000). Affect and pictographic image. *Int. J. Psychoanal.*, 81:1087–1099.

da Rocha Barros, E. M. & E. L. da Rocha Barros. (2011). Reflections on the clinical implications of symbolism. *Int. J. Psychoanal.*, 92:879–901.

da Rocha Barros, E. M. & E. L. da Rocha Barros. (2016). The function of evocation in the working-through of the countertransference: Projective identification, reverie, and the expressive function of the mind-reflections inspired by Bion's work. In: H. Levine & G. Civitarese (eds.), *The Bion tradition* (pp. 141–154). London: Karnac.

de Cortiñas, L. P. (2013). Transformations of emotional experience. *Int. J. Psychoanal.*, 94(3):531–544.

De Saussure, J. (1993). Two discussions of the mind of the analyst and a response from Madeleine Baranger. *Int. J. Psychoanal.*, 74:1155–1159.

Diamond, M. J. (2014). Analytic mind use and interpsychic communication: driving force in analytic technique, pathway to unconscious mental life. *Psychoanal. Q.*, 83(3):525–563.

Ferro, A. (2002a). Some implications of Bion's thought. *Int. J. Psychoanal.*, 83:597–613.

Ferro, A. (2002b). Narrative derivatives of alpha elements: Clinical implications. *Int. Forum Psychoanal.*, 11:184–187.

Ferro, A. (2002c). *In the analyst's consulting room*. London: Bruner-Routledge.

Ferro, A. (2005). Four sessions with Lisa. *Int. J. Psychoanal.*, 86:1247–1256.

Ferro, A. (2008). The patient as the analyst's best colleague: Transformation into a dream and narrative transformations. *Italian Psychoanal. Ann.*, 2:199–205.

Ferro, A. (2015). *Reveries*. London: Karnac.

Ferro, A. (2016). Changes in technique and in the theory of technique in a post-Bionian field model. In: H. Levine & G. Civitarese (eds.), *The W.R. Bion tradition* (pp. 189–200). London: Karnac.

Ferro, A. & L. Nicoli. (2017). *The new analyst's guide to the galaxy*. London: Karnac.

Flannery, J. G. (1979). Dimensions of a single word-association in the analyst's reverie. *Int. J. Psychoanal.*, 60:217–223.

Frayn, D. H. (1987). An analyst's regressive reverie: A response to the analysand's illness. *Int. J. Psychoanal.*, 68:271–277.

Freud, S. (1933). The dissection of the psychical personality. *S.E.* XXII:5780.

Green, A. (2000). The central phobic position: A new formulation of the free association method. *Int. J. Psychoanal.*, 81(3):429–451.

Green, A. (2005). *Key ideas for contemporary psychoanalysis*. London: Routledge.

Grinberg, L. (1987). Dreams and acting out. *Psychoanal. Q.*, 56:155–176.

Grotstein, J. S. (2009). *But at the same time and on another level*. London: Karnac.

Jacobs, T. J. (1999). Countertransference past and present. *Int. J. Psychoanal.*, 80(3):575–594.

Kernberg, O. F. (2011). Divergent contemporary trends in psychoanalytic theory. *Psychoanal. Rev.*, 98(5):633–664.

Levine, H. & G. Civitarese (eds). (2016). *The W.R. Bion tradition*. London: Karnac.

Ogden, T. H. (1997a). Reverie and interpretation. *Psychoanal. Q.*, 66:567–595.

Ogden, T. H. (1997b). Reverie and metaphor. *Int. J. Psychoanal.*, 78:719–732.

Ogden, T. H. (2001). Conversations at the frontier of dreaming. *Fort Da.* 7(2):7–14.

Ogden, T. H. (2007). On talking-as-dreaming. *Int. J. Psychoanal.*, 88:575–589.

Ogden, T. H. (2009). Rediscovering psychoanalysis. *Psychoanal. Perspect.* 6:22–31.

Ogden, T. H. (2011). Reading Susan Isaacs: toward a radically revised theory of thinking. *Int. J. Psychoanal.*, 92:925–942.

Ogden, T. H. (2017). Dreaming the analytic session. *Psychoanal. Q.*, 86:1–20.

Ogden, B. H. & T. H. Ogden. (2012). How the analyst thinks as clinician and as literary reader. *Psychoanal. Perspect.* 9:243–273.

O'Shaughnessy, E. (2005). Whose Bion? *Int. J. Psychoanal.*, 86: 1523–1542.

Schmidt-Hellerau, C. (2001. *Life drive and death drive*. New York: Other Press.

Schmidt-Hellerau, C. (2005). The door to being preserved and alive. *Int. J. Psychoanal.*, 86:1261–1264.

Stein, M. (1981). The unobjectionable part of the transference. *J. Am. Psychoanal. Assoc.*, 29: 869–892.

Taylor, D. (2011). Commentary on vermote's 'on the value of late Bion to analytic theory and practice'. *Int. J. Psychoanal.*, 92:1099–1112.

Vermote, R. (2011). On the value of "late Bion" to analytic theory and practice. *Int. J. Psychoanal.*, 92:1089–1098.

14 Telling stories

The capacity of patients to tell and own their stories is central to their developing a sense of well-being from analysis. It is the basis of an exhilarating freedom from stories neurotically imposed by internal and external sources—the stories remembered but never integrated; the stories experienced but never formulated; the stories experienced and remembered only in the language of action; the stories of unconscious fantasy and defense; and the importance of all of these in every other story. Another more technical categorization might be that these are the stories of compromise formations and screen memories; stories enacted due to unstable structures or to thoughts represented in preoperational terms (Piaget, 1930); and stories based on implicit memories (Fonagy, 1999).[1] In short, these are the stories of lives interrupted, manifested analytically in rigidly held and fearful unknown, or incomplete, stories.

Stories exist within a context, so the nature of a story told in analysis is at any time shaped by a multiplicity of factors (for example transferences in all their drive, object, and self-object configurations, all of which are influenced by psychic structures and counter-transference, and so on). Thus, we are always hearing a version of a story. Further, the understanding of every story is provisional, and leaves the way open for future stories.

One doesn't hear much about what I consider a fairly typical analytic experience—that is, the repetition of key stories throughout an analysis, while something new is always being added that allows for greater understanding of the stories within a story. A small kitchen utensil was involved in a story that ran through one patient's analysis. Early in our work Alex, a 20-year-old undergraduate, told me of asking his mother what this utensil was, and being impatiently told to leave her alone. Within the context of the analysis at that time, it seemed to represent how neglected he often felt by his mother as she struggled with depression. Later, though, Alex told me how furious his mother got at him when he and a friend were playing with this utensil. At that time, we understood it as an example of his mother's difficulty appreciating his curiosity. Still later in the analysis, after I had interpreted Alex's growing provocativeness with me, he remembered that his mother hadn't gotten mad at him until he and his friend started playing soccer with the utensil. Later still, after a sexual dream that took place in the kitchen, Alex finally identified the kitchen utensil as a V-shaped slicer. The last part of the story emerged as the analysis was ending, when Alex remembered this slicer had been a present from his father to his mother.

We can see how, over the course of analysis, the "kitchen story" became the "kitchen stories." Altogether they comprise some of the stories of Alex's difficulties in forming relationships with women. The emerging stories were not the result of repressed memories coming to consciousness; Alex always knew the different parts of his kitchen stories. But the parts emerged only in the context of current concerns.

Why do I call these stories when so many psychoanalytic terms exist already as a useful basis of clinical understanding and discourse? The word captures a way of thinking about the analytic process, especially the analyst's role in aiding or interfering with the patient's stories. This is something we all experience in everyday life—talking with people who help us to elaborate our stories, and with people who interrupt them. Some people, we feel, are interested in our stories, and we learn from them in the telling; some cannot wait to tell their own stories long enough to listen to ours.

This paper is about how we help to elaborate or interrupt our patients' stories. As psychoanalysts we always struggle with the task of sifting the patient's story from our own. I believe it is important to highlight this struggle, as intrusion by the analyst into a patient's stories is a problem across the theoretical spectrum. Those who proclaim the inevitability of the analyst's subjectivity have made it a virtual battle cry.

In fact, if we allow it, patients tell us their stories. In their words and actions, in their negations, denials, and intellectualizations, in the telling (or not) of their dreams, in the expression (or not) of their intense feelings—in short, in all the multitudinous forms of expression available—patients tell us their stories. In these stories we find the why of our patients' coming to us, and the roads by which they leave us. In between they tell us stories about why they shouldn't tell us stories, and vehemently deny that there are any stories to be told. Sometimes patients are happy to have us hear and understand their stories but will be uncomfortable owning them. Sometimes they can only tell their stories by a unique form of action, language action. And at some point, we become part of their stories.

There is nothing more inhibiting to the analytic process than for patient and analyst to believe they have discovered the patient's story. While psychoanalysis helps identify key stories that have inhibited the patient's life trajectory, the very fact of this identification should enable a deepening understanding of old stories, a readiness to understand old stories in newly configured forms, and the freedom to identify new stories.

Patients come to us because they are inhibited from living out their own stories. They live out somebody else's story instead, or they are afraid to see the story they're living out, or they cannot bear the consequences of the story they've constructed. They feel the pain of an unlived life, and they want to know whose life they've been leading and how they can learn to lead their own. The goal of analysis is to help patients discover the stories they've been living, and in this way find the stories they choose to live. Authorship of one's story is a crucial component in the "good-enough" analysis. While other people may play a significant role in the formation and continuation of our patients' stories, analytic progress toward well-being occurs only when authorship is accepted of the stories that emerge in the analytic process, and of their formation, continuation, and results.

Expanding stories

One way to conceptualize how patients come into treatment is that they *suffer from a dearth of available stories* about what brought them into an analyst's office. Reasons for this lack can range from a tendency to see one's symptoms lodged primarily in the actions of another, to psychological stories that are limited and limiting. Trapped in old stories (uncaring partners, dominating bosses, fear of authority, etc.), patients feel crushed by painful feelings and unable to move forward; they live with an attenuated sense of vitality and pleasure, while bringing misery to the people around them. Given an empathic, well-trained analyst who is open to his or her own multiple stories (the good-enough analyst, in other words), three guiding principles of psychoanalytic technique aid patients in telling their stories.

1. Resistance Analysis. This is a principle of technique agreed to by every school of analysis (Busch, 2001), although sometimes under different names; resistances are the major factor in the inhibition of stories. A resistance, from a technical point of view, always has at its center a fear, based on earlier adaptations, of unrevealed stories. Therefore, resistances always have their own stories. A resistance is the result of an unconscious process, not a descriptive term. If they are thought of in this latter fashion, however, their manifestations can often be confused with behaviors conveying other meanings (for instance a tendency to speak in generalities may be a way of being unthreatening, an invitation to be intruded on, or an expression of hostility), or with other forms of expressing stories (for example, the action language of unformulated experience, as described by Stern). There are ways of working with resistances that increase the capacity for storytelling; these have been described elsewhere, and therefore will not be gone into here (Busch, 1992, 1993; Gray, 1994; Pray, 1994).
2. Free Association. Free association is fundamental to storytelling in psychoanalysis. Freud's genius was to capture the possibilities of a naturally occurring process. Kris (1982) has stated it most succinctly: "Psychoanalysis does not create free association in the treatment setting. It merely provides an alteration in the condition of ordinary association... It replaces silent soliloquy with spoken words" (p. 14).

In the patient's use of the method of free association we can see unknown stories guiding them, inhibiting them, destroying them. We also come to understand the process by which patients guide, inhibit, and destroy stories. We see how effective our methods are in increasing the freedom to tell a particular story, and to tell stories in general. Sometimes the stories are told in words, sometimes in the absence of words. Primarily stories are told through a variety of processes.

Given the extraordinary power of the patient's use of the method of free association, why are there such resistances to its use among analysts? I have previously described some factors that account for this (Busch, 1994), but in my own experience and in listening to the work of others, I place high on the list the demands that free association makes on the analyst's psychic functioning. Unconsciously experiencing and trying to contain the patient's projections and projective identifications can give rise to sometimes unbearable tension; this may be experienced as the destruction of one's internal structures, and often leads us to act in a desperate attempt to stabilize our psychic equilibrium. We are always dealing with the fact that we are more or less vulnerable, based on our moment-to-moment thresholds and "capacities to tolerate helplessness, uncertainty, culpability, or affective closeness" (Schwaber, 1990, pp. 31–32). Schwaber (1992) succinctly captures the problem of listening for our patients' stories when she defines countertransference as a retreat from the search for the patient's vantage point. I have often wondered whether the need to stabilize ourselves, rather than help our patients, may have something to do with the recent insistence on the centrality of the analyst's story and actions in analytic practice.

3. Remaining "in the neighborhood." Another significant factor in facilitating analytic storytelling is the need for the analyst to remain "in the neighborhood" (Busch, 1993, p. 152). This term indicates that the analyst's interventions must be based on what the patient can hear and integrate, rather than what the analyst has understood and integrated. In technical terms, it means paying greater attention to the conscious and unconscious ego. While previously subsumed under the rubric of tact and timing, the technical implementation of this precept has remained hazy, and has been obscured by the tendency toward deep interpretations. Recent writings have attempted to close the gap between theory and practice (Busch, 1993, 2000; Gray, 1994; Levy & Inderbitzin, 1990; Paniagua, 1991, 2001), and have established a potential meeting ground between contemporary Freudians and contemporary Kleinians (Joseph, 2001; Kernberg, 1993, 2001; Schafer, 1994).

Clinical example

In this example I focus on how the emphasis on storytelling affects my clinical work.

Joan, an attractive middle-aged woman, began treatment fearful of having any story at all. The reasons for her failed marriages were externalized. Occasional spontaneous associations might lead her to think about what a thought could mean, but she handled this experience as if she were looking up a word in a dictionary. Sessions were filled with ruminations on the details of the previous day's events. Connections between thoughts, when Joan attempted them, were vague. Dreams, which she wrote down and studied, often filled entire sessions. Transference interpretations were often greeted with a "could be," and a protest that it was her real life that she needed to be concerned with. Links that I made in one session were destroyed by the next. Joan's rare expressions of sharp humor—sometimes sophisticated, sometimes bawdy, sometimes girlish—gave me a glimpse of her intelligence and potential for playfulness. Although she seemed to use those closest to her as self-objects, there were also expressions of compassion in which I could sense her warmth. Primarily she came across as someone tied in emotional knots. At times it was difficult for me to stay interested in what she was saying, which proved to be an important countertransference. So, at times, was my irritation at her slow pace, which sometimes led me to prod her with premature interpretations.

Over time, we could understand some of the stories that led Joan to need to feel that she had no stories: her belief that she had to keep her ideas and feelings, especially her rage, hidden as a way of holding onto her narcissistic father; her efforts to maintain her fragile omnipotence and protect herself against underlying feelings of shame and inadequacy; the fear/wish and the repetition in her way of speaking of compulsive masturbatory activity that she had and finally a repetition in the transference/countertransference of an exciting sadomasochistic relationship with her father, in which "who was who" was constantly changing. Over the first three years of analysis, significant changes occurred in Joan's openness to her own stories, but conspicuous by its absence was any story about Joan's relationship to women. Shortly before the session I will report, we had seen the possibility that a part of every relationship with a man was a desire to get closer to her mother.

The session

Joan began the session in a "proper" fashion, which in her usually indicated a defended stance. At such times the pitch of her voice and her clipped words sounded very British. I found myself playing with Jacobs's (1993) description of a patient; my version went, "Thinks Yiddish, talks British." The impulse to mock Joan was a familiar reaction of mine to this voice. It usually presaged a session in which I would experience her as lecturing me, explicitly or implicitly, about some problem with something I'd said, or with the psychoanalytic method. Sometimes it was an attack on linking (Bion, 1959). I often had the feeling that I was going to have to accept some "bullshit"; at the same time Joan would become increasingly desperate as to why I wasn't helping her. Up to the point of the session I will describe, we had understood this scenario mainly as a re-creation of an erotic sadomasochistic relationship with her father, who would sit Joan in a chair for what seemed to her like hours and lecture her about some misdeed. After that he would take her to the parental bedroom, tell her to take off her clothes, and spank her while her mother watched. Who was who in the transference-countertransference continually shifted.

Joan: In thinking about yesterday, I could consider what some of the issues might be that could lead me to want to get rid of the man to get to the woman. I know I always felt distant from my mother, but I'm sure she had her [brief pause] her reasons. I think it may have been because my father was so dominant in every way. He saw himself as the center of the household, and everybody was supposed to treat him as such. I'm sure he would have had a difficult time if my mother had a close relationship with me. She was expected to be there for my father, at home and at the office. [Joan's father was a physician, and her mother was expected to help out whenever there was a shortage of employees.]

FB: I wonder if you noticed that as you started to talk about how you felt distant from your mother, you paused, and then described what you saw as your father's reasons for keeping your mother distant. It's as if something made you uncomfortable about your feelings of distance.

In other words, Joan began a new story, which she immediately interrupted in favor of a familiar one. The interruption then became the new story. Why did her story of distance from her mother have to be stopped and replaced by her victimization by (what she saw as) her father's story—an old story she had told many times before, and already understood as one factor in her distance from her mother? Why is "I felt distant from my mother" unknowable at this moment? That question, that interrupted story, is the focus of my intervention. In fact, Joan's story of her relationship with her mother had been pretty much absent to this point. But now, when she brings it up and immediately inhibits it, we have an ideal opportunity to explore it. An active, observable conflict is much easier to understand than a hypothesized one.

When working from this perspective we have to make clear that we are interested in the reasons for the interruption, and not subtly encouraging the continuation of the story. It is my repeated experience that at this point patients are more willing to provide a defended version of a story than experience the fear implicit in the interruption.

Joan: [more spontaneous and genuine]: I did notice the pause but didn't feel like getting into it. When I paused, I just felt like I didn't want to take the time to get into the details. It seemed boring to me. I also had the thought that maybe my mother was put off by taking care of me. She just didn't want to take the time. Although I don't know what she did with her time. Did I ever tell you that full-time babysitters took care of me? [She hadn't.] They had other jobs in the house but did a lot of the caretaking of me. I knew I was being vague before, but the details didn't seem that important.

FB: It seems you didn't want to take the time with your own thoughts? Or felt like I wouldn't want you to take the time?

The first thing that happens after I point out the interrupted story is a change in Joan's affect (that is, greater spontaneity). Joan seems ready to be freed at least briefly from her previous story. In dynamic terms, as a result of previous work with her resistances, there has been a decrease in her anxiety about exploring a fearful thought. The interpretation of the resistance in this session was like opening a door that was latched, but no longer locked. Joan's spontaneity is typical of what happens when patients are freed from experiencing themselves as victims of another's story.

Joan's capacity to capture what was occurring right at the moment of resistance is an important analytic achievement (Busch, 1995) and indicates a readiness to face the exact moment of threat that led to the resistance. Just now, when she was associating to the moment of resistance, was one of those key times when there was a congruence between her actions (i.e., acting on the feeling that she couldn't take the time for her own thoughts), and her verbal associations (i.e., "I don't think my mother wanted to take the time with me"). My interpretation focuses on these two stories which occur in the here and now of the transference.

Joan: Maybe both. You know I get impatient sometimes, I must think you are the same. I've been noticing recently how impatient I am when talking with friends. I just want them to get finished so that I can say what I want. Actually, I always felt my mother thought I was a bit icky. An interesting word. But I don't know. Is this really worth spending time on? What difference does it make if my mother cleaned my diapers or someone else?

FB: You just started to feel interested in this icky stuff, and then it immediately became uninteresting to you.

   In Joan's initial response (that is, her implication that she is the irritable one, and might be projecting this onto me) it isn't clear to what extent she is making a necessary correction to what I said, or dealing with a safer topic (that is, her own irritability) that by identification brings her closer to her mother, or being resistant to my interpretation. The latter seems to be uppermost, as Joan then briefly approaches a possible story about why she finds it difficult to be interested in her thoughts or expects others to not be so interested. This brief leap into interest in the new story is quickly disavowed, which is a defense and also possibly an enactment of a prior adaptation.

   My interpretation is geared to what seems to me to be the most important story, Joan's conflict over her interest in her icky thoughts. While the deeper meanings of this are revealed in the disavowal (that is, "What does it matter if my mother cleaned my diapers or someone else did?"), we need to respect Joan's disavowal. To interpret the deeper meanings of the disavowal while it is still occurring is to risk bypassing the importance of the defense at that moment. After all, this need to disavow immediately what has just been said is a powerful demonstration of how uncomfortable Joan is at the moment. For analytic work to continue, it is crucial that patients feel safe to pursue whatever part of a conflict they can. It is a highly compacted, multi-layered, significant story that Joan is in conflict over telling. I think it is necessary, at these times, to point to the conflict; that way it is possible to see which part the patient is best able to deal with. I know that there are many who would be tempted to say, "You are afraid to say more because you felt that your mother saw you as a piece of shit," and would consider this defense analysis. However, I think this is an interpretation of an unconscious fantasy disguised as a resistance interpretation. It doesn't appreciate the possible importance to the patient of the disavowal at that moment.

Joan: You know I think my mother just handed my care over to others. But what was she doing? She was always around the house, but I don't remember interacting with her until I was much older. I remember in high school she would like it when I would come home and tell her entertaining stories about my friends and teachers. But you know I don't remember ever having brought a friend to my house. She never asked me why I didn't, and I just felt I shouldn't, or it would be more fun at someone else's house. But as I'm talking, I'm starting to feel disgusted. Like I'm filling the air with bullshit.

FB: It seems like you're feeling towards your own thoughts like you felt your mother viewed your icky diapers.

Here we begin to see more of the multilayered story behind the retreat from icky stuff. First there is an object-relations component in Joan's wondering about her mother's absence in her early memories. This is followed by Joan's memory of being a self-object for her mother. This had not come up before. The memory of not bringing friends home seemed an ambiguous association. While Joan meant it as another example of her home as unwelcoming, I also wondered whether it might be a wish not to disturb the dyadic relationship with her mother, or a rebellion against being a self-object. Her ending a story that I was finding interesting, calling it disgusting and bullshit, seemed to be filled with potential transferential and counter-transferential meanings. Defense, gratification, enactments of internalized self- and object relations, all seem condensed in Joan's response. Is her retreat from talking about this interesting stuff due to a sudden feeling she's getting close to something icky? Is the fear of touching this icky stuff imbued with the wish to fill the air with disgusting shit? Is she rebelling from experiencing my interest and feeling as if she is being used as a self-object?

As all of this is new material, I base my interpretation on the fact that at this point in the analysis Joan's fears are closer to the surface than her wishes, and the disappointing part of her relationship to her mother is closer to the surface than the drive derivatives or the transference. Again, as Joan's feelings towards her own thoughts are central in the analytic work (and in her life), in my interpretation I return to this issue, judging that this would be most helpful to the continuation of the story.

Joan: This was confirmed for me when I was much older. My mother had cancer of the bowels. Food would either go right through her, or she would get constipated. Once she was telling me of how she had to stick her finger up her rectum to unclog herself. She told me then that she used to find feces so disgusting, but now she doesn't. My mother was really narcissistic. I once had an aunt tell me that my mother went to New York with my father for some function but wouldn't leave her hotel room because she had a pimple. She always thought she was so important. She used to go into Lord & Taylor and say, "I'm Dr. K's wife," like anyone gave a shit. It was so embarrassing. She was the chosen one in her family. She was the most beautiful sister. She was the only one of her siblings to go to college, or to play the piano. She seemed to be worshipped. I remember another aunt saying to me once, "You may have the brains, but your mother has the beauty." What a horrible thing to say. [She suddenly stops talking.] But I don't know how I've come to this point. It's all a jumble.

FB: Jumble?

Joan: Like there's too much. I said too much. I don't know what I'm talking about anymore. There's too much there to make any sense of.

FB: As you start to express your anger towards your mother for the first time in here, you worry you're not in control of yourself, as if you're afraid of what has come out, like too much shit. For some reason, this leaves you confused.

Joan: But you know there is so much there, I don't know how it will all come out.

> *Here we see Joan's initial availability to a slew of new stories. They come tumbling out of her with an interest and liveliness I've rarely seen. Then she suddenly becomes disoriented. She feels that too much has come out of her, and possibly with too much pleasure; she becomes disoriented and has to stop. Here we see the sudden emergence of an inhibition of her stories, crucial to the lack of satisfaction in her life. In my interpretation of what stopped her I focus on the affect that I thought would be most available to her, while linking it to what I saw as its unconscious referent. I then return to the jumbled, disoriented feeling most immediately associated with the inhibition. This form of interpretation follows my thinking that while we need to interpret previously unconscious affects and fantasies, once an inhibition has occurred the route back to unknown stories is through the inhibiting affect, which itself is part of the story (Busch, 1993, 2000).*

In short, in this session I've tried to demonstrate how the principles of resistance analysis, the patient's use of the method of free associations, and being "in the neighborhood" inform my work in restoring storytelling. I want to emphasize that this was one of those sessions in which a convergence of the patient's associations, feelings, and actions lends new clarity to the work. This session was the culmination of many in which I saw only a glimpse of what was expressed in this one. It was the result of hard work on both our parts over a sustained period of time, not of magical interpretations.

Follow-up

Approximately 18 months later, Joan fell in love with a man who seemed very loving. Never having had an orgasm during intercourse became especially troublesome to her, and some analytic work led to her awareness that she became very excited until her lover entered her. At this point she lost all feeling. In a session much like the one just reported, Joan associated freely and became fascinated by a new story: that she fears letting go during intercourse as she unconsciously fantasizes urinating and defecating on her lover. In the following session, Joan talked with relish about her pleasure in a good meal the previous day. She didn't feel the usual self-imposed restraints in which etiquette triumphed over enjoyment. During dinner she and a friend had been talking about how their mothers had made them eat by reminding them of the starving children in Europe. Joan regretfully felt that this woman was able to be more directly hostile to her mother than she could. She then became very tired in the session, and lost interest in what she was saying.

As we began to explore the associations that ended in her tiredness, Joan briefly remembered a part of a dream, and told it in a dull fashion. She was at a wonderful restaurant with another woman, but all that was on the table were black olives. She remembered the woman as someone who had been especially critical of her in the past. She had no thoughts about the black olives. She became very tired again, explaining it now on the basis of external factors, and lost interest in the thoughts that came to her mind, which she expressed in a deadened fashion. I said, "You've come a long way from the gusto of taking in yesterday's meal and telling me about it."

After she saw the discrepancy between her enjoyment earlier in telling me about the meal and the way she was feeling now, Joan felt like crying. She blamed the early hour of our session for her tiredness and described how embarrassed she feels when leaving her lover to come to an appointment with me. She said, "I wouldn't feel the same way if I was going out to do business."

Joan laughed, remembering that this was the phrase her father used for taking a bowel movement: "doing your business." Joan then described how proud she usually is taking a bowel movement right after eating in the morning. This led to her thinking of the black olives, and how they reminded her of bowel movements when she's constipated. Her last thought before the session ended was that for the first time in a long time, she had had no interest in sex the night before.

As in any good story, the plot is thickening. Stories from previous sessions return as part of Joan's sexual inhibition. Her ability to share enthusiastically with me her experience of zestily taking in a good meal, which I in turn enjoyed hearing about, reminded me of the movie *Like Water for Chocolate*, which celebrates the sexuality of eating. However, the specter lurking in these feelings of hostility toward her mother caused her to clam up. That constipated state in turn reminds us of the unconscious fantasies of joyfully defecating on her mother that has unconsciously infiltrated her sexual pleasures. After I remind her of the pleasure she's inhibiting, and Joan experiences a sense of something lost, she brings us back to the many stories affecting the transference and keeping her from a pleasure now glimpsed, but never yet achieved.

De-emphasizing storytelling

We have always known that one important danger to a patient's storytelling is an overemphasis on the analyst's stories. We all struggle with this to varying degrees from day to day, and from patient to patient. Previously we over-emphasized the analyst's neurotic countertransference as the primary cause of this. It is my opinion that past problems with our theory of technique have contributed greatly to the analyst's stories becoming central (Busch, 1993, 1997, 1999). However, a current trend is leading to an institutionalization of clinical technique that enshrines the analyst's stories. The trend I refer to derives from the view that the analyst is irreducibly subjective, and thus any attempt toward objectivity is mere pretense. It leads to a deemphasizing of the patient's stories in favor of the analyst's reaction to them. These views contain some important insights, but it is important to keep them in context. As an example,I turn to Renik (2001), a provocative championing of the analyst's stories as central to analytic technique and successful analyses.

Ralph came to Renik with general malaise, problems at work, marital discord, feelings of being an inadequate father, and many other worries. In their first meeting, Renik asked him what he hoped to accomplish in treatment. To Renik's surprise, Ralph, a talented and passionate musician in his spare time, described how he would like to devote a year to studying the guitar, never having had any formal training. He feared that this would cause great privation to his family (in spite of their willingness to support the plan), and that he wouldn't be able to find another executive position when he returned to work. He felt himself to be in an impossible dilemma.

Renik says, "Listening to this I had the impression Ralph was not really describing a choice he was trying to make. It was more that he was describing his reluctance to act on a choice that he had already made" (p. 233). According to Renik, Ralph felt that he couldn't be happy pursuing his dream of studying the guitar, and that he couldn't do it without having his family make sacrifices. After Renik conveyed this impression to Ralph, and Ralph agreed, Renik asked him "if he felt he had the right to do what he wanted to do" (p. 234). Ralph thought for a while. At first, he said he wasn't sure, and then changed this to "probably," but even after reflecting on how miserable he was making himself and others, he still felt he couldn't act.

Renik outlined a number of issues Ralph could fruitfully explore in treatment, but he tells us that "it was also important to keep in mind that no amount of self-awareness was going to change the circumstances with which

Ralph had to deal, or the need for him to act, one way or the other, and to take responsibility for his actions" (p. 233). Another appointment was set, but Ralph called the next day to cancel it. About a month later he called Renik to say that he had decided to follow his dream, and from time to time Renik heard from Ralph that he was doing well. "In my view, Ralph's treatment was a successful clinical analysis, because for me, psychoanalysis is first and foremost a treatment method for bringing about life changes desired by the patient" (p. 234). As to whether this was a "cure" primarily through the analyst's influence, Renik states, "My experience over the years has led me to conclude that the distinction we have been used to making between a 'transference cure' in which important mutative experiences within the treatment relationship remain unexamined, and a 'psychoanalysis' in which they are adequately scrutinized during scheduled meetings, is based on an idealization of our capacities for objective self-awareness" (p. 235). While recognizing that his one-session "clinical analysis" may seem radical (p. 235), Renik ends up describing it as "an open-ended clinical analysis" (p. 235).

Renik's analyst-centered technique is based on his impression, after part of one session, of what he thinks Ralph wants. Given what we know about the complex, multidimensional nature of what patients really want, how could this appraisal, made in these first moments of meeting Ralph, be other than Renik's fantasy of what he thought was best for Ralph? There are so many stories unexplored. Central is Ralph's closely held fantasy that he will damage his family by following his musical quest, in spite of his family's assurances to the contrary. What about Ralph's other concerns, about marital discord, and about his belief that he's an inadequate father? It seems that Renik helped Ralph by reducing his sense of guilt. This is good supportive psychotherapy, but not clinical psychoanalysis, as I understand it. Clinical psychoanalysis gives people back their lives via an understanding of their multiple stories, and the inhibitions that have interfered with this understanding. It is very different from an analyst's decision about what a patient's life path should be and encouraging him to follow it. Whenever I feel I "know" what course a patient should take, I look for the transference/countertransference mix that leads me to this position, which seems like an odd one for an analyst to take. Clinical psychoanalysis is the only method I know that focuses on helping patients tell their own stories as a basis for greater freedom in choosing the stories they want to live, freer from stories neurotically imposed from within or from without. As far as I can tell, Ralph had barely begun his story before Renik reacted with his own.

Freud (1914) realized that at some point in all treatments patients who cannot tell their stories instead act them out. We have learned over the years that only by becoming free to explore and own their stories are patients able to engage in more effective action. Renik takes the opposite view with Ralph—that is, that the freedom to know the multiple stories leading to unhappiness doesn't help in taking effective action. My discussion with Aron on this issue (Aron, 2001; Busch, 2001, 2001a) also indicates what a wide gulf there can be between analysts even on matters that seem to me basic to psychoanalysis. While those who emphasize the analyst's subjectivity have given us a necessary reminder of our potential role in the analysis, the championing of subjectivity has had the effect of interfering with the stories of our patients. As I noted earlier, this is an issue analysts have struggled with throughout our history. Of course, we have our stories, both personal and theoretical, but at the very least we have an obligation not to let these claim our attention at the expense of our patients' stories. Our own stories will come into sessions unbidden, but our task as analysts, it seems to me, is to see if and how they fit with our patients' stories before making them the centerpiece of our work (Busch, 1998). Otherwise we ask patients to do what they've done their whole lives: to see their world in the context of someone else's story. This negates the most crucial potential of psychoanalysis, the possibility of finding our own unknown stories, so that we can choose the stories we want to live.

Note

1 Thick boundaries between these different kinds of stories are a useful device for categorizing, but they are not otherwise helpful. The mind, with its dynamic structures that serve multiple functions, is not easily categorized. It seems a daunting task to ascertain whether a complex series of thoughts or feelings in psychoanalysis represents an unformulated experience or one that was kept at an earlier level of thinking because of conflict. Further, there is rarely a sharp line in development between one phase and another. As Piaget (1930) has shown, this is especially true of thought processes.

References

Aron, L. (2001). Commentary on "are we losing our mind?" *J. Am. Psychoanal. Assoc.*, 49:758–767.

Bion, W. R. (1959). Attacks on linking. *Int. J. Psycho-Anal.*, 40:308–315.

Busch, F. (1992). Recurring thoughts on unconscious ego resistances. *J. Am. Psychoanal. Assoc.*, 40:1089–1115.

Busch, F. (1993). In the neighborhood: Aspects of a good interpretation and a "developmental lag" in ego psychology. *J. Am. Psychoanal. Assoc.*, 41:151–177.

Busch, F. (1994). Some ambiguities in the method of free association and their implication for psychoanalytic technique. *J. Am. Psychoanal. Assoc.*, 42:363–384.

Busch, F. (1995). *The ego at the center of clinical technique*. Northvale, NJ: Aronson.

Busch, F. (1997). Understanding patients' use of the method of free association. *J. Am. Psychoanal. Assoc.*, 45:407–424.

Busch, F. (1998). Self-disclosure ain't what it's cracked up to be, at least not yet. *Psychoanal. Inq.*, 17:518–529.

Busch, F. (1999). *Rethinking clinical technique*. Northvale, NJ: Aronson.

Busch, F. (2000). What is a deep interpretation? *J. Am. Psychoanal. Assoc.*, 48:237–254.

Busch, F. (2001a). Are we losing our mind? *J. Am. Psychoanal. Assoc.*, 49:739–751.

Busch, F. (2001b). Reply to Aron's commentary on "Are we losing our mind?" *J. Am. Psychoanal. Assoc.*, 49:773–777.

Fonagy, P. (1999). Memory and therapeutic action. *Int. J. Psycho-Anal.*, 80:215–223.

Freud, S. (1908). Creative writers and daydreaming. *Stand. Edn.*, 9:143–153.

Freud, S. (1914). Remembering, repeating, and working through. *Stand. Edn.*, 12:145–156.

Gray, P. (1994). *The ego and analysis of defense.* Northvale, NJ: Aronson.

Jacobs, T. (1993). The inner experiences of the analyst: Their contribution to the analytic process. *Int. J. Psycho-Anal.*, 74:7–14.

Joseph, B. (2001). The psychoanalytic method and the analyst's listening. Presented in the Panel *"What is the Psychoanalytic Method?"* at the July 2001 meetings of the International Psychoanalytic Association, Nice, France.

Kernberg, O. F. (1993). Convergences and divergences in contemporary psychoanalytic technique. *Int. J. Psycho-Anal.*, 74:659–673.

Kernberg, O. F. (2001). Recent developments in the technical approaches of English-language psychoanalytical schools. *Psychoanal. Q.*, 70:519–548.

Kris, A. O. (1982). *Free association.* New Haven: Yale University Press.

Levy, S., & Inderbitzin, L.B. (1990). The analytic surface and the theory of technique. *J. Am. Psychoanal. Assoc.*, 38:371–392.

Paniagua, C. (1991). Patient's surface, clinical surface, and workable surface. *J. Am. Psychoanal. Assoc.*, 39:669–685.

Paniagua, C. (2001). The attraction of topographic technique. *Int. J. Psycho-Anal.*, 82:671–684.

Piaget, J. (1930). *The child's conception of physical causality.* London: Kegan Paul.

Pray, M. (1994). Analyzing defenses: Two different models. *J. Clin. Psychoanal.* 3:87–126.

Renik, O. (2001). The patient's experience of therapeutic benefit. *Psychoanal. Q.*, 70:231–242.

Schafer, R. (1994). The contemporary Kleinians of London. *Psychoanal. Q.*, 63:409–432.

Schwaber, E. A. (1990). The psychoanalyst's methodological stance: Some comments based on a response to Max Hernandez. *Int. J. Psycho-Anal.*, 71:31–36.

Schwaber, E. A. (1992). Countertransference: The analyst's retreat from the patient's vantage point. *Int. J. Psycho-Anal.*, 73:349–361.

15 I love you that's why I ignore you

It is not an uncommon clinical experience for the analysts to tell a patient about an unusual interruption in the treatment (e.g., a sudden break to deal with a family emergency) and, after a brief moment, to have the patient go on to talk about whatever was on his or her mind before coming into the session. This apparent lack of reaction also occurs with the more usual absences that we know have some meaning to the patient (e.g., vacations). With certain patients all the time, and with all patients some of the time, anything that causes a break in the treatment is seemingly treated as a nonevent. Similarly, when the analysand returns to treatment, there is always some incident that occurred during the break that fills his or her psychic space. Attempts to make a bridge between the analysand's state of mind and the separation from the analyst are greeted, at best, with mild interest, but have little emotional meaning for the patient.

Patients' lack of reaction to breaks have been interpreted in various ways. These include: that the patient's anxiety over the separation is too over-whelming and thus the feelings must be split off; any feelings stirred up by the analyst's being gone are experienced as an attack on the patient's omnipotence and to reestablish omnipotence the analyst is blotted out; and the idealizing transference is shattered and the patient regresses to a mirror transference so that the analyst is only there to function as a self-object to bolster the frag-mented self. Obviously, there is merit in all these explanations, and many more that I have not covered. However, experience with several patients has led me to consider still another possible explanation for these nonreactions. That is, *they can be a caring response to keep alive a dead mother or to at least not drive her further into deadness.* This dynamic seems to occur when a sensitive child senses his or her mother's depressed, narcissistically absorbed state, leading the child to "realize" that to worry about his or her own needs would only drive her into further deadness. To react with concern for him- or herself arouses feelings of extreme danger, ranging from aloneness to annihilation. Thus, in the analysis it is important for the analysand to react as though the analyst's comings and goings have no effect on him or her. *In the patient's mind, it is the only way to keep the analyst close, especially at a time of a real separation.*[1] Typically in these patients' backgrounds, there is a taboo against noticing anything unusual, peculiar, or bizarre. A typical example is a patient who, at age nine, discovered his mother after she made a suicide attempt by an overdose. Throughout her subsequent hospitalization and afterward, no one talked about what happened. Life just went on. The child perceived his role as needing to pretend as though nothing was going on as a way to protect the weakened object. In analysis, whatever event threatens the connection to the analyst, the analysis just goes on.

With the patients I am describing, our usual interpretations of their seeming non-responsiveness is to unwittingly "accuse" them of exactly what they are defending against-that is, any feeling of concern for themselves, which in their mind will drive the mother-analyst even further away. These interpretations can cause the patient severe anxiety because in the patient's mind he or she is attempting to enliven the analyst.

Clinical example

I begin exploration of the dynamic I have described with what I consider a typical example of this phenomenon. The patient, Jim, was in his 40s and very smart, but a chronic underachiever. He had been underemployed since graduating from college, and his primary investment in adulthood was in being there for his mother during a 20-year illness. He was married, with no children, and came to treatment because of his rages at his wife. He was supported by a trust fund.

Jim seemed to be developing normally until his mother went back to work when he was three years old. It was reported that he had a severe regression in speech and toilet training. It seems as though over time Jim's mother became increasingly depressed, resulting in several hospitalizations starting when he was in latency. Although he had an older sister and brother, for some time I thought he was an only child because he seemed to be alone much of his childhood. In addition to depression, his mother struggled with alcoholism, resulting in angry, seemingly irrational outbursts. At the beginning of treatment, his father, a successful businessman, was devalued, although as it turned out he was the more consistent maternal presence in the home.

It was a week before I was to have surgery that was going to keep me out of the office for 4–6 weeks. The surgery came up suddenly, so I felt it was important to tell my patients the reason for this unplanned, lengthy absence. Jim, in his characteristic manner, said a few formal words of sympathy and good wishes. Then he immediately began to talk about what happened the previous weekend, which took up most of the session. This was his usual manner of dealing with absences, but I was struck by his nonreaction to what I had just told him.

I felt deadened and withdrawn from what Jim was telling me. I wondered about a projective identification or an unconscious attempt to angrily or defensively deaden me. However, I also realized I was narcissistically vulnerable at this time, so who was contributing what to my countertransference reaction was unclear. In sorting through countertransference reactions, I often find it helpful to listen simultaneously to the patient and my associations. I think it is useful to consider that there are times when an analysand is more into an enactment mode, more into an associating mode, or more into a combination of enacting and associating. These latter patients are those with whom we experience a variety of countertransference reactions and can listen to the patient's associations as one guide to our experience.

As I returned to listening, Jim was talking about a meeting he was at during which he was highly attuned to what others were thinking of him. His preoccupation revolved around whether others were thinking he was too loud, too brash, or putting himself forward too much. As Jim elaborated on this story, I found myself thinking of his narcissistic, alcoholic mother, whom he took care of throughout most of his early adult life. *For him, it was a matter of life and death. He had to be what his mother wanted him to be so that she could be enlivened. He was her self-object.* He first came to analysis shortly after his mother died. One of the first things he told me was that when people came up to him to tell him what a wonderful job he did taking care of his mother, he would inwardly shrug off the compliment because he "couldn't keep her alive." According to Jim, he felt his mother wanted him to be a "potato," and she would call him "my little potato." For Jim, this represented how his mother wanted him to be "silently growing" out of sight, causing no problems.[2] These thoughts led me to say the following:

FB: In the meeting you're worried that you're drawing too much attention to yourself. I wonder if this is similar to concerns you had when I told you about my surgery?

Jim: I felt selfish. You were the one having surgery, and my thoughts should be more about you. But I got scared. This bad thing was happening, and how would I do? Then I told myself you would be fine, and I calmed down.

FB: So, reassuring yourself that I would be OK blotted out your feelings of being scared, which worried you because you felt you weren't focusing enough on me.

Jim: [through tears, which were very unusual] I just had another thought. When I saw you today, you seemed to be holding your arm in an awkward position, as if you were in pain. As I thought that, I felt some pains in my chest.

FB: Maybe we can say you were drawn to even feel my pain.

Jim: I remember, near the end of my mother's life, how I felt sick to my stomach all the time. [His mother died of stomach cancer.] But I felt I had to be chipper and upbeat, pretending like I didn't know the end was near.

FB: It reminds me of the times your mother was hospitalized, and everyone kept going on like nothing was happening. [His mother was hospitalized for depression several times in his latency.]

Jim: [Sobbing for several minutes] I don't know why I keep thinking this. [He then tells an elaborate story of a very expensive trip he is planning for his wife's birthday even though it is not at a good time for him.]

FB: Just like you felt you had to sacrifice your own worries to take care of me, you do the same with Robyn [his wife].

Jim: When you say that, I start to feel anxious. I know Robyn doesn't feel like she needs this kind of extravagant vacation, and it's the worst possible time for me. Yet I still feel like I have to do it.

As we can see, Jim's unresponsiveness to my informing him of my impending surgery was, in fact, the result of a complex reaction. Jim's concern for his own welfare immediately aroused anxiety over being selfish, and his focus shifted to how he should be concerned about me. However, showing concern also seemed to be threatening, and the resultant compromise formation was silence, as Jim reassured himself that I would be OK. Jim ended up having no concerns about himself or me, and the analysis went on as if nothing had happened. This "nothing happened" is what we frequently interpret as an attack against the analyst when in this instance it can be seen as an attack against the self (i.e., Jim's worries for himself need to be discarded because of anxiety) and, as we shall see, a protection of the object.

Listening to Jim's associations, we hear that he is afraid others are seeing him as self-centered. When I am able to connect this concern with his unresponsiveness, Jim is able to feel pain he first ignored. However, it is another's pain. It is what he imagines as my pain, just as he was only able to feel his mother's pain as she was dying. He cannot easily feel his own pain because it is frightening and dangerous. Selfish is the word he uses to describe being scared when I tell him of my operation. He must turn his attention to the object and pretend like nothing happened, or his tenuous connection to the object will be shattered.

Jim's thoughts then lead us to see another meaning in his "not noticing"; that is, caring for the object. Thus, he needs to "not notice" when his mother is dying, just like he did not notice when his mother was hospitalized, and like he did not notice his mother's narcissistic self-involvement or angry tirades from an earlier time. His associations lead him to how he is driven to care for his wife, even recognizing that it has little to do with her. In Jim's mind, caring for a woman is to literally keep her alive, and thus to feel enlivened himself. Here it is useful to remember Jim's discomfort when, after his mother's death, her friends would tell him what a wonderful caretaker he was during her illness. What he would think to himself was something like "Yes, that's all well and good, but I couldn't keep her alive." This was his job in life: to keep his mother alive. Not noticing became one way he did this, thus its manifestation in the transference when I told him of my impending surgery.

Follow-up

Jim returned to analysis almost four weeks later.[3] He seemed glad to see me, and after a few words of sympathy for my having to go through an operation, he said he was pleased I was back. His thoughts immediately turned to three situations in which he felt that if he said what was on his mind, others would be critical of him or retaliate against him. For example, because of his productivity at work, he was in line for a significant salary hike. However, he was sure that if he went to his section head to mention this, this woman would put him down. So once again, Jim's fear was that expressing his own needs or wishes would lead others to turn away from or retaliate against him.

After a while, Jim wondered whether he was avoiding thinking about what it was like to be back in analysis. His first thoughts were about how busy he was during the last month and how he was glad to have had the time. Jim then described a meeting he arranged for his colleagues to alert them to new legislation that would affect their way of doing business. He was angry with the people who were not there and those who left in the middle of the meeting. Jim then remarked again that he was glad I was back because so many things had gone on. He had been thinking about the fact that I lost a month's income and thought he would pay me for the month anyway. In this, I felt that Jim was saying he had no need for me while I was gone (i.e., he was so busy), but that he was angry with these other people who were not there. This feeling triggered unconscious anxiety because it was probably too close to how he felt about my absence, and Jim once again had to take care of me. After I pointed this out to Jim, his thoughts turned to the previous weekend where he made the plans for Saturday evening with another couple. Although everyone seemed to be having a good time, he worried that he "dragged" everyone into what he wanted to do. Finally, he associated to how everyone at dinner was talking about what was happening with mutual friends and how out of it he was. All these things were going on, and he just did not notice them.

In Jim's return to analysis, we see a repetition of his relating to me as if I was his dead mother. He fears his own needs will lead to disapproval or retaliation so he becomes a "potato" and can only say what it is like to be back, not what it was like for me to be gone. In fact, he can only be aware of how convenient it was that I was gone. When he gets close to feelings of anger over being abandoned (by his colleagues), he becomes anxious and immediately needs to care for me by thinking about paying me for the time I was away. Thus, any need to care for himself or wish to be cared for must be obliterated, replaced by the need to care for the other. As noted previously, in the cases I am describing part of caring is to not notice any disturbance in the other, so that one's sense of being ignored is a special form of caring.

Love, hate, care

As Schmidt-Hellerau (2002) has pointed out, there are a number of un-fortunate consequences of Freud's (1920) move to the drive theory of libido and aggression. Primary among these is that the concept of self- preservation as a drive was lost, and aggression was put in the position of a primal drive rather than as a force in obtaining gratification. Schmidt-Hellerau (2001, 2005) has made an impressive case for the retention and exploration of Freud's pre-1920 view of a preservative drive. She expanded this view to include not only preservation of the self, but also preservation of the object. However, after 1920 the preservative drive was subsumed under the libidinal drive, which contributed to a skewed view of certain clinical phenomena.[4]

In the context of Jim's dynamics, what becomes an obvious clinical problem derived from the continued primacy of aggression, put in its simplest terms, is the analyst's stance of "if you're not invested in me, you must hate me." It has led to a view of analysis in which the analyst is primed to see hostility toward the analyst or analysis.[5] If focused on exclusively, it can lead to blind spots in understanding the analysand's attempts to preserve him- or herself and/or the object. For many years, it led to a view of resistances as an attack on the analysis rather than as an attempt at self-preservation (Busch, 1992).

The utility of the concepts self- and object preservative become clear in understanding the clinical material. Jim's immediate response to my an-nouncing my surgery was self-preservative (i.e., he became scared and won-dered how he would do). However, we see that being self-preservative made Jim anxious, and he immediately felt the need to be object preservative. Part of being object preservative means pretending like nothing untoward is hap-pening, and the analysis goes on, seemingly as though nothing happened. To care for himself, he must care for the object. Self-preservation is entirely dependent on object preservation.

The dualities of libidinal versus preservative strivings and self-versus object preservation, as Schmidt-Hellerau (2005a) has demonstrated, are useful clinical dimensions to keep in mind, and they have important clinical utility in a variety of situations. For example, it is striking how many relationships that start out as libidinal end up as preservative. Caretaking overwhelms libido, leading to a diminution of the lively, zesty dimensions of the relationship that brought the couple together in the first place. Jim's need to give Robyn an extravagant birthday vacation, when it was inconvenient to him and unim-portant to her, is a good example of how the need to take care of another can dominate a relationship.

The dead mother

Few concepts have as much evocative power as Green's (1972) dead mother. As described by him, she is a mother who is "psychically dead in the eyes of the young child in her care" (p. 142). The central dynamic of the dead mother complex described by Green is the following: The transference will reveal a significant depression and state of emptiness, which is a repeat of a childhood depression. This is brought about by the mother's depression, leading to sudden withdrawal of her libidinal cathexis and involvement with the child. *Before that time, there had been a lively, vital interest in the child.* The literature is filled with examples in which the analyst describes the emptiness and deadening nature of the transference with these patients.[6] Green saw the child as interpreting the loss of the object as being caused by his or her drive toward the object.

Although the dynamics Green (1972) described fit what I have noted in my non-responsive patients, there are two outcomes that Green mentioned in passing that come closer to the immediate dynamic when Jim seemingly ignored my mentioning the operation. Green noted that the child may link the suddenly dead mother "with *his manner of being* rather than with some forbidden wish; in fact, it becomes forbidden for him to be" (pp. 151–152, italics added). We get a glimpse of this when Jim is able to tell me what went on at the moment of nonreaction. He is not able to just be, especially when it comes to concerns for himself and his well-being. It is selfish and associated with loss of the object. Jim has interpreted his mother's depression and narcissistic preoccupation as resulting from his needs to be cared for.

Green (1972) outlined three objectives in the child's internal mechanisms to deal with the dead mother. One succinctly captures the dynamic I have described: "to reanimate the dead mother, to interest her, to distract her, to give her a renewed taste for life, to make her smile and laugh" (p. 155). Although moments of countertransference deadness were an important component of my earlier work with these patients, characteristically there was also a constant attempt to reach the analyst-dead mother, albeit in ways that were not always easy to recognize. At first, patients' attempts to animate the analyst seemed like resistances, and only later could the repetition be seen (Freud, 1914). For example, Jim would often come into the analysis in a chatty mood. He would tell me what he had done since our appointment the previous day, usually some small accomplishment, on the basis of what I might have observed or interpreted the previous day. After I made the observation one day, early in the treatment, that Jim became depressed after he became angry, Jim proudly came in for a number of sessions afterward noting how he started to become depressed, then realized he had been angry, and felt much better. It seemed less an analytic achievement than I had helped him find the "Holy Grail." It took me a while to realize that analysis had become a daily progress report. It seemed to be Jim's way of bolstering me up, letting me know how meaningful and useful my interpretations had been. His unconscious fantasy was that without such rewards, I would withdraw, stop talking, and sink into depression.

A note on the analyst's narcissism

Although there are innumerable rewards in our work as analysts, when we are working well enough, we invest a lot of energy in our analysands, and it comes with a relative ease. Bolignini (2004) has captured our investment when he describes the analyst's need for sharing, by which he meant the analyst's capacity to dive into the turbulent waters of our patient's thoughts and feelings in an experience-near fashion. In addition, he highlighted the necessity for us to be empathic with all sides of our patients, including their narcissistic rage, sadism, masochism, and sociopathic tendencies, and I would include the patient's wish to remain distant from us. However, there are ordinary and extraordinary days, and days when our own narcissistic vulnerability makes it difficult for us to appreciate the patient's perspective. It is my impression from my own work and that of others that it is at these times we tend to understand the patient's non-responsiveness as something they are doing to us (usually something hostile).[7] In my work with Jim, I could have understood my initial countertransference feeling of deadness in his non-responsiveness as hostile, with a good deal of merit. To sort through what is most affectively meaningful and understandable in what Jim may have unconsciously invited me to feel, versus my own narcissistic vulnerability to not having my own plight recognized, was a central and crucial psychoanalytic task with Jim, but also with all of our patients.

Another component of our countertransference response to being ignored is that at the times I've described, the analysand is relating to the analyst as a primitive internalized object. The problem for the analyst, at these times, has been captured by Kohut (1971):

> True alertness and concentration during prolonged periods of observation can be maintained only when the observer's psyche is engaged in depth. Manifestations of object-directed strivings always tend to evoke emotional responses in those toward whom they are directed. Thus, even while the analyst is still at sea about the specific meanings of his patient's communications, the observation of (object-instinctual) transference manifestation is not boring to him. (p. 274)

In short, although the patient is attempting to engage us, it is not us the patient is attempting to engage in an object-directed manner. Unless we are narcissistically balanced, it is difficult to follow Schlesinger's (2003) aphorism that "the patient is doing the best he can" (p. 36). What Schlesinger means by this is that the patient is always attempting to keep some sense of safety and equilibrium, no matter how it strikes us. In this way, a patient who seems to be ignoring us can be attempting to keep us close. In such cases, our countertransference response may need more analytic thinking to become a guide to understanding.

Notes

1 In this chapter I focus on separations; however, with these patients anything that brings the analyst's existence into the analysis is treated as a nonevent. This includes such things as the analyst's having a sneezing attack, the analyst's dropping a pen on the floor; or seeing the analyst outside the office.
2 In this, one can also see the symbolic meaning of Jim's mother seeing him as food or nourishment, where his presence had to feed her.
3 I had been in e-mail contact with him three times, the first to let him know I was OK after my operation. In the second e-mail, approximately two weeks later, I told him I was progressing well. Jim responded to both e-mails with pleasure at the good news. I also let him know a week before I was to start work.
4 See Schmidt-Hellerau (2005b) as an example.
5 See Spillius (1994, pp. 1123–1124) as an example.
6 See Bach (2001) and Eshel (1998) as examples.
7 Of course, we also have to recognize there are times when patients will attempt to undermine, attack, and destroy us.

References

Bach, S. (2001). On being forgotten and forgetting oneself. *Psychoanal. Q.*, 70:739–756.
Bolignini, S. (2004). *Psychoanalytic empathy.* M. Garfield (trans.). London: Free Association Books.
Busch, F. (1992). Recurring thoughts on unconscious ego resistances. *J. Am. Psychoanal. Assoc.*, 40:1089–1115.
Eshel, O. (1998). "Black holes," deadness, and existing analytically. *Int. J. Psycho-Anal.*, 79:1115–1130.
Freud, S. (1955). Beyond the pleasure principle, group psychology and other works. In: J. Strachey (ed. & trans.), *The standard edition of the complete psychological works of Sigmund Freud* (Vol. 18, pp. 5–64). London: Hogarth. (Original work published 1920)
Freud, S. (1957). Remembering, repeating, and working-through (Further recommendations on the technique of psycho-analysis II). In: J. Strachey (ed. & trans.), *The standard edition of the complete psychological works of Sigmund Freud* (Vol. 12, pp. 145–156). London: Hogarth. (Original work published 1914)
Green, A. (1972). The dead mother. In: *On private madness* (pp. 142–173). Madison, CT: International Universities Press.
Kohut, H. (1971). *The analysis of the self.* New York: International Universities Press.
Schlesinger, H. (2003). *The texture of treatment.* Hillsdale, NJ: Analytic Press.
Schmidt-Hellerau, C. (2001). *Libido and lethe: A formalized consistent model of psychoanalytic-drive and structure theory.* New York: Other Press. (Original work published 1995)
Schmidt-Hellerau, C. (2002). Why aggression? Metapsychological, clinical and technical Considerations. *Int. J. Psycho-Anal.*, 83:1269–1289.
Schmidt-Hellerau, C. (2005a). The other side of Oedipus. *Psychoanal. Q.*, 74:187–218.
Schmidt-Hellerau, C. (2005b). We are driven. *Psychoanal. Q.*, 74:989–1028.
Spillius, E. B. (1994). On formulating clinical fact to a patient. *Int. J. Psycho-Anal.*, 75:1121–1132.

Endmater

The chapters in this book originally appeared in the following journals and are reprinted with their permission.

Busch, F. (1992). Recurring thoughts on the unconscious ego resistances. *J. Am. Psychoanal. Assoc.*, 40:1089–1115.

Busch, F. (1993). In the neighborhood: Aspects of a good interpretation and a 'developmental lag' in ego psychology. *J. Am. Psychoanal. Assoc.*, 41:151–176.

Busch, F. (1994). Some ambiguities in the method of free association and their implications for technique. *J. Am. Psychoanal. Assoc.*, 42:363–384.

Busch, F. (2000). What is a deep interpretation? *J. Am. Psychoanal. Assoc.*, 48:238–254.

Busch, F. (2001). Are we losing our mind? *J. Am. Psychoanal. Assoc.*, 49:739–779.

Busch, F. (2003). Telling stories. *J. Am. Psychoanal. Assoc.*, 51:25–42.

Busch, F. (2005). Conflict theory/trauma theory. *Psychoanal. Q.*, 74:27–46.

Busch, F. (2006). A shadow concept. *Int. J. Psychoanal.*, 87:1471–1485.

Busch, F. (2007). 'I noticed': The emergence of self-observation in relationship to pathological attractor sites. *Int. J. Psycho-Anal.*, 88:423–441.

Busch, F. (2009). Can you push a camel through the eye of a needle? *Int. J. Psychoanal.*, 90:53–68.

Busch, F. (2009). I love you that's why I ignore you. *Psychoanal. Psycho.*, 26:335–342.

Busch, F. (2010). Distinguishing psychoanalysis from psychotherapy. *Int. J. Psychoanal.*, 91:23–34.

Busch, F. (2015). Our vital profession. *Int. J. Psycho-Anal.*, 96(3):553–568.

Busch, F. (2016). The search for psychic truth. *Psychoanal. Q.*, 85:339–360.

Busch, F. (2018). Searching for the analyst's reveries. *Int. J. Psychoanal.*, 99:569–589.

Published Papers and Books (In Chronological Order)

Ekstein, R., Busch, F., Liebowitz, J. L. Perna, D., & Tuma, J. (1966). Notes on the teaching and learning of child psychotherapy within a child guidance setting. *Reiss-Davis Bull.*, 3:68–98. (Also see Book Chapters section.)

Busch, F. (1968). Transference in psychological testing. *J. Project. Tech. Personal. Assess.*, 32:509–512.

Busch, F. (1970). Basals are not for reading. *Teachers College Rec.*, 72:23–30. (See also Book Chapters section.)

Busch, F., Nagera, H., McKnight, J., & Pessarossi, C. (1973a). Primary transitional objects. *J. Am. Acad. Child Psychiatr.*, 12:193–215.

Busch, F. and McKnight, J. (1973b). Parental attitudes and the development of the primary transitional object. *Child Psychiatr. Human Dev.*, 4:12–20. (Also see Book Chapters section.)

Busch, F. (1974). Dimensions of the first transitional object. *Psychoanal. Study Child*, 29:215–229.

Whiteside, M., Busch, F., & Horner, T. (1976a). From egocentric to cooperative play in young children: A normative study. *J. Am. Acad. Child Psychiatr.*, 15:294–313.

Horner, T., Whiteside, M., & Busch, F. (1976b). The mutual influence of the positive cohesive self, mental representational structures, and interactive behavior in the child's involvement with peers. *Int. J. Psychoanal.*, 57:461–475.

Busch, F. (1977). Theme and variation in the development of the first transitional object. *Int. J. Psychoanal.*, 58:479–486.

Busch, F. (1978). The silent patient: Issues of separation-individuation and its relationship to speech development. *Int. Rev. Psychoanal.*, 5:491–500.

Busch, F. (1986). The occasional question in psychoanalytic assessments. *Int. Rev. Psychoanal.*, 13:453–461. (Also reprinted in *Libro Annal De Psicoanalisis*, 1986.)

Busch, F. (1989). The compulsion to repeat in action. *Int. J. Psychoanal.*, 70:535–544.

Busch, F. (1992). Recurring thoughts on the unconscious ego resistances. *J. Am. Psychoanal. Assoc.*, 40:1089–1115.

Busch, F. (1993). In the neighborhood: Aspects of a good interpretation and a 'developmental lag' in ego psychology. *J. Am. Psychoanal. Assoc.*, 41:151–176.

Busch, F. (1994). Some ambiguities in the method of free association and their implications for technique. *J. Am. Psychoanal. Assoc.*, 42:363–384.

Busch, F. (1995a). Resistance analysis and object relations theory: Erroneous conceptions amidst some timely contributions. *Psychoanal. Psychol.*, 12:43–53.

Busch. (1995b). Do actions speak louder than words? A query into an enigma in psychoanalytic theory and technique. *J. Am. Psychoanal. Assoc.*, 43:61–82.

Busch, F. (1995c). An unknown classic: N.M.Searl's (1936) "Some queries on principles of technique". 64:326–344.

Busch. (1995d). Beginning a psychoanalytic treatment: Establishing an analytic frame. *J. Am. Psychoanal. Assoc.*, 43:449–468.

Busch. (1996a). Reply to "commentary on the special section". *Psychoanal. Psychol.*, 13:133–135.

Busch. (1996b). Reply to Brenner. *J. Am. Psychoanal. Assoc.*, 654–655.

Busch, F. (1996c). The ego and its significance in analytic interventions. *J. Am. Psychoanal. Assoc.*, 44:1073–1100. (also appeared in 1999, *Psicoterapia e Scienze Umane*, 33:23–53.

Busch, F. (1997). Understanding the patient's use of the method of free association; an ego psychological approach. *J. Am. Psychoanal. Assoc.*, 45:407–424.

Busch, F. (1998). Self-disclosure ain't what it's cracked up to be, at least not yet. *Psychoanal. Inquiry*, 17:518–529.

Busch, F. (2000). What is a deep interpretation? *J. Am. Psychoanal. Assoc.*, 48:238–254.

Busch, F. (2001). Are we losing our mind? *J. Am. Psychoanal. Assoc.*, 49:739–779.

Busch, F. (2002). Back to the future. *Psychoanal. Q.*, 72:201–216.

Busch, F. (2003). Telling stories. *J. Am. Psychoanal. Assoc.*, 51:25–42.

Busch, F. & Joseph, B. (2004). A missing link in psychoanalytic technique: Psychoanalytic consciousness. *Int. J. Psychoanal.*, 85:567–577.

Busch, F. & Schmidt-Hellerau, C. (2004). How can we know what we need to know? Reflections on clinical judgment formation. *J. Am. Psychoanal. Assoc.*, 51:689–708.

Busch, F. (2004). JAPA books: The long and short of it. *Hanna Sachs Libr. Archiv. Newsl.* 5:4.

Busch, F. (2005). Conflict theory/trauma theory. *Psychoanal. Q.*, 74:27–46.

Busch, F. (2005). Analysts on the loose. What I did on my summer vacation. *Psychol.-Psychoanal.*, 25:7–8.

Busch, F. (2006). Countertransference and defense enactments. *J. Am. Psychoanal. Assoc.*, 54:67–86.

Busch, F. (2006). Talking with strangers. *Psychoanal. Rev.*, 93:463–476.

Busch, F. (2006). Un anello mancate nella tecnica psicoanalitica: La conscienca psicoanalytica. *L'Ann. Psicoanal. Internazionale*, 2:15–27.

Busch, F. (2006). A shadow concept. *Int. J. Psychoanal.*, 87:1471–1485. Also appearing as Un oncerto ombra, *Psycoanalisi*, 11:5–26.

Busch, F. (2007). 'I noticed': The emergence of self-observation in relationship to pathological attractor sites. *Int. J. Psycho-Anal.*, 88:423–441.

Busch, F. (2007). An optimistic turn. *Psychoanal. Q.*, LXXVI:609–615.

Busch, F. (2007). O analista trabalhando: Modelos e teoria da tecnica no momento atual. *Rev. Brasil. Psucanaal.*, 41:151–160.

Busch, F. (2008). Ego psychology: Reports of my demise have been greatly exaggerated. *Libre Cahiers Pour Le Psychanal.*, 18:23–33.

Busch, F. (2008). Witnessing: A particular form of the analyst's love. *Int. Psychoanal.*, 17:8.

Busch, F. (2009). Can you push a camel through the eye of a needle? *Int. J. Psychoanal.*, 90:53–68. Also published in *Revista de Psicoanalisis de APA*, 69:41–56.

Busch, F. (2009). I love you that's why I ignore you. *Psychoanal. Psycho.*, 26:335–342. Also published as: (2009). "Te amo, por eso te ignoro" Docta. Revista de Psicoanálisis. 7:207–217.

Busch, F. (2009). On creating a psychoanalytic mind. *Scand. Psychoanal. Rev.*, 32:117–124. Also published in *Psicoanalisis.* 32:407–426.

Busch, F. (2009). Conversando com estranhos. *Alter: Revisita de Estudos Psicanaliticos.* 17:13–24.

Busch, F. (2010). Distinguishing psychoanalysis from psychotherapy. *Int. J. Psychoanal.*, 91:23–34. Also reprinted In *Uluslararasi Psikanaliz Yilligi*, (2011), 11–24; Busch, F. (2013). Podermos diferenciar el Psicoanalisis de la Psicoterapia? *Revista de Psicoanalitica de Madrid.* 68:109–124.

Busch, F. (2010). Fred Busch's response to H. Kächele and D. Widlöcher. *Int. J. Psychoanal.*, 91:51–54.

Busch, F. (2011). Zur frage der Entwicklung einer psychoanalytischen Denkweise. *Jarbuch Der Psychoanalyse*, 62:167–190.

Busch, F, (2011). Por qué el aquí y ahora? *Temas de Psicoanalisis.*, 2:5–12.

Busch, F. (2011). Un freudien nord-américain peut-il penser en français. *Psychiatrie Française*, XLII:37–55.

Busch, F. (2011). The workable here and now and the why of there and then. *Int. J. Psychoanal.*, 92:1159–1181.

Busch, F. (2012). La creation de la pensee psychoanalytique in séance. *Tribune Psychoanal.*, 19:121–142.

Busch, F. (2012). Response to Jacqueline Amati Mahler's paper, "A plea for the survival of psychoanalysis." IPA Forum in *IPA E-Newsletter*, June 2012.

Busch, F. (2012). An invitation to a conversation like no other. *Eur. Feder. Bull.*, 66:86–93.

Busch, F. (2012). Συζήτηση Απάντηση του Fred Busch στον H. Kächele και στον D. Widlöcher. *Greek Annn. Psychanal.*, 1:80–83

Busch, F. (2012). Διακρίνοντας την ψυχανάλυση από τηνψυχοθεραπεία. *Greek Ann. Psychanal.*, 1:49–62

Busch, F. (2013). Changing views of what is curative in 3 psychoanalytic methods and the emerging, surprising common ground. *Scand. Psychoanal. Rev.*, 31:27–34.

Busch, F. (2013). Reflections on supervision. *Cand. Connect.*, 15:4–5.

Busch, F. & J-L. Baldacci (2013). Debat on L'analyse des resistances. *Rev. Franç. Psychoanal.*, LXXXVII:781–810.

Busch, F. (2013). O aqui-e agora trabalhavel e o porque do la e entao. *Livro Ann. Psicanalise.*, XXVII(1):119–139.

Busch, F. (2013). Transforming the under-represented: The unacknowledged influence of ego psychology. *Canad. J. Psychoanal.*, 21:292–312.

Busch, F. (2015). *Working through sarah polley's stories we tell* (and the issue of creative expression). *Int. J. Psycho-Anal.*, 96(2):477–491. Also in Busch, F. (2015). Ensayo de un film. *Int. J. Psycho-Anal. Es.*, 1(2):526–544.

Busch, F. (2015). Our vital profession. *Int. J. Psycho-Anal.*, 96(3):553–568. Reprinted in Busch, F. (2015). La nostra professione vitale. *Rivista Psicoanal.*, 61(2):435–456; Busch, F. (2015). Nuestra profesión vital★. *Int. J. Psycho-Anal. Es.*, 1(3):605–627; Busch, F. (2015). Nuestra profesión vital1. *Rev. Psicoanál. Asoc. Psico. Madrid*, 75:131–153.

Busch, F. (2016). Methods of understanding: Revisions to a Freudian model. *Psychoanal. Inq.*, 36:548–557.

Busch, F. (2016). The search for psychic truth. *Psychoanal. Q.*, 85:339–360.

Busch, F. (2016). Unraveling an enigma. *Psychoanal. Inq.*, 36:295–306.

Busch, F. (2016). Transforma la countertrasferencia amorfa en un forma representable. *Rev Psicoanal. Assoc. Psico.*, 78:141–157.

Busch, F. (2017). Discussion of the case of Bento. *Int. J. Psychoanal.*, 98:1423–1431. Also reprinted in: Busch (2017) Discusión del caso de Bento,*The International Journal of Psychoanalysis (en español)*, 3:5, 879–888.

Busch, F. (2018). Searching for the analyst's reveries. *Int. J. Psychoanal.*, 99:569–589. Also published as: À la recherche des rêveries de l'analyste. *L'Année psychanalytique international.* 2019: 17–49: Also, as, Auf der suche den reveren des analytikers. *Int.Psychoanalyse*, 2019: 17–49. and Busch, Fred (2019): Auf der Suche nach den Rêverien des Analytikers. In: Karsten Münch (Hg.): Internationale Psychoanalyse Band 14: Gedachtes fühlen – Gefühltes denken. Ausgewählte Beiträge aus dem International Journal of Psychoanalysis. Gießen: Psychosozial-Verlag (Internationale Psychoanalyse), S. 1–35.

Busch, F. (2019). Un enigma chimato reverie. Revista di Psicoanalysis. LVX (3):615–636, Un enigma chimato reverie. *Revista di Psicoanalisi.* LXV:615–636.

Busch, F. (2019). El trayecto que recorrí para convertirme en psicoanalista. *Revista de Psicoanalisis*, 85:83–101.

Books

Busch, F. (1995). *The ego at the center of clinical technique*. Northvale, New Jersey: Jason Aronson Press.

Busch, F. (1999). *Rethinking clinical technique*. Northvale, New Jersey: Jason Aronson Press. Ripensare La Tecnica Clinica. Milan, Italy:FrancoAngeli and Russian translation of

"Rethinking Clinical Technique". St.Petersberg: Eastern European Psychoanalytic institute.

Busch, F. (2013). *Creating a psychoanalytic mind: A psychoanalytic method and theory.* Routledge: London. Also translated into Italian, Spanish, Portuguese, Japanese, and Farsi.

Busch, F. (2019). *The analyst's reveries: Explorations in Bion's enigmatic concept.* Routledge: London.

Busch, F. (2020). F. Busch (ed.), *Dear candidate: Analysts from around the world offer personal reflections on psychoanalytic training, education, and the profession.* London: Routledge (In press).

Book Chapters

Busch, F. (1972). Basals are not for reading. In: S. L. Sebesta & C. J. Wallen (eds.), *The first R: Readings on teaching reading.* Chicago: Science Research Associates.

Busch, F. (1972) Interest, relevance and learning to read. In: S. O. Zimet (ed.), *What children read in school: A critical analysis of first grade reading textbooks.* New York: Grune & Stratton.

Heinicke, C. M., Busch, F., Click, P., & Kramer, E. (1973). A methodology for the intensive observation of the preschool child. In: J. C. Westman (ed.), *Individual differences in children.* New York: John Wiley and Sons.

Heinicke, C. M., Busch, F., Click, P., & Kramer, E. (1973). Parent-child relationships, adaptation to nursery school, and the child's task orientation: A contrast in the development of two girls. In: J. C. Westman (ed.), Individual differences in children. New York: John Wiley & Sons.

Busch, F. & McKnight, J. (1975). Parental attitudes and the development of the primary transitional object. In: D. H. Olson & N. S. Dahl (eds.), *Inventory of marriage and family literature* (Vol. 3). St. Paul, Minnesota: Family Social Science, University of Minnesota.

Ekstein, R., Busch, F., Liebowitz, J. L., Perna, D., & Tuma, J. (1976). Notes on the teaching and learning of child psychotherapy within a child guidance setting. In R. Ekstein (ed.), *The search for love and competence.* Brunner/Masel.

Busch, F. (1996). Free association and technique. In: M. Goldberger (ed.), *Danger and defense.* Northvale, NJ: Jason Aronson Press.

Busch, F. (1999). Carlton Fredericks, the republican party and me. In: J. Reppen (ed.), *On becoming a psychotherapist.* Northvale, NJ: Jason Aronson Press.

Busch, F. (2006). In the neighborhood. In: A. Cooper (ed.), *Contemporary psychoanalysis in America; leading analysts present their work.* Washington, DC: Am. Psychiatric Press.

Busch, F. (2007). Il controtransfert negli enactment difensivi. In: A. Nicoli (ed.), *Attualita Del Transfert.* Milano, Italy, FrancoAngeli.

Busch, F. (2016). Second thoughts on Freud's two principles. In: G. Legorreta & L. Brown (eds.), *On Freud's "formulation on the two principles of mental functioning".* London: Karnac.

Busch, F. (2017). The fate of conflict and the impoverishment of our clinical methods. In: C. Christian, M. Eagle, & D. Wolitsky (eds.), *Psychoanalytic perspectives on conflict.* London: Routledge.

Busch, F. (2018). Lest we forget: A Freudian perspective. In: R. Tuch & L. Kuttenauer (eds.), *Conundrums and predicaments in psychotherapy and psychoanalysis.* London: Routledge.

Busch, F. (2019). The problems of a traumticentric view. In: T. McBride & M. Murphey (eds.), *Trauma and the destructive-transformative struggle.* London: Routledge.

Index